Track of Sohar

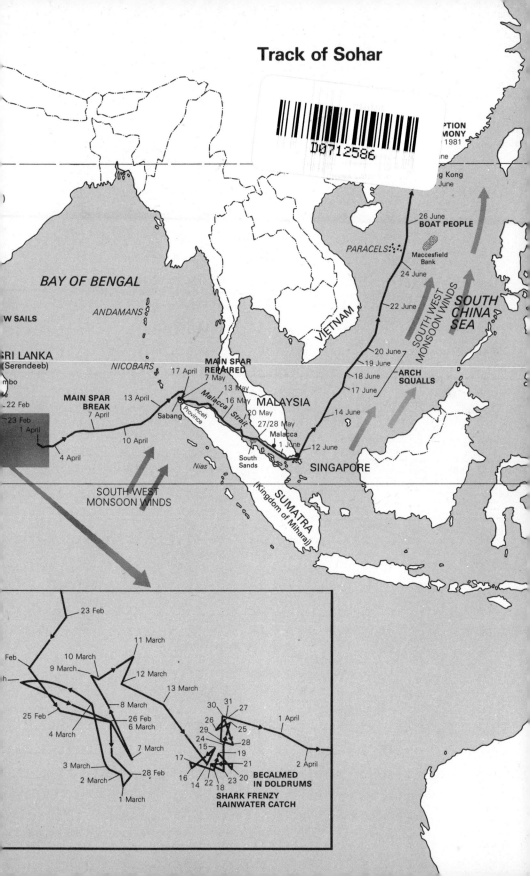

Viscount
Gibson-McConnell.
Gordon Gibson Kintail
1986

THE
SINDBAD
VOYAGE

By the same author
Tracking Marco Polo
Explorers of the Mississippi
The Golden Antilles
The African Adventure
Vanishing Primitive Man
The Oriental Adventure
The Brendan Voyage

THE SINDBAD VOYAGE

Tim Severin

HUTCHINSON

London Melbourne Sydney Auckland Johannesburg

Hutchinson & Co. (Publishers) Ltd
An imprint of the Hutchinson Publishing Group
17–21 Conway Street, London WIP 6JD

Hutchinson Group (Australia) Pty Ltd
30–32 Cremorne Street, Richmond South, Victoria 3121
PO Box 151, Broadway, New South Wales 2007

Hutchinson Group (NZ) Ltd
32–34 View Road, PO Box 40-086, Glenfield, Auckland 10

Hutchinson Group (SA) Pty Ltd
PO Box 337, Bergvlei 2012, South Africa

First published 1982
© Tim Severin 1982

Set in Linotron Sabon
by Input Typesetting Limited

Colour plates printed in Great Britain
by Jolly & Barber Ltd of Rugby
Text printed in Great Britain by The Anchor Press Ltd
and bound by Wm Brendon & Son Ltd,
both of Tiptree, Essex

ISBN 0 09150560 7

Contents

Illustrations

*Photographs by Bruce Foster.
†Photographs by John de Bry.
All other photographs by Richard Greenfield.

The Crew of Sohar

Captain: Tim Severin

Omani Sailing Crew – Muscat to Canton

Khamees Humaid al Araimi *Abdullah Mubarak Salim al-Salhi
*Musalam Ahmed Saleh al-Shaiady Eid Abdullah Saleh al-Alawy
*Khamees Said Sbait al-Mukhaini Saleh Usif Saleh al-Alawy
Jumah Matar Mubarak al-Saad Jumail Marhoon Jameel al-Saad

Specialists

*Peter Dobbs: British, diver and weapons specialist – Muscat to Canton
Andrew Price: British, marine biologist – Muscat to Canton
*Tom Vosmer: American, radio operator – Muscat to Sri Lanka, detached
    duties Sumatra, Sumatra to Canton
David Bridges: British, film cameraman and director – Muscat to Sumatra,
    detached duties Sumatra, Singapore to Canton
Terry Hardy: British, sound recordist – Muscat to Sumatra, detached
    duties Sumatra, Singapore to Canton
Bruce Foster: New Zealand, stills photographer – Muscat to Sri Lanka
Shanby al Baluchi: Pakistani, 'cook' – Muscat to India
John Harwood: British, marine biologist – Muscat to India
Robert Moore: British, oceanographer – Muscat to India
Trondur Patursson: Danish (Faeroe Islands), artist – Muscat to India
*Mahomed Ismail: Indian, shipwright – Muscat to India
Dave Tattle: New Zealand, diver – Muscat to India
Ibrahim Hasan: Indian, cook – India to Canton
Peter Hunnam: British, marine biologist – India to Sri Lanka, Sumatra to
    Canton
Nick Hollis: British, doctor – Sri Lanka to Canton
Tim Readman: British, diver and purser – Sri Lanka to Canton
Richard Greenfield: British, stills photographer – Sri Lanka to Canton
Dick Dalley: British marine biologist – Sri Lanka to Canton

*Denotes watch leader during part of voyage.

Foreword

The funds for the Sindbad Voyage were provided by the kindness of His Majesty Sultan Qaboos bin Said. Official sponsorship came from Oman's Ministry of National Heritage and Culture, whose Minister, HH Sayyid Faisal al Said, gave his unwavering support to the venture. Rarely can any expedition have received such whole-hearted backing, and I hope that the success of the Sindbad Voyage repays in some measure this outstanding generosity which was in the very best Arab tradition.

It took nearly five years to plan and carry out the voyage, and to present its results in words, pictures and film. During those five years one remarkably competent person did the work of an entire support team – Sarah Waters. She ran the nerve centre of the project. Across her desk passed all the paperwork. Single-handed she dealt with the telexes, organized and shipped the supplies, met the aeroplanes, and kept in touch with the families of crew members. Anyone who had anything to do with the Sindbad Voyage owes her a great debt, particularly myself.

Gulf Air, the airline owned by Bahrain, Oman, Qatar and the United Arab Emirates, carried all the stores and personnel for the project without charge – yet another example of Arab munificence. Petroleum Development Oman placed its technical resources at our disposal during the hectic last-minute preparations before sailing, as well as giving a grant-in-aid to get the film of the voyage started. Their gift was promptly matched by the British Bank of the Middle East; and during the voyage I was happy to discover that the bank's parent organization, the Hong Kong and Shanghai Banking Corporation, could provide facilities which Sindbad himself would have envied. The bank's hospitality and assistance reached its zenith in Hong Kong, where the bank even acted as our local agent.

Only a selection of the characters and events which made up as complex a project as the Sindbad Voyage can be included in this single book about the venture. Yet I hope that the selection I have made gives a fair – and entertaining – view of the voyage, and will not disappoint anyone who may have been omitted. At the end of the book is a list of some of those people who assisted the project. Even this list is far from comprehensive, but it does give some idea of just how much help and enthusiasm is needed if one is to build a medieval Arab ship and then sail her all the way to China. To be the captain of that ship was an unforgettable experience for me, and I hope that, through this account of the Sindbad Voyage, my readers will enjoy the entire project as much as I did.

Tim Severin

Courtmacsherry
Co. Cork
Ireland

Spring 1982

Back to the Arabian Nights

The shark must have swallowed the bait in the early hours of darkness the previous night, because the animal was utterly exhausted by the time we noticed the wire-taut fishing line in the first glimmer of dawn. With a whoop of triumph several men ran to the rail of the ship, grabbed the fishing line, and began to haul it in hand over hand. When the 7-foot-long torpedo shape of the shark broke the surface of the sea, the creature began to thrash back and forth in desperation as it suffocated in the thin air. The water churned up into a foam around the shark's flailing body, and as the fishing line was not strong enough to pull the shark vertically out of the water, a long pole with a crude hook on its end was poked cautiously towards the writhing animal. The hook slithered back and forth on the shark's glistening wet skin, seeking one of the vulnerable openings, an eye, a gill slit, or the mouth. But there was an error. Heaving with a final burst of panic, the shark threw the whole weight of its body down on the pole just as it lay across the fishing line. The taut line snapped under the strain, and the shark fell back into the sea, hung there for an instant, and with a slow exhausted roll sank back into the ocean.

'Blast!' said a voice. 'I was looking forward to fresh shark steak for breakfast.'

'Did you see the remora fish sticking to its belly?' asked someone else. 'It must have been at least 16 inches long.'

'I wonder how long we've been towing him behind us,' said a third voice. 'It looked like a white-tip shark to me.'

The group of men who had been standing at the rail of the ship began to disperse. They were a strange-looking band by any standards, I thought to myself as I watched them. The colours of their skins ranged from a rich ebony black to a raw sunburned pink. Most of them were naked to the waist, and all had bare feet. A few wore shorts, but the majority were dressed in loincloths. At least half their number were heavily bearded, and this, together with the fact that they wore turbans and carried sheath knives dangling at their belts, gave them a distinctly piratical air, so that once again I marvelled at the romantic, almost unreal, nature of my surroundings. Was I really in the twentieth century, or was I imagining myself back in an earlier time? Despite the solid feel of the wooden planking beneath my feet, the whole situation had a dreamlike quality. A tropical sea of startling blue stretched out to the horizon on every side, and was marked by the clean wake of the ship drawn across it. Ahead of the vessel a small flock of seabirds was wheeling and calling out exitedly as they peered down into the depths, hoping to catch the glint of small fish disturbed by the motion of our passage. A warm monsoon breeze filled the graceful curves of the three distinctive sails, triangular in shape, which billowed above my head. The largest of these sails was immense, a great expanse of canvas held aloft by a single spar as long as the ship herself, which slanted dramatically upward at a rakish angle. In the centre of each sail was a bright scarlet emblem – two crossed swords and a hooked dagger – which showed that the ship belonged to an Arab sultan, and his country's flag, green, red and white, fluttered at the ship's flagstaff mounted on the rudderhead behind me.

My ears registered the constant background noises of a great sailing ship pushing through the water, the unending creaking of ropes, the occasional splash and hiss of the bow wave caught and magnified in the curve of the mainsail and thrown back to me like an enormous sound reflector, and the soft thump and murmur of timber. My eye followed the intricate tracery of the rigging, past the sweep of the bulwarks to the prow of the ship where the long slender lance of a jib boom was pointing eastward, dipping and rising rhythmically to the swell of the sea as the ship cruised forward. I knew every inch of that vessel, every splinter of wood and every fibre of rope, and yet I never ceased to wonder at her elegance and grace. She was a classic Arab merchant vessel which could have sailed straight from the pages of the Arabian Nights, and she was unique. She was the only vessel of her kind in the world, and this remarkable ship was carrying us, all twenty of her crew, across the Seven Seas to China. It all seemed too far-fetched to be true, a fantasy, a mirage, and I found myself thinking back to the precise moment when this extraordinary adventure had started to take shape.

It had struck root three years before, at the end of a quite different voyage, in a distant and far colder sea, and in a much smaller boat. At that time with three companions, I had been approaching the coast of Newfoundland in a small, open boat made of ox-hides. The purpose of that voyage had been to test whether it was possible for Irish monks to have reached North America nearly a thousand years before Columbus. Our little craft was a replica of the original skin boats used by the Irish monks, and was named *Brendan* in honour of the most famous of the Irish sailor saints, St Brendan the Navigator, the hero of a popular medieval saga that tells how he and his monks sailed across the ocean to a land far on the other side. On that day back in June 1977 it was evident that, barring accidents, my companions and I were about to prove that the saga of St Brendan was probably founded on real Irish voyages into the North Atlantic in the sixth century. Although we had not yet sighted the coast of North America, we could already smell the pine forests of Newfoundland quite distinctly; and in a day or two I knew we would prove that a skin boat could cross the North Atlantic. So, at that moment, my thoughts had turned to what other experimental voyages might add to our knowledge of early exploration and seafaring.

The Brendan Voyage had demonstrated that the technique of building a replica of an early vessel was a useful research tool. It had taught us how the early skin boats were built, what materials were used, and how the boats were handled. It had also given us a taste of what life aboard an open skin boat must have been like for the early sailors. What attracted me was the idea of using the same technique to investigate another, apparently mythical, figure connected with the sea. If St Brendan had stood up to the test, was there another, equally famous, legendary figure whose exploits might also be based on real voyages by real people? At that instant the answer came to me: why not investigate the most famous sailor of all time, a sailor known to every child who has read *The Thousand and One Nights*, a man whose very name is synonymous with seafaring: why not examine the legend of Sindbad the Sailor?

Even there, sitting 50 miles off the coast of Newfoundland, I knew enough about the extraordinary record of Arab seafaring to wonder if the figure of Sindbad the Sailor might be something more than pure legend. Soon after the foundation of Islam in the first quarter of the seventh century the Arabs had launched upon a dazzling geographical expansion. Their armies conquered by land as far as Morocco and Central Asia; and at sea their ships had reached the coasts of Zanzibar and China. Arab merchants had established the most widespread seaborne trading network that the world had ever known, a network that was not to be matched for another seven hundred years when the globe was first circumnavigated by a European ship. The Arabs are generally considered to be a desert people, whose lives and culture have been shaped by the deserts of their homelands. But this is only partly true. The Arabs have also provided some of the most adventurous and skilful sailors recorded in history. Twelve centuries ago, Arab sailors were embarking on voyages that might last as long as three or four years before they returned to their families. Some Arabs, in fact, were as much at home on the sea as in the desert; and by coincidence their philosophy was something which the Irish monks would have understood. The monks of St Brendan's time had written that they sought 'a desert in the ocean', meaning that they were looking for spiritual experience in the vast expanses of the seas. Similarly, the Arabs took to the sea with that same philosophy of devotion which helped them cross the great deserts. They set out trusting in the destiny which Allah would provide them, and both camel caravaneer and Arab shipmaster used the same stars to guide them on their courses, believing that God had placed the stars there for that very purpose. Aboard *Brendan* I had only to glance upwards to appreciate the heritage of Arab seafaring: of the major navigation stars used by sailors, most bore Arabic names because it was Arab savants who had developed the art of astronavigation.

So at the very first opportunity I began to research the background of Sindbad the Sailor. His stories appear in *The Thousand and One Nights*, the collection of traditional folk tales which first began to be published in Europe at the start of the eighteenth century after they had been discovered in manuscript form in Syria by a French literary scholar, Antoine Galland. Galland also managed to copy down other tales which were still being told in the Near East. The stories themselves were obviously far older than any of the manuscripts – and none of the literary scholars would even hazard a guess as to when the stories had begun. The tales in *The Thousand and One Nights* had been collected from a number of sources – some from India, others from Persia, and many from the Arab world. They had been passed down by word of mouth over many generations, and the earliest of the tales seemed to have been in circulation for at least fifteen centuries. The group of stories known as 'The Voyages of Sindbad of the Sea', as the Arabic version calls him, were supposed to have taken place when Haroun al Rashid was Caliph of Baghdad, between AD 786 and 809.

It is more likely that the adventures were compiled by a single author in the late 800s or early 900s, using a variety of sources including Arab geography books, travel books, and sailors' tales.

It did not take long to confirm that the stories of Sindbad of the Sea were closely connected with the golden age of Arab geography which flourished between the eighth and eleventh centuries. When I compared the locations which Sindbad visited on his adventures, with the lands described in the early Arab geography books, it was obvious that many of Sindbad's adventures took place in countries which the Arab geographers also described in their texts. Indeed in some cases the geography books and the Sindbad stories used almost identical sentences to describe particular features. Now the interesting fact is that the Arab geographers obtained a great deal of their information about distant countries by interviewing sailors who had returned from long-distance voyages. So either the places where Sindbad of the Sea had his adventures were borrowed from the early Arab geography books, or the author of the Sindbad stories used the same sources. In particular there was one book of sailors' yarns, the *Marvels of India*, written down in the tenth century, which shared much of the material found in the Sindbad stories. It even named several of the sea captains who had made long-distance voyages. Had one of these sea captains been the original Sindbad? And had Sindbad existed at all? My research might not answer that particular question, but at least I could try to establish a dividing line between truth and fiction in the adventures, and try to discover just how much of Sindbad the Sailor's voyages was based on the real achievements of Arab seamen.

To do this, however, I would have to widen the scope of my investigation to include all the source material relevant to the creation of the Sindbad stories. I would need to experiment with the art of early Arab navigation to find out how they steered their ships. I would have to learn about the nature of early Arab seaborne trade. And I would have to cross-check the Sindbad stories with other Arab tales. In short, Sindbad the Sailor was a symbol for the whole extraordinary phenomenon of early Arab seafaring in the same way that the author of the adventures of Sindbad had used the figure of Sindbad, whether real or imaginary, as a peg on which to hang a whole series of escapades drawn from many sources. In *The Thousand and One Nights* Sindbad goes on seven voyages. Each time he is shipwrecked, marooned, or in some fashion cast away so that he is propelled against his wishes into an adventure. This device allowed the storyteller to turn his material into a serial and hold the attention of his audience, episode by episode. Now I proposed to reverse the process and make a single voyage to see how it might link together the various elements in the stories and place them in relation to the great days of Arab maritime expansion. And here one fact was obvious: on re-reading *The Thousand and One Nights* it was clear that the majority of the locations mentioned in the Sindbad text lay on the sea road eastward from the Arabian Gulf. And it could not be a coincidence that this sea road was the great achievement of early Arab navigation. It was nothing less than the 6000-mile voyage by way of Ceylon and South-east Asia to the fabled ports of China.

At this stage I began to realize the daunting scale of such a project. This voyage would not be like the Brendan Voyage in a little, open boat, small enough to build with the help of a few friends. The Sindbad Voyage was much more ambitious. It needed the research, design and construction of a full-sized sailing ship. It required a place to build her, a port to fit her out, and a large crew to sail her. On board we would have to carry enough spare materials to maintain an early medieval ship at sea for at least eight months of voyaging, with enough food and water for each stage of the journey. And there was no point in making the journey unless I could record it properly, so that meant finding a photographer, a film cameraman and a sound recordist. I would also need to find men who knew how to sail an Arab-rigged ship, and before that was possible I would need to learn to speak some Arabic . . . the list was endless. Also, I had to admit that the venture was a risk. My research turned up the chilling fact that in the first part of this century one Arab sailing ship in ten had failed to make its landfall on passages across the Indian Ocean, and had disappeared at sea. And in Sindbad's time the voyage to China had been considered so dangerous that an experienced sea captain who returned safely was regarded as an exceptional navigator. A successful voyage to China made a man rich for the rest of his life, but the chances of such a trip were very slim. Many ships never returned to their home ports, and the losses were horrendous. All in all, the Sindbad Voyage would not only require massive financial backing, but whoever put up the money for the project would be placing a great deal of faith in the ship and her crew.

Feeling rather overawed, I put aside the problem of finding funds for the voyage and concentrated on the type of ship that would be historically correct for the project. Fortunately the history of Arab ships has attracted the attention of a number of maritime historians, and there were several good studies on the design of early Arab vessels. The most important point was that the scholars believed that the design of Arab vessels had changed radically after the first European exploring fleet, led by Vasco da Gama, arrived in the Arabian Sea in 1498. Soon afterwards the Arabs began to copy European ship design by building their ships with square sterns, whereas the earlier Arab vessels had been double-ended, that is, they came to a point at both bow and stern. The only double-ended, ocean-going Arab ship still to be seen widely in the Arabian Gulf was a type of vessel which the Arabs call a *boom*. It was a design which almost exactly fitted the specification I had in mind: it was a cargo vessel; it was designed to be driven by sails; and the double-ended shape of the hull appeared to have changed little over the period of time for which records existed. But there was one snag: some maritime historians believed that the *boom* had only been invented in the nineteenth century – in other words the *boom* was a modern design, and unsuitable for my purpose. I was puzzled. The *boom* appeared to be such a straighforward solution to the need for a long-distance trading vessel that it should have had a long history. The ship was simple, elegant and capacious. It was an ideal merchant ship. But how could I check that the *boom* had been in existence before the Europeans arrived in the Arabian Sea? The early Arab texts contained a few scattered references about their ships which were useful to establish size, construction and so forth, but there was no specific mention of their hull shape. I found one or two pictures by Arab artists of early Arab ships, and these pictures certainly looked more like *booms* than any other vessel I could identify. But the pictures were too highly stylized to be much help. Who could have drawn a picture of an Arab ship from the pre-European era? And who would have had the special eye for design? The most likely candidate seemed to be another sailor, someone who had seen Arab ships before they came under European influence, and the most obvious place to look was in the Portuguese archives, for the Portuguese had been the first Europeans to round the Cape of Good Hope and enter Arab waters. So I consulted the earliest Portuguese charts of the Indian Ocean, and there I found the answer I was looking for: on the open spaces of a 1519 map of the Indian Ocean was drawn a whole fleet of ships. Some of the ships were Portuguese caravels, identified by the Christian crosses on their sails. But there were also Arab vessels, with the crescent moon of Islam on their sails . . . and most of them were *booms*.

So a *boom* it was, and I had moved a cautious step forward in the project. All the little Arab ships drawn on the old chart carried the vast, triangular sail which is so typical of an Arab ship even to this day. Such sails are immense. The spars which hold up the sails are often as long as the ship itself, and to change the direction of the vessel, from one tack to another, requires shifting the entire sail and all its gear from one side of the mast to the other in an operation which seems both delicate and dangerous. Just how dangerous this operation was, my crew and I would find out for ourselves.

But before then there was one huge problem to be solved – my vessel would have to be built without a single nail in her construction. This was a real challenge. All the early texts make it abundantly clear that early Arab ships were not nailed together, but that their planks were sewn together with cord made from coconut husks. It seemed a flimsy way to make an ocean-going ship. Yet all the early authors agreed that this extraordinary method of construction had been the most distinguishing feature of an Arab ship. Some offered reasons for it. It was claimed that the sewn ship was more flexible, so that when it hit a coral reef it did not split apart but flexed its way out of trouble. One early traveller even claimed that the Arabs sewed their ships together because they feared there was a great magnet at the bottom of the sea which dragged the iron nails out of the hull when the ship passed over it. To me this tale sounded like a good sailor's yarn, and I wondered who was fooling whom. But Marco Polo himself, a notably accurate and reliable observer, had remarked on the stitched hulls of the ships of the Arabian Sea, though he was not impressed. He wrote:

> Their ships are very bad, and many of them founder, because they are not fastened with iron nails but stitched together with thread made of coconut husks. They soak the husks until it assumes the texture of horse hair; then they make it into thread and stitch their ships . . . this makes it a risky undertaking to sail in these ships. And you can take my word that many of them sink, because the Indian Ocean is often very stormy.

Modern naval historians were not much more encouraging. They wrote of Arab ships breaking into fragments in storms, and literally falling apart; of men endlessly baling leaking bilges, of capsizes and shipwrecks; and that Arab shipwrights had abandoned sewn construction because stitched ships could not withstand the recoil shock of deck cannon but shook themselves apart. It was a long and gloomy tale, and even if I ignored the warnings, how did one actually set about sewing together the thick wooden planks of an ocean sailing ship? How could it be done? I read that coconut thread is considered to be the weakest of all natural fibres, and it seemed foolhardy to embark on a voyage one-fifth of the way round the world in a ship held together with a type of string that one would hesitate to use to tie up a parcel. Yet I also remembered how my experience with the skin boat *Brendan* had taught me not to reject the evidence of early texts. After all, *Brendan* had been another sewn boat, her ox-hides stitched together with flax thread. Critics had said that neither thread nor stitches would survive immersion in sea water, yet *Brendan* had survived the North Atlantic and collisions with ice floes. So I knew that the most far-fetched and apparently illogical statement found in an early text might be true, and that every such statement should be noted, considered, and if possible put to a practical test. They could make the difference between a ship that swam and a ship that sunk. And I also knew that if one searches hard enough, it is often possible to discover a modern example of what is, at first sight, a lost shipbuilding technique. The obvious place to start looking for the evidence of early sewn Arab boats was on the shores of the Arabian Sea.

So I went to the Sultanate of Oman, a country on the extreme south-eastern corner of the Arabian peninsula, whose existence since the earliest times has been intertwined with the sea. Oman sits on the maritime crossroads of the Arab world. Ships must pass close by if they are *en route* to India, to Africa, or into the Arabian Gulf, and Omani sailors are famous. Omani ships drove the Portuguese out of the Indian Ocean. A seaborne Omani empire once extended from the shores of Persia to the island of Zanzibar. And, perhaps more important, Oman still preserved a living heritage of Arab seafaring because until 1970 the country had kept itself isolated from the outside world. Eight years later it was still not easy to arrange a visit to Oman, since the Sultanate still had a very strict policy concerning visitors. To enter Oman one needed a special visa which was only given to people with a good reason to go there. Helped by Oman's urbane Ambassador in London I applied for a visa, and on the Ambassador's advice wrote to the Ministry of National Heritage and Culture in Oman's capital, Muscat, asking if the Ministry would support my visit to look at traditional boats. There was the inevitable long delay while the application went from London to Muscat, passed from one Ministry to the other, was processed, passed back again, and finally the visa was stamped in my passport in London. So it was not until several months later that I actually arrived for the first time in the country that was to become my home for the next twelve months, and where the Sindbad Voyage changed conclusively from a dream to a reality.

Even that first moment, as I arrived at the airport, gave me an encouraging premonition. Seeb Airport outside Muscat gleamed. It lay crisp and clean and almost silent. Everything glistened: the rows of service trucks waiting to attend to the aircraft, the marble floors of the arrival building, the plate-glass windows of the airport control tower, the buttons of the starched British-style uniforms of the Royal Oman Police who manned the immigration desk. Everywhere was calm, control, and a high degree of polish. It is true that the Immigration sergeant who examined my visa looked a little odd with pierced ears beneath the black-and-white chequered band on his immaculate cap. But his well-pressed turn-out would have been the pride of any police college. After I collected my bags, I took a taxi to the cheapest hotel in Muscat. That was not difficult to find. My guide book listed only five hotels in the whole of the Sultanate. For the next ten days I existed in a curious state of limbo. Out of courtesy I telephoned the Ministry of National Heritage and Culture to let them know that I had arrived, and to thank them for agreeing to my visit. But as yet speaking no Arabic, I failed to make myself understood. Also I suspected that since my visa application was so out-of-date, my file had gone to the bottom of the pile. So I was left to my own devices, and contentedly walked the beaches of Oman looking for traditional Arab vessels.

The scenery was spectacular. Within sight of the sea dramatic hills reared up in rock formations that were a geologist's dream. Sometimes the minerals in the rocks gave them striking colours – dark mauves, greys, and olives. Dense green palm gardens contrasted with golden yellow sandstones and limestones along the lines of boulder-strewn watercourses. The buff-coloured houses of the villages, faced with dried clay, were so cunningly built into the contours of the hills that they seemed like coral colonies clinging in a living relationship to the rock. At every strategic point the villages and passes were guarded by crenellated fortresses and watch towers, and over every battlement or village square fluttered the red, white and green flag of the Sultanate. It was as if the entire country was waiting for a medieval pageant.

On the sandy beach that stretched for mile after mile north-west from Muscat I found a style of beach boat that could not have changed in two thousand years. It was called a *shasha*, and was made from the central spines of the leaves of the date palm. These leaves were cut at a particular season, stripped and then dried. The spines were then tied together at both ends with a rope lashing to form a bundle, rather like a child's bathtub toy. On this half boat, half raft, a single fisherman would sit while he rowed out to tend his nets or his fish traps, until the palm fronds became too waterlogged and heavy and he had to return to the shore, drag his cockleshell on to the beach and leave it to dry. I actually found one old man in the process of making a new *shasha*. He was trimming the palm fronds with a curved knife, weaving together the frame, and lashing in place the side lathes of the strange hull. He was, I learned much later, the best of the regular *shasha* builders, and fishermen came from miles around to place orders for his boats. His reputation was explained to me more than a year later, while we were halfway across the Indian Ocean, by his nephew, who had then become a member of my crew and left behind that quiet beach in order to sail all the way to China.

Along the same beach I also came across my first example of stitched construction in an Arab boat. The vessel was a derelict, lying canted over on its side on the beach. The planks of the hull were bleached grey by the sun, and its seams gaped. But it was still an extraordinary-looking craft. About thirty feet long, it was shaped like a dagger. The long, slim, shallow hull came to a sharp needle-nose like the ram of an ancient war galley. The stern post swept upward a good 10 feet above the ground in a flamboyant curve. On closer inspection I saw that the bow and stern projections, and the topmost plank, were all held in place by stitching. The boat was very old, and the stitching had been replaced many times. Mingled with the original coconut fibre cord were lengths of fishing line, old nylon rope, even household electric flex. It was a *bedan*, one of the rakish coastal vessels that had once fished and traded all along the Omani coast. *Bedans* are scarcely used any longer, for they require a crew of ten or twelve men to row them, yet I was to find the hulls of *bedans* at nearly every fishing village and to come across the same stitch pattern, the same type of knots, and the same fastenings on other types of boats, not only in Oman but on the other side of the Arabian Sea on the Malabar Coast of India.

On the same stretch of coast lay the town of Sohar, and there I stumbled on a charming echo of Sindbad the Sailor himself. In the days of the great Arab voyages the city of Sohar had ranked among the leading ports of the Arab world. The tenth-century Arab geographer, Istakhri, stated that it was 'the most populous and wealthy town in

Oman, and it is not possible to find on the shore of the Persian Sea nor in all the land of Islam a city more rich in fine buildings and foreign wares than Sohar'. He said it was the home of many merchants who traded with other countries, while his contemporary, Al-Muqaddasi, described Sohar as being 'the hallway to China, the storehouse of the East'. So it was all the more intriguing to discover that Sindbad the Sailor was reputed to be a native of Sohar. It was one of those claims which are impossible to check. There is no written evidence to support it, simply the assertion that Sindbad of the Sea had originally been a man from the city of Sohar.

According to the texts, Sindbad was the son of a rich merchant. When his father died, Sindbad foolishly squandered all his inheritance in riotous living with his young friends. When all his personal fortune had been wasted he sold his last possessions, invested in trading goods, and went to sea as a merchant venturer. *The Thousand and One Nights* says that Sindbad lived and traded from Baghdad, then the metropolis of the Arab world and the capital of the Caliph Haroun al Rashid. But the Caliph himself was such a glittering figure of semi-mythical proportions that it was the habit of later storytellers to ascribe to the reign of Haroun al Rashid all manner of great adventures and marvels, including, naturally, the exploits of Sindbad the Sailor. So I found it intriguing that Sindbad should also be associated in Oman with the city of Sohar by people who were probably unaware of the historical coincidence that Sohar was a leading Arab merchant community just at the time when the Sindbad stories are most likely to have been compiled. Did that mean that Sindbad the Sailor had really been a Sohari merchant whose exploits and residence had been transferred back a century to the reign and capital of the semi-legendary Haroun al Rashid? Or was Sindbad a Sohari who had gone to live in Baghdad?

The answer may lie in the actual process of myth-making, the way in which the figure of Sindbad himself was moulded by the storytellers. There was probably no one single person who was Sindbad. It is much more likely that there was a renowned foreign-going Arab merchant about whom travel stories were told. Gradually the journeys and exploits of other men were credited to him, and the hero-figure was established. This is the normal development of a story cycle. The deeds of a real person are taken, exaggerated, and then embellished with the feats of other men until the entire assembly is presented as a story sequence. This was the process which created both the voyage of

Ulysses and the sea journey of St Brendan. It was quite probable that the same process created the voyages of Sindbad of the Sea, to which the experiences of Sohari merchants trading in strange foreign lands contributed.

Those first days walking the beaches of northern Oman produced a strange effect on me. I felt I was living in a time warp that flickered on and off intermittently, now keeping me in the twentieth century, now projecting me back into the Middle Ages. The reason for this odd sensation was that Oman itself was oscillating between the past and the present. Until eight years previously, the Sultanate had been among the most archaic and isolated countries in the world. For thirty-eight years it had been ruled by a sternly conservative Sultan who saw no merit in modern inventions. He was an autocratic ruler who deliber-ately cut off his country from the outside world. In the countryside most Omanis knew nothing of electricity, cars, or the world beyond their tribes. Even in the capital they lived virtually as they had done in biblical times. If a man tried to visit the capital after dusk, he would find the main gate of the city locked and bolted for the night on the Sultan's orders. And anyone moving around inside the city walls after dark had to be accompanied by an escort carrying a lantern which illuminated the traveller's face.

This historic sleep lasted until 1970 when a new young Sultan came to the throne. Sultan Qaboos was dynamic, foreign-educated, and decreed that it was time for the land to modernize. The next few years were astonishing. Paid for with money from relatively modest discov-eries of oil, superbly engineered highways were slashed through the mountains. Hospitals were built in every town. An educational system was set up, beginning with primary schools for everyone because vir-tually the entire population was illiterate. In the days of the old Sultan, there had been three schools, two post offices, and twelve hospital beds to serve a population variously estimated at between 750,000 and 1,500,000 – no one knew the exact number because there had never been a census. Eight years later the number of schools and hospital beds had increased a hundredfold, and there was an earth satellite station to handle radio and television links. The contrasts between old and new were often startling. Driving down a fine black-top road in Oman one might be watching a string of camels in a nearby wadi, each beast loaded with its burden of firewood, and a wild-looking tribesman striding out in advance, carrying a rifle, when suddenly the spectacle would be blotted out by the massive wheels of a convoy of forty-ton trucks roaring down the highway, taking concrete girders to a new construction project. Or one would be admiring the magnificence of an old Omani fort, its huge wooden double doors studded with nails, and the sun sending shafts of light through the embrasures as if on a film set, when the scream of jet engines would break the silence and war planes of the Sultan's air force would come pouncing over the palm tops and then roll away jauntily into the sky, leaving the observer with a quick glimpse of the Sultanate's crest painted on their fuselages.

There was, I felt, a sense of excitement in Oman. The country vibrated with confidence and vigour. It had the feel of a place where life had not yet settled down to a cosy rhythm. Above all, it was a place of style. The Omanis themselves loved the swagger and gleam of display. Whether in the bright red sashes of the Sultan's soldiers or the triumphal arches they erected across the roads to celebrate the National Day, every Omani seemed to have a great sense of theatre: they enjoyed making an effect. In their national dress they were magnificent – a spotless white cotton gown, the *dishdasha*, worn with a coloured turban tied in any number of fancy ways, and a thick silver-filigree belt to hold the silver-mounted dagger, the *khanja*, in the centre, with perhaps a gold-fringed cloak of the finest wool to add swirl to the ensemble.

I also went to take a look at the Omani port of Sur just inside Cape Ras al Hadd, the most easterly point of the Arabian peninsula. Here, within living memory, a large fleet of wooden merchant ships had been built and maintained, which had operated from Sur up into the Arabian Gulf, eastward to the ports of India, and south towards Zanzibar. More than a hundred sailing ships had lain at anchor off the sand bar at Sur, waiting for the change in the monsoon wind that brought a new trading season. The ships and seamen of Sur were famous as far afield as Kuwait, Bombay and Dar es Salaam. In the oasis towns of the Wahiba sands which lie behind Sur there still stand great houses which were built by Omani families who made fortunes in the clove trade with East Africa, or whose ships regularly brought timber and spices from the Malabar coast of India. And far up in the mountain villages there were people who spoke not only Arabic, but also Swahili, the language of East Africa where the ships of Sur regularly made their annual voyages. Then everything had changed. Political upheavals in East Africa closed the ports of Tanzania to the Arab ships. The prosperity brought about by oil meant that Omanis need no longer face the hardships of life at sea to make their living, and soon afterwards the government of India imposed such crippling taxes and stringent export controls that it was no longer worthwhile to sail to Bombay for trade. In less than a decade the entire merchant fleet of Sur went out of existence, sold or sunk, and was never replaced. The town itself languished into torpor.

To visit Sur, therefore, was a rather unsettling experience. Along the banks of the inlet that connects Sur's lagoon with the sea, where once dozens of large merchant ships had been under construction, I found only about ten small fishing boats being built. The Suri shipwrights still used their traditional tools – adze, handsaw, and the bow drill operated like a violin – and they were still building their boats entirely by eye, never needing a naval architect's drawings. But their work was a pale shadow of Sur's former shipbuilding glory, when Suri craftsmen had been capable of building the great *baghlahs*, wooden merchantmen up to 400 tons burthen that were as massive and stately as Spanish galleons. One last *ghanja*, a ship very like the *baghlah*, was still to be seen in Sur, propped up on stilts in the shallows of the lagoon. It had been placed there by the son of a prosperous Suri merchant family as a monument to the memory of his father. The vessel was magnificent, from its bird's head motif which decorated the prow, along the tremendous run of deck, to a lovingly carved stern castle. But the ship would never sail again. Her planks were split, and on every tide the water rose and fell in her hold. The same sad desolation could be seen all along the foreshore, a graveyard of abandoned native boats like pages scattered from a picture book of Arab shipping. Arabs do not use the word 'dhow' – though it is a convenient term, possibly of East African origin, to describe Arab ships in general – but refer to each particular ship by its special type and design. Here at Sur was a ruined *sambuk* that once plied the run to Bombay; there an Indian-built *kotia* with the land crabs running in and out of her frames; the wreck of a blunt-prowed *dhangi*; and a strange, rakish craft that somebody told me was a gun-runner out of Yemen that had been abandoned at Sur. Rock herons perched on the rotting timbers to give themselves a better view of the shallow water. Even the old customs house was being lost. Where the former Sultan had stayed on his visits to Sur, no one lived now. The great double entrance door was half submerged under a sand dune, and the wind was slowly piling up more sand against the outer walls.

I rode the little ferry that set out from the beach next to the forlorn customs house and crossed a hundred yards of sparkling blue water to disembark at Al Aija, the little town on the other side. A small mosque, beautiful in its whitewashed simplicity, overlooked the landing place, and there was a crescent beach that fringed the bay where Al Aija's fleet had once sheltered. Here I found a single *sambuk* under construction. It was being built well and truly, but there were only three shipwrights to do the work. Two were mere helpers, and the third man was obviously the real craftsman: he had a splendid physique, evidently with much African blood in his veins, and he greeted me with a delightful, slow smile. He was speaking Swahili to his companions. For more than an hour I watched him, fascinated and unaware that this shipwright's family would also provide me with a crew member, the youngest of my team.

On the second to last day of my visit to Oman I received a message from the Ministry of National Heritage and Culture. The Minister himself asked if I would give a lecture to a small invited audience on the subject of the Brendan Voyage; I could only suppose that one of the Minister's advisers had told the Minister about my voyage in the wake of St Brendan. Luckily I had brought with me a copy of the film of the Brendan Voyage which I was planning to show in London on my way back home to Ireland. The Minister, a member of the ruling family of Oman, arrived promptly with his friends, sat down in the front row, and waited expectantly. This, I reflected, was a bizarre situation. Here was I about to describe a journey of investigation in the wake of an Irish Christian saint, in a leather boat across an icy sea, to an audience composed mostly of devout Moslems dressed in *dishdashas*, turbans and daggers. On the screen would be scenes filmed among the ice floes of Greenland, while here in Oman the temperature stood well over 100 degrees. The audience listened patiently, and when the talk was over everyone filed gravely out of the room, leaving me to ponder on the unlikely turns that life can take.

Next morning was my last in Oman; when I went to pay my hotel bill, however, I found that it had vanished. The desk clerk told me that the Ministry had paid the bill, and there was a message for me to call to see the Minister. I went to his office where he questioned me closely about my research and my project for the Sindbad Voyage. Then he thanked me for the lecture and presented me with a splendid antique Omani battle sword. It was a gesture that touched me deeply. With typical perception the Minister had guessed what gift I would most appreciate. That evening, with the sword in my luggage and a letter from the Ministry authorizing me to take it out of the country, I was on my way back home to Ireland.

I had spent two weeks in Ireland when two telegrams reached me on the same day: they were both from the Minister in Muscat, and had been held up by the quirks of the Irish postal system. The two telegrams said the same thing: the Sultan had approved my project, and would I return at the earliest opportunity to Oman to discuss the matter. Twenty-four hours later I was back in the offices of His Highness Sayyid Faisal, the Minister of National Heritage and Culture.

'I am glad to tell you that I have talked with His Majesty about your project, and His Majesty has approved,' the Minister began. 'The Ministry of National Heritage and Culture will sponsor it.'

I did not know what was meant by 'sponsoring' the project, or quite what was involved, so I said nothing. The Minister went on.

'We want the project to be for Oman, and the ship to be an Omani ship, sailing under the Omani flag. Oman has a long and famous history as a seafaring nation. In fact it was the first Arab state ever to send a ship to the United States – that was in 1840. Next year will bring our tenth National Day, and the ship should be ready by then.'

'When is National Day?' I asked.

'The celebrations will last for a week, beginning on 18 November.'

I made a quick mental calculation. That gave me only fifteen months to find the material for the ship, a task which I knew could be extraordinarily difficult, build her, select and train her crew, and conduct the necessary sea trials. It was a very tight schedule indeed.

'Your Highness,' I said, 'I think I can manage to have the ship ready by then if there are no major hold-ups. Also November will be a good time to begin the voyage, because the winds will be favourable at that season.'

'Good. Let me know what you will want, and we will do everything we can to help you.'

I must still have been looking puzzled, for I had no idea exactly how much help the Minister, with the approval of Sultan Qaboos, intended to provide for the Sindbad Voyage. Sayyid Faisal must have sensed my bewilderment, because he repeated his offer that the voyage would be sponsored by the Ministry. Yet I was still confused and unclear. The more he tried to explain, the more puzzled I became. The interview seemed to be drifting to an embarrassing halt.

'Would you like a letter about this arrangement?' the Minister finally suggested.

Anything to clear up the confusion, I thought. 'Yes, please, Your Highness.'

He pulled open the drawer of his desk, selected a sheet of his crested ministerial notepaper, and slid the blank sheet across his desk to me. 'Perhaps you would like to draft the letter for me to sign?' he said.

Suddenly it dawned on me. With the backing of Sultan Qaboos, the Ministry of National Heritage and Culture was offering to pay for the entire cost of my Sindbad Voyage. The extent of the generosity was breathtaking. I had not asked for this help: it was being offered because the history of Omani seafaring was very close to the hearts of the people of Oman. The Minister was trusting me to build a ship for his nation, and then sail her to the farthest end of Asia. Such confidence and magnanimity were more than I could have dared hope for. It seemed that the world of the Arabian Nights still existed.

From *The Arabian Nights' Entertainments*,
trans. Edward William Lane, 1877

—2—

The Coast of Malabar

The timber for building Omani ships is brought nearly 1300 miles from the Malabar coast of India. It is a trade which goes as far back as the earliest records, because Oman lacks trees large enough to provide first-class boat timber. So it was to Malabar that I now travelled in search of the massive trees that would be needed to build the replica ship. Over the next seven months I was to make half a dozen trips to India to track down and purchase all the materials I would need; and in that time I saw a side of India that had little to do with the twentieth century, taking me back to a bygone era which blended squalor with beauty, craftsmanship with chicanery.

I went to India with three very colourful companions provided by the Ministry of Culture and National Heritage in Oman. First there was Said al Hatimy, a genial, portly figure in a gleaming white turban and splendid jutting beard that denoted his status as a religious and learned man. On account of his education Said was often called by the honorific title of Sheikh; and as he had once been a schoolmaster in Zanzibar he spoke impeccable English with an Oxford accent in a rich *basso profundo*. He was to be the interpreter and to represent the Ministry. Next there was Hoodaid, a master shipbuilder from Sur, whose job it was to advise on the quality of the timber we might find. He was a tall, gentle man with a gleaming gold tooth in the centre of his smile, and a liking for beige-coloured *dishdashas*. He did not speak a single word of English, and was never certain whether the pious Said al Hatimy approved of his smoking. So Hoodaid was forever edging away into quiet corners for a cigarette, and giving me a sheepish grin when he caught my eye. The fourth member of our team was its most surprising. He was the palace victualler from Muscat, by the name of Dharamsey Nensey. A very spry gentleman at least seventy years of age, he had been appointed paymaster to the project. Dharamsey was a gem. He was a deeply respected Indian *banyan* or merchant, orig-

31

inally from Gujerat, who had lived for forty-six years in Muscat, close by the Palace. Originally his shop had supplied the Palace kitchens with groceries, but as the Sultan's wealth and power expanded so too had Dharamsey Nensey's role. Now, at a minute's notice, he might be called upon to supply anything from a Rolls Royce to a handful of pistachio nuts, and he kept a small army of Indian clerks labouring away over their ledgers in a counting house behind the Muscat Palace to satisfy the royal commissariat. Dharamsey's three sons could run the business while he was away in India, so when the Minister entrusted my project's finances to him Dharamsey decided that he himself should accompany the timber-buying expedition. Dressed in a long white shirt, with his spindly legs emerging from his loincloth, Dharamsey made an enchanting travelling companion. He and I conversed in a strange mixture of English, Arabic and Hindi, and his sharp eyes never missed anything. At the end of an eighteen-hour travelling day he would hop about as alert and active as a sparrow, always clutching what appeared to be a magic handbag. This bag was no more than a simple pouch made of white cotton, about 8 inches by 10, hardly bigger than an office envelope. Yet by some sleight of hand, out of this bag, which never grew grubby nor left his person, Dharamsey would produce everything that was necessary – tickets, reading materials, diary, and any amount or type of currency that was required, and always in cash. Dharamsey's cotton purse was apparently bottomless, and its contents never ceased to amaze me.

We made a totally incomprehensible group in the sight of the Indians, as we travelled up and down the length of the Malabar coast. Whenever we stopped to eat, the restaurant staff would be thrown into a state of confusion. They recognized immediately from his dress and manner that Dharamsey was a strict vegetarian, so they knew he observed his own dietary rules. They also knew that the two turbaned Arabs did not eat pork and ate with their fingers, while as a European I would expect to have a knife and fork. So the usual reaction in a restaurant was to seat us at separate tables, and we always attracted amazed glances as the four of us insisted on sitting together, happily sharing a table while we went about our food in our own particular ways. In a series of decrepit taxis we rattled up and down the atrocious, potholed roads of the Malabar coast from one seaport to the next. The vehicles broke down; the monsoon rain fell in sheets; and we were crammed together in soggy discomfort. In short, the quest for timber could have been a hellish experience. But my travelling companions made the event fascinating. Three times a day we halted for Sheikh Said to say prayers, and at least twice as many times a day we would stop in the bazaars while the two Omanis dived into the back-street shops and haggled for knick-knacks and curios. Perfume was in great demand, and I got used to being swept into perfume shops to have my sleeve rolled back, and several blotches of rosewater and other scents dabbed on the skin for trial sniffs. I particularly enjoyed the gleam of antici-pation in the shopkeeper's eyes as he thought he had two rich Arabs to fleece, and the way the gleam died the instant that Dharamsey Nensey chirpily came in sight, his little white purse in hand and his shrewd brown eyes calculating the percentage profit on every item.

The hub of our activity was Calicut, the port which gave calico its name. When Vasco da Gama, leading the first European trading fleet ever to enter the Indian Ocean, reached Calicut in 1498, Arab mer-chants had already been trading there for at least seven centuries. Today a handful of Arab ships continue to come to Calicut to load spices, timber and general cargo. Formerly an entire community of Indians lived off the pickings of the Arab trade: there were sailmakers, shipbuilders, moneylenders, ropemakers, and a hopeful colony of Mos-lem Indians whose womenfolk often married visiting Arab seamen. This last contact was not totally lost, for as we approached Calicut Hoodaid, who had once been a sailor himself, began to look distinctly furtive. I asked Sheikh Said if anything was the matter with Hoodaid, and he gave a deep, throaty chuckle.

'Oh yes!' he said. 'He is worried that he will be recognized. He still has a wife in Calicut from his days as a sailor. He's not been back for several years, and he has not sent her any money. Under Moslem law he should look after her. If her family finds out that he is in town, Hoodaid will have to pay up for all the time he has been away.'

As it turned out, Hoodaid did the decent thing. On the evening of our arrival in Calicut he went off to find his wife and surrender the arrears. He reappeared the next morning, a subdued and doubtless poorer man.

Today Calicut's merchant community, which caters to the Arab trade, has withered to just two merchant houses – the Baramys and the Koyas. The two families occupy almost identical houses strategically situated on the beach which overlooks the anchorage. Each house is a large, low bungalow. Behind it are a courtyard and various sheds in which lie boxes of ship's nails, coils of rope, tins of clarified butter, mysterious packing cases, and a jumble of homemade anchors. The focus of life is the long, elegant veranda. Here at all hours of the day, but especially at the time of sunset prayers, can be found a sprinkling of Arab merchants, taking their ease on benches and cane chairs, sipping cups of tea or coffee, and gazing out over the roadstead, where the waves of the Arabian Sea crash and rumble on the beach, and an occasional beggar sidles up to the railings to seek alms in the name of Allah. The head of each trading house, Baramy or Koya, is a man of considerable standing in the Calicut community. He virtually controls all the contact between the Arabs and their suppliers of timber, spice and trade goods. Abdul Kader Baramy, whom we went to see, had all the world-weariness of a harassed international business executive. He had seven brothers – a sure sign of Allah's favour – but in the tradition of such enterprises, nothing could be done without his consent. His brothers, all in identical smart white robes, were strategically scattered: one ran the Baramy shipyard ten miles down the coast at Beypore, where they built modern motor dhows for the Arabs. Another travelled regularly to the Gulf to visit Arab clients. A third might be sent off to negotiate with the civil servants in Delhi. The others were kept on hand, hovering expectantly to run errands. Abdul Kader himself knew as much about the timber trade and boatbuilding as any man on the Malabar coast. He was distinctly pessimistic about our chances. It would be extremely difficult to find teak logs of the large size we were looking for, and impossible in the time available. Moreover, the Indian government had banned the export of teak: Abdul Kader produced a government notice which carefully listed a whole range of hardwoods, including teak, which could not be sent out of the country as unworked timber. As for constructing a sewn ship, he had heard of such vessels, but it was out of the question to build one nowadays. The men who knew such work, the shipwrights in rope, simply did not exist any longer. Abdul Kader recommended that we drop the idea of a sewn ship, and of building it in Oman. He could build us a nailed ship in India, and it would be ready in a year's time. Of course we were free to keep on looking for timber, but he held little hope for us.

It was a disappointment, but not a final one. The previous year, while on a trip to India to look at Indian traditional ships, I had found my way to a small creek north of Mangalore in the State of Karnataka. It was an isolated, sad place, a graveyard for ships that were hauled up on the mud in retirement. What had rewarded my visit was the fact that three of the beached vessels were sewn ships, fastened together exactly like the boats I had seen on the beaches of Oman. The timber of these ships was not teak, but a very similar wood call *aini*; I looked into the characteristics of *aini*. The tree is a cousin to the breadfruit, and the timber can be used for fine housebuilding, for doors and window frames – and for ships. Technically it is virtually identical to teak – it has very nearly the same strength, density and weight. It grows to a good size, and is easily worked, but it has a major drawback: it tends to split if nails are driven into it. But of course I was not intending to nail my ship together – I was building a sewn ship, and this was precisely why Indian sewn ships were often built of *aini*. I also chanced on the fact that *aini* contains a very high proportion of lime in its fibres, which makes the timber difficult to paint because the lime burns away the paint. For a ship, however, the lime in the timber may actually help discourage attacks by teredo shipworms. Indian shipwrights told me that *aini* lasted far longer in water even than teak. To make *aini* even more attractive, it was only about half the price of best teak. But the deciding factor which made me select *aini* for the replica ship was that the Indian government had omitted it from the list of banned exports – Abdul Kader Baramy carefully scrutinized the entire inventory of timbers the government had forbidden for export. The list included nearly every hardwood, but by an oversight, or because it was an obscure timber, the Indian authorities had failed to ban the export of *aini*.

Encouraged, my companions and I found the timber we were looking for in the hills behind Cochin. There, fine stands of *aini* were being felled for logs by Indian timber merchants. Our arrival in the hills caused a sensation. On the one hand the timber merchants joyfully anticipated making huge profits from any Arab customer; but on the other hand they were totally unused to their customers coming up into the hills and tramping around the forests, measuring trees, banging the logs enthusiastically with a hammer to try to detect hidden flaws by the sounds of the reverberations, and chatting with the foresters. Hoodaid, Sheikh Said and Dharamsey had to go back to Oman, but I stayed on in the forests, determined to find the very best logs for my ship, and also to receive an education in the tricks of the timber trade.

By reputation the timber dealers of India are the biggest rogues in the country, and in a curious way they are almost proud of their fame. I was warned never to take anything on trust, to check every log for faults, and to make sure that the logs I bought were actually the same logs which reached the sawmill and were not substituted on the way, and so forth. To my secret delight I discovered that the timber merchant

I was dealing with was steeped in the rules of the game. On the very first day, at his office on the edge of the forests, I produced my own brand-new tape measure, with which I intended to check the measurements of every log. The tape measure was still in its box, and the timber merchant asked to look at it, expressing admiration. Five minutes later I noticed that the tape measure had vanished. I made an excuse, left his office, and went round the back of the building. There I found the timber merchant's foreman carefully laying out my tape measure on the ground so he could check that its markings matched those on his own tape. It seemed that the merchant suspected me of bringing along a fake, specially marked tape measure of my own in order to cheat him!

The excursions into the forests were great fun. I enjoyed homing in on the ringing blows of the axes of the woodsmen as we pushed our way through the undergrowth, or hearing the huge, rending crash as a large tree toppled and fell. Then, for a moment, the whole forest went silent except for the eerie pattering sounds of hundreds upon hundreds of twigs and leaves raining to the ground, torn adrift by the giant's fall. I spent hours watching the elephants at work as they tugged the logs out of the forest and down to the logging paths. The intelligence and grace of the huge animals never ceased to amaze me. An elephant would move up to the fallen log with almost catlike grace, and wait with its ears fanning steadily back and forth while the axemen stripped the larger branches and cut a hole in the butt of the log for the hauling chain. Then, nudged by the heels of its driver, the elephant would move deliberately into position. The trunk would reach out, the tip curl round to pick up the chain, and tuck the fat, soft end-rope into the great jaws. Then the elephant's massive feet would shuffle into a good hauling position. The trunk slid back down the chain like a black python and wrapped itself around the links in order to hold the chain at just the right angle. Then the elephant would lean back to put its whole weight into the heave. Charmingly, just before the animal gave a mighty tug, it would screw up its eyes tight shut, just like a child. Then with one smooth jerk of its whole body the log was sent skidding ten yards through the mud. A few ponderous moments later, and the elephant was at a different angle to the log. Another jerk of the chain, and the log was angling down between the obstructions and roots to land on the roadway in front of us.

'Elephants are very costly,' murmured the timber merchant, who was standing prudently clear of the great beast and obviously saw no romance in its performance. 'I must hire them by the hour from the elephant hire company, and so much time is spent washing them. They must be bathed three times each day, or their skins will trouble them, and they will not work. Also I must pay their food. But,' and here he brightened up, 'I am just purchasing my own elephant, and it will work for many, many years. If it does not get sick and die, maybe it will be working too for my sons. An elephant is better than a tractor. I have looked into this matter. Tractors cannot work on such steep slopes, and in the forest there is no one to look after the engines. Also spare parts are very difficult. Yes, an elephant is better.'

Eventually I came to be quite fond of Mr Sunny, the timber merchant, as he made a valiant effort to keep up with his eccentric customer. He would accompany me on each of my timber-buying trips, bouncing along in an ancient car which squelched up the muddy tracks. His courage only failed in the late evening, when after dark I insisted on visiting the log parks to try to pick out a few more fine pieces of timber.

As I scrambled out of the car on to the squelching mud, and the rain rattled down, Mr Sunny would wind down the window, hand me a torch, and call out mournfully as I disappeared: 'Be careful for snakes. You will see many poisonous snakes. They come out after darkness, looking for frogs . . . cobra, krait, viper . . . there are many types of viper, and over two hundred species of snake in India.'

But despite much stumbling and slipping in the darkness I never saw a single snake.

I carried a shopping list for my timber, an inventory of every plank, beam and frame, its size and curve. The list was worked out from the technical drawings of a replica *boom* which had been produced by Colin Mudie, the brilliant naval architect who had also prepared the lines plans for *Brendan*. I had complete confidence in Colin, and he had begun by making a preliminary set of lines plans based on the shape of surviving *booms* and the historical data that I had been able to glean from the early texts. Then I showed a scale model of this preliminary version of the replica to the Omani dhow-builders at Sur, and obtained their suggestions for modifications, which Colin had incorporated in his final drawings. All agreed that the keel of the ship was the key to its construction. The keel of a *boom* is long, straight and massive; it is the very backbone of the vessel, and its dimensions dictate the remainder of the ship, for an Arab shipwright builds mathematically. Once the keel is laid, every other timber relates to it at a particular angle or size, so that if one tells an Arab shipwright the type of vessel – *boom* or *sambuk* or whatever – and the length of its keel, he will know exactly the final size and shape of the finished ship. Where European shipwrights measure the size of a vessel by its length overall or on the waterline, the Arab shipbuilder calculates a ship by the length of its keel.

The problem was that the keel piece to my replica needed to be 52 feet long, 12 inches by 15 inches in cross-section, and dead straight. Also Colin wanted it to be cut from a single baulk of wood, which meant a superb log, of a size in hardwood virtually unobtainable in Europe. Even the Indian timbermen shook their heads in astonishment when they heard that I was looking for such a log, but in the end my persistent search was rewarded. In July I found the great tree that would provide the keel of my ship. It was a magnificent tree, owned by a family who had tended it for half a century, trimming away the lower branches so that the main trunk kept pushing upward. What is more, the family had a daughter who was about to get married, and they were willing to sell the tree to find her dowry. I bought the tree where it stood. A forester shinned up it to attach a rope that would guide its fall, two axemen came forward, and within two hours the giant had been cut down. The branches and bark were stripped away to reveal the characteristic banana-yellow colour of fresh-cut *aini*, which would change to a dark reddish brown in the next few weeks. The timber, I had been assured, did not need to be seasoned. Fresh *aini* could be used for boatbuilding. It needed two elephants to manoeuvre the great log down to the road. There it was put on trestles, and cut square by two men working a huge double-handed pit saw. One man stood on the log, while his partner crouched underneath on his knees to pull down the blade, showered by the rain of damp sawdust. It took four days of solid labour to trim the log, but at last it was ready, and with two extra feet in length to spare. It was loaded on a lorry and, accompanied by an elephant to manoeuvre it around the hairpin bends, the keel piece began its journey down to the coast.

By now my visits to India had produced for me a small, permanent entourage. This was the nature of the country: I was discouraged from being too self-sufficient, and my presence was a chance to create jobs for other people. Thus I found I needed a driver who knew the roads and could look after the car; a carpenter who would talk with the foresters about timber; and an interpreter-cum-assistant who could make all the thousand and one arrangements, from finding overnight accommodation to calculating the correct amount for bribes. For instance between Cochin and Goa, the stretch of coast where I was hunting for materials, at least four different languages were spoken by the local villagers, and my quest was constantly taking me into small hamlets and quiet backwaters where strangers were rare, and foreigners unknown. So my interpreter had to be versatile – and he was. He came with a letter of introduction from an Indian marine biologist who had encountered him while collecting marine samples on the remote coral islands of Minicoy some 220 miles off the Indian coast. 'He is a man in a million,' announced the letter. 'He can speak fourteen languages, and will follow up any subject that interests him.' Man in a Million, as I tended to think of him from that moment onward, lived up to his recommendation. His real name was Ali Manikfan, and he was the son of the last headman of Minicoy island. Now he lived on the mainland, having found the island too restrictive for his talents. He had a well-honed sense of his own dignity and abilities, and could be very haughty towards other Indians, but at a pinch he could cook and sew, sail a boat, mend an engine, or make up a book of accounts. From his marine collecting days he knew the Latin name of every fish and shell on his islands, and spoke a certain amount of classical Arabic, because like all the Minicoy islanders he was a Moslem and had studied at the Koranic school. He also shared with Dharamsey Nensey the ability to travel light. Every time I arrived in India Ali would be there to meet me, smiling broadly under the little white cap perched on his head, and holding a small briefcase which was his only luggage.

The men of Minicoy have an excellent reputation all along the Malabar coast. Living in isolation on their island, which is only 40 miles square, they have developed a remarkable self-reliant culture. Every man is expected to be able to look after himself, to fish and tend the coconut trees, build his own house, cook and swim, and work as a member of a team. Minicoy men are also said to be the best seamen in India, and were the original Lascars who, for generations, have signed on as deck hands with foreign ships. Often they served long years abroad before returning to their island home. Even in the huge, pullulating port of Bombay the men of Minicoy were renowned: almost exclusively they staff the boats of the Bombay Pilot Service, and it is said that not only are the Bombay pilot launches the smartest, best-handled boats in the whole of the port, but whatever happens, in foul weather or emergency, the Minicoy men keep their boats on station.

Moreover, in perhaps the most remarkable claim of all, it was said that in Bombay's labour-troubled port the Minicoy men never go on strike.

Minicoy is one of a group of islands where medieval Arab ships picked up the coconut rope used for shipbuilding, and until this century the only export from the Laccadives was coir, the rope made from coconut husks. So it seemed logical for me to try to obtain coconut rope for my replica sewn ship from the same source as the Arabs. But the Indian government restricts foreigners from visiting the Laccadive Islands on the grounds that intruders would disturb the fragile native culture. This was where Ali Manikfan was doubly important: he could put me in touch with Laccadive Islanders when they came to the mainland on rare visits to buy rice, cigarettes and provisions. The key islander I ambushed on such a visit was a genial rogue from Agatti Island named Kunhikoya. Quick-witted, active, and with an engaging grin, he was a likeable scoundrel. Kunhikoya also possessed an encyclopedic knowledge of the coconut rope trade and had done a bit of sewn boatbuilding himself. He told me that what I needed for shipbuilding was a very special quality of coconut rope. It had to be hand rolled from the best-quality coconut husks. These husks had to be soaked, or retted, in sea water to loosen the fibres. Most coconut fibre is retted in fresh or brackish water, said Kunhikoya, and this type of fibre was useless for my purposes – it was not strong enough for a ship. After retting in sea water, the coconut husks had to be dried in the sun, then pounded with wooden clubs on wooden blocks to loosen the powder. If metal hammers were used for the pounding, the fibres would be crushed and damaged and the rope would again be too weak. After that, the fibre should be twisted by hand into string. If twisted by machine, the threads would be too feeble.

Kunhikoya announced that I would need about fifteen hundred bundles of coconut string to build the ship I needed. I calculated the total length, and it came to four hundred miles! This seemed a colossal amount, but events proved Kunhikoya right. With his help, Ali and I tried at first to buy good-quality coconut string in the little villages hidden along the backwaters of the Malabar coast. It was highly entertaining to watch the two islanders at work. They were experts. They knew exactly what they were looking for, and they also knew most of the ruses which would be used to trick them. Offered a sample piece of coconut twine, Kunhikoya would grimace theatrically, take the sample between his hands and with a quick twist of his wrist would unravel the spiral of string. Then, with a seemingly effortless flick, he snapped the string like a cotton thread, and let the two broken ends drop to the ground with an expression of total disgust. Of course there was a trick to the way of snapping a piece of thread, but Kunhikoya was such a good actor – and he had immensely strong forearms – that he could make even the strongest twine look fragile. Nor would he accept the vendor's protestations that the twine had been retted in salt water. Snatching up a sample he would stuff it into his mouth like spaghetti and chew on it, trying to detect the characteristic salty flavour of sea water-prepared coir. Not finding it, he would turn to me, and offer me a sample to taste. Reluctant to spoil the pantomime, I too would munch solemnly on the coconut rope, trying not to think of the stagnant ooze of the fetid backwaters where the coconuts were retted.

Eventually I had to accept that the only place I could get proper sea water-prepared coconut string was the Laccadive Islands themselves, via Kunhikoya as my agent. I was not altogether surprised to discover four months later, when the bundles were delivered and Kunhikoya was safely many miles away, that Kunhikoya had included some machine-made string in the consignment. But it was worth it: in India Kunhikoya had saved me from far greater swindles.

Some of the items he said I would need for the construction of a sewn vessel were truly bizarre. There were the husks of 50,000 coconuts to be used as a kind of wadding, two particular thicknesses of string, and forty bundles of a curious knobbly wood from the islands which I suspected was mangrove root. This wood was immensely strong and hard, and Kunhikoya said it would be used for the levers which the ropeworkers would need when they were tightening up the lashings of the ship. There was also a quarter ton of a tree gum called *chundruz*, a natural resin which is more usually employed for making cheap incense. The boatbuilders would use it as a type of shellac, painting it between the planks. To select his *chundruz*, Kunhikoya would take a handful of the granules of resin, and set them alight in order to see how they burned. It took almost a day of these fiery tests before he was satisfied with the selection of the *chundruz* but, alas, our efforts were in vain. We bought six large sacks of *chundruz*, sealed them, marked them, and stored them in a bonded warehouse. But when the sacks reached Oman and we opened them, we found that two-thirds were filled with pebbles: we had been victims of the notorious 'substitution'.

Kunhikoya also wanted half a dozen barrels of fish oil, which was to be mixed with melted sugar and painted on the outside of the completed hull. The oil came from tiny fish which were boiled down in vats near Mangalore and the grease skimmed off. The stench of the oil was indescribable. Next there was half a ton of lime to be plastered to the underwater surfaces of the ship as a form of anti-fouling. To obtain the lime, we went to a lime burner near the fish oil vats. It was like a scene from Hell. A long file of women carried buckets of seashells on their heads to dump them in a heap outside a long, low hut, which had smoke billowing up through the thatched roof. Inside a very old man, a mere skeleton, pedalled a wheel to force air into the charcoal-fired tubs of burning shells. More gaunt men, with cloths bound around their heads, stirred the tubs with long wooden spades. Two children staggered back and forth in the choking heat to dump more shells into the tubs. Every worker dripped with sweat, coughed whenever the wind changed, and was red-eyed with the acrid fumes, all for a subsistence wage.

Item by item, we assembled the ingredients in Kunhikoya's recipe for building a stitched vessel: six augers; soft iron chisels for wood-cutting; a hank of flax rope, purpose unknown; four large crowbars; two sledge hammers; an old-fashioned beam balance scale; several large boxes of assorted tools. The only items I was utterly unable to find were the tails of six stingray fish.

'What do you want those for?' I asked Kunhikoya.

'For making the holes in the planks when they are drilled for stitching.'

'But what do you actually do with the rays' tails?'

'We use them for making the holes smooth so they do not cut the rope.'

I realized what he meant. The Laccadive islanders were so isolated that they used the rough tails of rayfish instead of wood rasps. Relieved, I explained to Kunhikoya that I could get metal files to do the same job.

Kunhikoya's final triumph, and his ultimate disaster, came when we went back to Beypore to purchase the masts and spars for the ship. Now we were looking for a very special timber which the Indians call *poon*. Like a tremendous spearshaft, a mature *poon* tree sometimes rises 50 feet before it puts out a single branch. For centuries seamen have known that *poon* makes superb masts and spars. Indeed the Royal Navy used to send agents to India to purchase what the Royal Navy called 'poonspars' for its sailing vessels. The *poon* grows, not in stands like *aini*, but usually as an isolated tree difficult of access. Today such trees are chopped up to go to plywood factories, but at Beypore logs are still floated down river and held in the shallows for the occasional Indian sailing craft that may require them. Along the river bank lie rafts of *poon* logs, half submerged like soggy crocodiles in the backwaters. The water itself is putrid, foul with slime and rotting vegetation and the sewage of the upriver settlements. On a hot day the smell is gagging, and hangs like a miasma over the backwaters, but the stench did not deter Kunhikoya. He was at his most cheeky that morning, skipping from log to log like a squirrel, followed by the foreman of the timber yard, clutching the skirt of his loincloth to prevent it being soiled in the disgusting water. Kunhikoya was brandishing a little hatchet, and whenever he came to a possible log he chopped out a small piece from the timber so as to inspect the inner surface. The foreman's assistant carried the measuring tape because the spars would be sold by length, and fortunately I remembered my last experience and asked to inspect the tape. Sure enough, the first 3 feet of the tape was missing, so I would have been buying a non-existent yard of timber every time. The foreman was quite unabashed: the end of the tape had rotted away in the damp conditions, he explained. But I also noted that he had another cunning technique. As we stood on a floating log to inspect a flaw, the foreman would spin the log under his bare feet so I had to dance about like an acrobat to avoid falling into the foul soup of the river, and was distracted from looking too closely at the quality of the logs.

By lunchtime we had found the spars we were looking for, marked them with Kunhikoya's hatchet, and bought them. All we lacked was a log for the main mast. The rest of that day we hunted, nosing around the sawmills and the holding yards until finally, on the beach itself late that night, we came across the perfect log, 65 feet long and tapering to exactly the right dimensions: it would scarcely need to be trimmed to make the main mast of my ship. Jubilantly Kunhikoya ran up and down the log, banging it with his hatchet to produce solid thumps that showed the timber was perfect. It was so late in the evening that even the timber sellers had gone home. So Ali and I crouched by the butt end of the log while Kunhikoya struck matches so we could copy down the reference mark which the timber merchant cuts into every important log he owns. Just as we were making our notes there was a terrific commotion, and a mob of angry Indians came charging up the beach at us. There were shouts of rage and menacing gestures, and some were waving sticks threateningly. I wondered what on earth we had done wrong, what local custom had we offended? It was a very ugly scene. The mob swept up to us. Screaming and yelling they pounced on Kunhikoya, ignoring Ali and myself. Then the mob dragged Kunhikoya away, haranguing him and threatening him with violence.

To my surprise Ali was shaking with laughter. 'What's he done wrong? What's the matter?' I asked. 'Will he be all right?'

Ali grinned in pleasure. 'Oh, he will be all right,' he replied. 'Someone has recognized Kunhikoya. Those men are relatives of his wife. He married her in Calicut, and then ran away. He hasn't been seen since. Now the wife's brothers and cousins are taking him back to his wife. He will have to go before the judge – he will have to pay dearly for all the time he has been away.'

First Hoodaid from Sur, and now Kunhikoya from Agatti Island, I thought to myself. I seemed to have a knack in bringing back the runaway husbands of Calicut. Perhaps the abandoned wives should employ me to return other truants. Quite how prophetic those thoughts were, I was to find out a year later. On that occasion I was to provide not truants but a fine crop of new husbands for the apparently insatiable ladies of the seaport.

The most delicate phase of my work on the Malabar coast was the hiring of carpenters and rope workers to come across to Sur to help build the sewn ship. The Sur shipowners had told me that they frequently employed Indian carpenters because their workmanship was excellent. Also there was the matter of hard economics. It was going to be far cheaper for me to employ Indian carpenters than Omani shipwrights, and my visit to Sur had shown quite clearly that I could neither find nor afford enough Omani shipwrights to build the vessel in the six months that I had allowed myself. The best carpenters in Sur were already working on other jobs, and there were only a very few of them. Not for a decade had any oceangoing ship been built in Sur; nowadays when a Suri shipmaster wanted to build a new vessel he usually ordered it directly from Beypore. Among the seething masses in the Beypore shipyards I had already noticed the white *dishdashas* and head-dresses of Omanis and Bahrainis, watching over their motor dhows being built by Indian labour. By taking my carpenters across to Sur I intended to go one step farther back in the chain, to the days when Omanis, Zanzibaris and Indians had all worked together on the trading vessels being built on Sur's beaches.

Hiring shipwrights to come to Oman from Beypore was easy enough – there were several good men available – but the real challenge was to find ropeworkers who could sew the ship together with coir. Abdul Kader Baramy had been right in saying that such men could not be found on the Malabar coast. I had tried an experiment: I announced that I was looking for men skilled in sewing boats. Of course I received scores of eager applicants, all of whom promised me that they knew the work and were eager to go across to Oman. I gave them a practical test on the beach, and asked them to try to stitch together some sample planks. The results were catastrophic. Not one of the applicants knew what he was doing. They fumbled the strings, their knots slipped, and they made cat's cradles of the rope. The performance greatly amused one little wizened man, squatting on the sand nearby, puffing away at a cigarette. I asked him to have a try. Taking the most deft of the charlatans to help him, the stranger promptly put in half a dozen good, tight stitches. Where did he come from? I asked. From Chetlat Island in the Laccadives, he replied. He was only visiting the mainland for a few days. Would he like to come to Oman to help sew together a big ship? He shook his head vehemently. He would never leave his island to go to a foreign land. Coming across to India was bad enough. People always cheated and exploited the islanders. They would find jobs and be promised their pay, but when the job was over they were dismissed without receiving any money. With nowhere to stay and no influence, they could only go back to their islands. Even now he was waiting for a boat to go back home.

This deep-rooted distrust of strangers was endemic to the inhabitants of the Laccadives, yet they were vital to me. Effectively they were the only men left in the world who still retained the ancient art of sewing boats of oceangoing size. Even in the Laccadives this skill had almost vanished. I heard of only two sewn boats under construction in all the Laccadives, and I was told that no work had been done on one of them for the last four years. Time, materials and interest had petered out, and that particular boat would probably never be finished. Hoping against hope, I sent Ali on a recruiting trip to the islands. He came back with a list of some twenty ropeworkers, experienced sewn boat-builders, who had promised him that they would come to the mainland to talk with me. But only ten of the men actually showed up in Calicut, and of these ten it was clear that two of them were only interested in the excursion to the mainland. I was beginning to feel a little like an eighteenth-century recruiting officer, with Ali as my sergeant trying to coax men to join the colours of the regiment. Laboriously I held meeting after meeting with the islanders to try to explain to them my project. The concept of going to a foreign country was so new to them that it took several hours of discussion to persuade them that they would not be enslaved. I offered them a small sum of cash in advance as an inducement, and promised them that they would be housed, fed, their health looked after, and their tickets paid for; in return they would sew together a ship that was larger than any boat they knew. I coaxed and waited, and coaxed again. Without these simple, wary men it would be impossible to build a true replica. Looking at them, I wondered if I was not being over-optimistic. One man was so elderly that I didn't know whether he would survive the journey; another had only one eye; and there was a gentle little simpleton with a perpetual happy smile on his face who obviously did not have all his wits about him. Finally it was Kunhikoya who tipped the balance. He promised that his brother, Abdullakoya, who was as chirpy and opportunist as he was, would lead the group to Oman to help me. But first they would have to return to the islands, gather together their tools, obtain passports, say goodbye to their families and then come to join me in Oman. Worried that they would get lost in the chaos of Bombay Airport, I arranged for all the volunteers to be given bright green shirts so that they could stick together on the journey.

There remained one last hurdle. I had located the materials and the men, but I still had to find a way of sending 140 tons of timber, much of it in odd shapes and sizes and angles, to Sur. It was out of the question to use regular transport. In the old days such timber was simply shipped directly across in Arab dhows, but this trade was virtually closed, and only an occasional Indian motorized country craft crossed from Calicut. What I had to do was charter a ship with a captain who would load my cargo and chug across to Sur, and dump the timber on the beach in the manner of a thousand years ago. When I put this suggestion to the Malabar timber men, themselves rogues of the first order, they rolled up their eyes in horror. Didn't I realize that by comparison to shipowners, the timber dealers were angels of honesty? Any legitimate shipmaster was kept busy on the regular coasting trade. The only shipowner who would even contemplate my charter to Sur would have to be either the owner of a vessel on the point of sinking and looking for the insurance, or someone who was confident he could bring off a first-class swindle. The classic trick, I was warned, was that my timber would be loaded, taken a few miles up the coast and dumped overboard where it would be towed ashore by accomplices in small boats and sold without trace. The ship would then sail on to her destination, and arrive with a tale of woe, of a great storm which had threatened the vessel, and of being forced to jettison the cargo to lighten and save the ship. I made a few inquiries. The story was true. It was impossible to insure any deck cargo of timber on an Indian country craft.

I hunted up and down the coast for weeks and finally found a shipmaster of such apparent villainy that, sitting cross-legged in his office above a spice warehouse where coolies sweated over their loads, he could have passed for a villain in a comic opera. Yes, he would be able to provide a ship and carry my cargo, he said shiftily. But I would have to pay the full freight in advance. Deeply suspicious, I haggled over the price and inspected the vessel. She looked as if she could just about make the crossing without foundering. It was a horrible risk, but I had no choice. I made one stipulation in the charter contract – on board would be one crew member, selected and paid by me. The condition was accepted and, trusting only Minicoy men, I put aboard a young man from Ali's island. The timber, resin, fifty thousand coconut husks, fish oil, bags of lime, and all the other paraphernalia were loaded. I was presented with a final bill, which to my amusement actually included in black and white one item listed as the bribe for the local leader of the dockers' union. Then, with my Minicoy guard aboard, the charter vessel wallowed off towards Sur.

From *The Arabian Nights' Entertainments*,
trans. Edward William Lane, 1877

—3—
The Greenshirts

I next saw the precious cargo of timber and materials in mid-December when the unkempt, ugly little Indian country craft, painted a bilious light green and optimistically named the *Mahomed Ali*, sidled into the bay off Sur and dropped anchor. A police patrol craft took me out to her, and I clambered on to the filthy, cluttered deck. The ship reeked of knavery. The furtive expressions on the faces of her crew warned me that something was wrong, and I caught sight of my Minicoy islander lurking in the background, obviously wanting to talk to me privately. The hangdog crew told me that the third son of the ship's owner was on board. Although it was his first voyage, he was in charge because there was no captain, only a first officer who had managed the ship. It was clear to me that everyone was trying to duck out of any responsibility. Someone went below to roust out the shipowner's son. He groped up a companionway ladder and emerged on deck, rubbing the sleep from his eyes. He was an unprepossessing specimen, about twenty-five years old, with a fawning manner and over-fed – already he had a soft paunch hanging over the belt band of his flared trousers, and his flowered shirt was bursting at the buttons over his plump body. He had a sickly smile on his face as he wobbled along the deck towards me on an incongruous pair of shoes with platform soles. The voyage had been terrible, he whined. He had feared for his life; the ship had almost foundered; the charter had not been worth the time and trouble; he would need more money because the charter had taken so long; they had received no co-operation from the dockers when loading the timber; and so forth. The wretched creature was looking so shifty that by now I was certain that he was leading up to his main stratagem. In a burst of bad breath, he told me: because of the trouble with the dockers, the ship had been unable to load all the timber. Some of the wood had been left behind.

The news shook me. Looking around the deck, I noticed it was half empty. Why hadn't he loaded more deck cargo? I asked. The young man shrugged. He did not know, he replied, he was a merchant not a sea captain. His moist brown eyes examined me carefully for my reaction. Now I realized what he was up to. Part of the cargo had been deliberately left behind so that I would be forced to re-charter the vessel and send her back for a second, equally lucrative, run. I was furious. Turning to the police inspector with me, I explained the situation.

'He's trying to cheat the government,' I concluded.

'That's easy, then,' the inspector replied briskly. 'We'll place the boat under arrest. Tell him he's not to move without permission. You can hold the passports of the crew, and let me know when you think they should be allowed to proceed.'

So for the next three weeks the *Mahomed Ali* lay at anchor, idle. The Minicoy islander who was my agent on board slipped ashore and in floods of tears told me the story. Apparently the *Mahomed Ali* had not even attempted to load all the timber. The crew had deliberately stacked the timber in the ship's hold so as to waste space, then they had refused to load a complete deck cargo. The Minicoy man had protested, but had been unable to make them change their minds. On the way over to Sur the crew had threatened to kill him if he told the truth. One night the deck cargo had shifted mysteriously as he slept, and he had been badly bruised by falling logs. He begged not to be sent back aboard the ship. Anything, he pleaded, rather than have to return aboard the *Mahomed Ali*. He was sure that on the way back to India the crew would tip him overboard in revenge for the information he was giving me.

I sent the Minicoy islander back home by plane, and avenged his bruises by keeping the *Mahomed Ali* at anchor even after her cargo of timber had been unloaded. Once, pleading a dangerous wind, she tried to sneak off down the coast. But a helicopter of the Royal Oman Police soon found her hiding up a creek and hovered menacingly over her, and the *Mahomed Ali* returned meekly enough to Sur. Only then did I return the passports, and *Mahomed Ali*'s revolting green hull dwindled over the horizon as ship and crew sought another swindle.

Shortly before Christmas my shipwrights and ropeworkers arrived by air. They looked very smart in the new bright green uniform shirts that I had issued them in India, and their first job was to tidy up the house which had been rented for me by the Ministry of National

Heritage and Culture and which would be our home for the next eight months.

By any standards it was a mansion. It had been built some two hundred years ago by a wealthy Suri merchant family around a large open courtyard to a traditional Omani design. The courtyard was carpeted with crushed coral which crunched pleasingly underfoot as one walked in through the iron-studded double doors which guarded the main entrance. At ground level the sides of the courtyard were pierced by a number of doors leading into a warren of rooms built in the shelter of the outer wall. Here were rooms of every shape and size, some large enough for dormitories, others small enough for a kitchen or a larder. There was a room with drainage to be used as a wash house. Other rooms were suitable for storehouses. In fact whenever I needed a room for a particular purpose the great mansion seemed to provide exactly what was needed. It was perfect, for the house might have been designed exactly for the use to which I now put it – the home of a shipbuilding team. There was a separate lodge for the foreman and senior carpenters. There was a long, low, cool room for the fifty thousand coconut husks. There was a strongroom to hold all the valuable stores, and there was one suitable corner where we set up a small forge to make ironwork for the ship. A separate staircase led up from the courtyard to a series of upper rooms arranged around two sides of the courtyard. Here, where the original owners had lived, I now installed myself. Each of four large rooms had its own small room adjacent, suitable for bathroom or kitchen; and even in the hottest month the 3-foot-thick walls kept the rooms cool, while a gentle breeze could filter in through the wooden shutters. The windows looked out across the lagoon where I could see the heads of turtles as they basked in the lukewarm water. In the middle distance sand flats sloped gently to a small knoll crowned by the remains of a battlemented fortress, and behind it I could see the line of hills which divided Sur from the baking wasteland of the Wahiba sands. On most evenings the distant hills would make a deep magenta and purple horizon against the setting sun.

In short, the house was magnificent, and it was a pleasure to be able to return it to its former glory as a living, thriving establishment. The greenshirts laboured for ten days to recover the house. When they arrived, its condition was lamentable: goats browsed in the rooms, dirt and filth were everywhere; even a cow was tethered in the corner of the yard. The greenshirts swept and cleaned. Five truckloads of new crushed coral were brought up from the beach and spread in the courtyard; Dharamsey sent three dozen iron bed frames, and several of the rooms became dormitories. Upstairs I put down rugs and cushions in traditional style, for it seemed an insult to the elegance of the building to do otherwise. Three-quarters of a ton of whitewash was painted on the walls, inside and out. The great double entrance doors were scraped and oiled. By the end of our efforts the great house was transformed. To celebrate the occasion, I gave the greenshirts a party. Under a velvet sky in the cool of the evening, the figures of the men moved like fireflies as they distributed the hurricane lamps which hung around the walls of the courtyard. A single bright shaft of light streamed out from the door of the cookhouse where the two Indian cooks, hired locally, were preparing a chicken curry, and the light emphasized the fine curves of the arches and niches of the courtyard. The only sound was the muted conversation of the men, and the soft scuff of their feet moving over the crushed coral. It was a scene of great contentment.

The great house had another advantage: it was exactly the right distance from the spot where I proposed to build the ship. That is, it was close enough for the men to walk to work, but too far away for them to sneak back to their dormitories unobserved during the day. For I was becoming canny in the ways of my labour force. The place I had picked to build this new ship was no more than a slightly raised mound on the foreshore. It was one of three possible building sites that I had noted as I walked along the beach, and I was not surprised to be told that each of the three sites was exactly where the Suri shipbuilders had built their largest ships in the old days. The particular site I chose had only one major disadvantage: it flooded during the high spring tides. In the old days this had not mattered – the original shipwrights would simply have waited until the tides eased, and then gone back to their work. But I could not afford even a day's lost work. I was racing against time to have the ship ready by Oman's tenth National Day in mid-November, and I calculated that to give an uninterrupted workflow I would need a low gravel platform about a metre high in order to raise the ship above high tide level.

The building of that platform was an example of the speed and efficiency with which matters could be arranged in Oman when the need arose. On the first day I went to Muscat to visit the relevant planning ministry for permission to build the platform. Twenty-four hours later permission was granted, and I called upon a large construction firm whose vehicles I had noted working in the desert near Sur. Could they help me? Yes, of course they could. Their resident manager made a sketch on the back of an envelope and estimated that 300 tons of hard-packed gravel would be needed for the platform. All he asked me to do was to mark up the site with pegs. In three days' time, he promised me, his machinery would arrive to do the job. I returned to the waterfront at Sur. There, right in the middle of my projected platform site, stood a very rickety hut knocked together from sheets of plywood and painted with a peeling slogan advertising the local fizzy soft drink. This shack belonged to a pair of Suri mechanics who repaired boat engines; in it they kept a jackdaw jumble of rusty tools, broken engine parts, half-used tins of grease, and old rags, hoarded against the time when they might be needed. I spoke to the two mechanics. As the land belonged to the Ministry, would they mind if I moved their hut a few yards away to a better site of their own choosing, so that I could build my platform? The two mechanics were entirely agreeable. It was no problem at all. They assured me that they would move the hut themselves, the very next day. I advised them to be certain to do so, for the lorries would be arriving in only three days' time. That would be no problem, they said. It would be done.

The next day came, and by evening the hut had not moved an inch. There was not the slightest trace of any activity. I found one of the mechanics, and spoke to him again. I warned that I had to begin work on the platform in two days' time because the lorry-loads of gravel were already arranged. No problem, no problem, he assured me. The hut would vanish next day.

The second day was exactly like the first. The hut stayed.

The third day, the day of action, I found the mechanics by their hut, relaxing in the sunshine, smoking and chatting. I told them that the trucks of gravel would come that same morning, and that their hut still sat in the middle of the square marked out by my pegs. They shrugged amiably. Clearly they did not believe anything could happen so quickly. I went back to the house for breakfast, and returned an hour later to find two very shaken mechanics. Looming over their hut was an immense earth-moving machine, so vast that the driver, his mead muffled in a scarf and goggles like a spaceman, seemed no larger than a child's toy doll. The throb of the immense machine's engines seemed to shake the flimsy hut, and over everything lay a cloud of fine dust from a 15-ton pile of gravel which the giant had just dumped. The two mechanics were hysterical. Stop the machines, they begged.

Our hut will be buried. We will move it this morning. Please call a crane to help us. I told them there was no crane available, and anyhow it was too late. Along the road leading to the site I could see plumes of dust as more giant earth-movers came bearing down on us, each loaded with its tons of gravel. I offered to move the hut for the mechanics. Yes, anything, anything, they replied; and the older of the two mechanics threw his turban on the ground, and began beating on his head with his hands.

I signalled to my twenty greenshirts, who were watching the whole performance with broad grins on their faces. Gleefully they ran towards the hut and poured inside. Like ants rescuing eggs from a broken antheap, the greenshirts reappeared clutching various rusty mechanical bits and pieces which they carried off out of danger. One more trip, and the hut was empty. Back came the greenshirts with sledge hammers. Bang, bang, bang, and the corrugated iron roof flew off, and was carried away. Thump, thump, thump, and the plywood walls of the hut literally fell outward like the sides of a house of playing cards. Five greenshirts per side picked up a wall, and the various sections of the hut went scurrying off like multi-legged insects. The four corner posts were uprooted, and twenty minutes later the hut had disappeared.

The convoy of giant lorries kept rolling inexorably in, dumping their loads into the pegged square with shattering roars, and growling off back to the desert. A bulldozer clanked down off its transporter and began spreading and compacting the gravel. On all sides there was dust and noise and bedlam. Four hours later the bulldozer pushed the final bladeful of gravel into place, and directed by a greenshirt it crawled off to be shackled up to the great keel piece of the ship. Backing cautiously up on to the platform, the bulldozer pulled the keel piece behind it, manoeuvred it into position, and went off. The whole operation of building a worksite had taken three and a half days from start to finish, and I had earned a nickname on the waterfront. From that time onward, longshoremen referred to me as Mr Alyom, 'Mr Today'. The local joke was that it was pointless to ask me when I wanted a job done. The answer was always the same – 'today'. The two displaced mechanics were delighted. The greenshirts had re-erected their hut for them; now it stood on its own miniature platform of gravel, above high tide level and 300 yards away from the spot where it had been just eight hours earlier. The work platform was built on New Year's Day 1980, and was the best New Year's present I could have wished for.

As soon as the 52-foot-long keel piece had been raised on wooden blocks buried into the gravel, Hoodaid, the senior Omani shipwright, asked if he and his colleagues could sacrifice a goat to bring good luck to the new ship. I had heard that in some Arab communities it is believed that if a barren woman jumps over the keel of a new ship she will bear children. But shipwrights say that this puts an evil spell on the vessel, and try to keep women away. I never knew what Hoodaid and his men felt about this belief, but I did notice that a guard was posted overnight on the keel. Next morning a goat, purchased from the Beduin, was sacrificed, and its blood was daubed on the keel; the meat provided a feast for the Omani shipwrights. Then I called together Hoodaid and the two senior Indian shipwrights to discuss Colin Mudie's lines plans of the ship. Normally, of course, neither Hoodaid nor the greenshirts would have used any drawings for building a ship; they worked only from their experience and by eye. But Hoodaid had never built a sailing *boom* before, only *booms* whose hulls were adapted for being driven by engines. Colin Mudie's drawings, on the other hand, were based on data which had been laboriously culled from the historical texts and from my observations of sewn craft on the shores of the Arabian Sea.

While we were poring over the technical drawings, I discovered that one of the greenshirts not only understood Colin's drawings, but could translate them into the practical necessities of sewing a ship together. This was a tremendous bonus and, not surprisingly, the man was a Minicoy islander. He was called Mohamed Ismail, and it was quite by luck that he was in Sur at all. Ali Manikfan, my Man in a Million interpreter, had originally recommended Mohamed's father, Ismail, to be my foreman, because the family were renowned in Minicoy as shipbuilders. But when Ismail turned up, bringing his son with him, it turned out that it was the son who had inherited the family talent. Mohamed was a born craftsman. He was only in his late thirties, yet he was already so sure and so perceptive in his judgements that the other greenshirts looked to him as their natural leader. For example, Mohamed's eye immediately detected a very slight curve in the keel piece, a curve so slight that I myself could not see it. But Mohamed was a perfectionist. He told four greenshirts to dig a large hole under the defect, buried a boulder in the hole, and then, using the boulder as a strong point, wrapped a heavy rope around the keel and tightened the rope with a handbar, until it had pulled the keel down flat so that he was satisfied.

Hoodaid too accepted Mohamed's skill at the very first technical discussion. They talked about how to fit the massive bow and stern pieces to the keel, and with a few quick sketches drawn in the sand were soon in complete agreement. A complicated mortise joint was cut by the greenshirt carpenters, the 36-foot-long stem piece was fixed in place, and at that point I had my first inkling of just how good Mohamed was at his craft. The baulk of timber I had selected for the stern post was missing – it was one of the lengths of timber deliberately left behind in India by the rogues of the *Mahomed Ali.* Mohamed Ismail was unruffled. He carefully searched through the timber pile, measured several pieces of timber, and told me that he could put together a substitute stern post by joining together two other baulks of wood. He had already calculated how to replace these two baulks in their allotted places. As for the rest of the missing timber, Mahomed Ismail worked out how it could be replaced by planks and beams short enough to fit inside large containers; and the indefatigable Dharamsey Nensey arranged a complicated delivery from India by way of his friends in Bombay and Dubai.

In the next few days I also began to appreciate just how delicate and painstaking would be the task of forming the hull. The ship had to be constructed like an eggshell; that is, we would have to put the planks in place and form the complex curves of the hull before we were able to fit the inside supporting ribs. The reason for this apparently roundabout technique was simple – we could not stitch the planks on the inside if there were ribs in the way. The necessity of assembling the planks before the ribs made for an infinitely painstaking task: it meant that we could not bend the planks into shape against the strength of the ribs, but had to pre-shape every plank before we put it into position. Thus the twist and curve of each plank had somehow to be formed into the wood before it was offered up and stitched into place. It was a method of shipbuilding that had been common in Europe three centuries ago, but had largely been abandoned because it was so difficult, delicate and time-consuming. Now we were preparing to build a large merchant ship in this fashion.

The difficulty of the task made itself clear with the very first plank which we attempted to fit. The plank was only 12 feet long, merely the centre section of the garboard strake, the first plank next to the keel. But this piece of timber was 3 inches thick, and it took us four days to twist, bend and chisel it into exactly the right curve. Next we had to smooth down the edge of the keel itself, shaving it off millimetre

by millimetre to make a perfect fit. Then we carefully gouged out a
line of stitch holes with a hand auger, and temporarily held the plank
in place against the keel with wooden dowels. Finally Mohamed pronounced himself satisfied. The first plank was ready to be sewn. Like
the master mason of a medieval cathedral who chiselled his name on
the keystone, Mohamed leaned over the plank, and with his pencil
wrote in the hour, day and year on which the first plank of the new
ship was put in place. It was three o'clock on the afternoon of 4
February 1980.

As if on cue, a strange sight now appeared across the sand flats
leading to the house. A dozen of the ropeworkers, walking in single
file, were carrying on their shoulders what seemed like a long python.
It turned out to be a 52-foot-long thin sausage made of coconut husks,
pounded out, placed end to end, and then wrapped around with string
to make a sort of wadding about the thickness of a firehose. This
'python' they placed into the angle between the keel and the first plank,
on the inside of the hull. Then they stretched thick coir string up and
down the length of the python, covering it entirely. The operation was
very precise – there had to be exactly the right number of strings, and
at the correct tension. When Kasmikoya, the senior ropeworker, was
ready, he divided his men into pairs, an inside man and an outside
man. Each pair worked at passing a strand of the finest-quality coir
cord out through a hole in the plank, back through the opposite hole
in the keel, round the python, and out again. There the outside man
took a turn of the cord around his lever of stout wood, put his feet
against the hull, leaned back and hauled the string as tight as he could.
On the inside, his partner tapped on the string to help it tighten, and
pounded on the python with a mallet to compress the coconut fibres.
The string grew tighter and tighter; the python was gradually squeezed
smaller and smaller until it could compress no more. The stitch was
temporarily locked with a light wooden peg, and then the whole
process began all over again with the next pair of holes. Up and down
moved the teams of men to a steady rhythm of hauling, pounding and
tapping. Three times, stitch and overstitch, they lashed together plank,
keel and python until finally the last stitches were plugged with little
tufts of raw coconut fibre. It took them the best part of a day, but by
the time they had finished the 'python' was as hard and stiff as a shaft
of wood, and the first plank was firmly held in place. The Sur shipwrights gathered round and stroked the stitching with approval.
'*Tamam, mazboot*,' they murmured in admiration. 'Good, correct.'

The ropeworkers were a strange group. They kept themselves very much apart from the other greenshirts, perhaps because they were timid or perhaps because they came from a single island and preferred to stick together. In India these islanders had a reputation for being lethargic, and it was true that most of them moved with an almost sloth-like deliberation. Yet their apparent lack of speed was deceptive. I noticed that they were merely pacing themselves to the work of the carpenters. When a plank was ready to be stitched, the ropeworkers were ready too, with their python, the correct length of string, and pegs. And when the ropeworkers tapped home the last plug of coconut husk on that plank, it would be at just the moment when the carpenters had finished preparing the next plank for them. Abdullakoya, Kunikoya's brother and virtually his twin in appearance, was the driving force behind the ropeworkers. A ferocious grumbler and complainer, he was always haranguing the others in a buzzsaw voice that could be heard clear across the courtyard of the great house, but scarcely made a dent on the lethargy of his workmates. More than half the ropemakers were men in their fifties and sixties, which was very old indeed by the standards of their island, where life expectancy was less than fifty years. Sur must have seemed very strange to them, with its invasion of modern amenities, such as cars and television sets. I discovered that even the younger Agatti men had no notion of how a telephone worked. When the telephone at the house went wrong, I asked Man in a Million who was the best coconut tree climber in the workforce, and he pointed out a muscular young ropeworker from Agatti. Together we walked across the sands, following the telegraph poles until I spotted the fault: it was a broken wire. But the Agatti man had never joined two wires together before in his life, so I gave him a demonstration of how to do it. He then strolled up to the telegraph pole and produced a small loop of coconut rope which he placed around his feet. Placing one hand behind the pole, and the other in front, he pressed his feet against it and went straight up the vertical, smooth telegraph pole as if he was strolling down the street. At the top of the pole he clung there, apparently in complete comfort, while he made the joint.

'That's impressive,' I remarked to Ali.

He sniffed depreciatingly. 'He should not have needed the rope around his feet. He is out of practice. Any islander can do what he is doing.'

The carpentry for the ship was as remarkable as the stitching. The

Arab shipwrights, led by Hoodaid, were responsible for preparing the main frames of the vessel. They sat in the shade of a canvas awning, chopping razor-sharp adzes against the 6-inch-thick baulks of timber which had been marked out for the frames. As always they worked entirely by eye, in a happy, carefree manner. It was a complete contrast to the greenshirts. Inside the shed of palm thatch which we had erected to give shade around the hull, the greenshirt carpenters worked with a frenzy that it was difficult to imagine possible in the blazing heat. Their tools were hammer and chisel. Whether cutting a foot-thick lump of timber to size, or shaping the finest sliver of wood for a delicate joint, 90 per cent of the greenshirts' work was done with hammer and chisel; only very reluctantly did they pick up a saw or a plane. The soft iron chisel was their tool, and with it they could work wonders. They could carve a plank into delicate curves, or they could shape the 60-foot spar into a taper as if it had been turned on a giant lathe. They were craftsmen whose original caste in India had been carpenters. Their fathers, grandfathers and great-grandfathers, and untold generations before that, had been carpenters. There had never been any question as children but that they would also become carpenters; and they had begun work as soon as they were big enough to pick up a mallet. Now, as grown men, they performed like well-oiled machines. It was as if Mohamed could point them at a piece of work, switch them on, and leave them to run until they were told to stop or the job was finished. No piece of work seemed to bore them, however repetitive, or to deter them, however difficult. Much of the time they scarcely seemed to look at the job in hand, even to glance at the tip of the chisel before it sliced into the wood. They could turn their heads to chat to a friend or gaze around at the rest of the boat shed, while the unwatched hammer rose and fell with steady accuracy, never missing the chisel handle, while nervously I watched and waited for the mis-aimed blow which would crush a finger. It never happened.

The accuracy expected of the carpenters was extraordinary. Because the hull was being stitched together, it could not be caulked: that is, it would not be possible to stuff filling material into any small cracks between the planks before the ship was launched, as is the normal practice when building large wooden ships. The action of hammering in a filling material would merely stretch the stitching and force the planks wider apart. So the hull of the new ship had to be made a perfect shell before it was ever put into the water. This meant placing planks edge to edge, without even a hairline crack, along a length of as much as 80 feet. It was an achievement which some European engineers who came to visit the worksite considered virtually impossible, and which would have been prohibitively expensive in a European boatyard because it required the most minute attention to detail. To achieve the required accuracy, each plank was fitted into place at least three times before it was finally stitched. Before each fitting the carpenter would smear blue powder on one plank edge, push the two planks together, and then pull them apart to inspect where the blue powder had transferred from one face of wood to the other, showing up the slightest imperfection. Only when the two faces matched perfectly would Mohamed permit the final phase: a thin coating of melted tree gum was painted on both faces of the wood, and a single strip of light muslin patted down on to the tacky resin so that it would be sandwiched between the planks when they were pressed together ready for stitching. As a last check, Mohamed would then take the protruding edge of the muslin strip, and give it a sharp tug. If the muslin slipped, he would order the job to be done again. A visiting engineer calculated that this work demanded an accuracy of better than $1/_{64}$ inch along the full length of the plank.

The penalty for this exquisite care was paid in the number of hours required to build the ship. Stitching a vessel together was perhaps two or three times slower than conventional shipbuilding using nails. Baramy's best shipwright in India had guessed that it would take eighteen months to sew together a vessel, and after the first, slow plank had been fitted at Sur, the local critics estimated that it would be two or three years before we would launch our ship. But no one had taken into account the sheer hard work of the greenshirts. They tackled the job like marathon runners who intended to sprint all the way. They began at six o'clock in the morning with a vigour and enthusiasm that seemed undiminished twelve hours later as they began to approach the end of the working day. Sometimes, unasked, they would work through till nine o'clock at night to complete a particular job. And they never filtered away, one by one, in the evening. If one man had not finished a task, all the other eleven stayed on to help him, and they went home in the darkness in a gang. In the sapping heat of Sur, the carpenters' shirts were wringing wet. Half an hour after beginning work most of them were so sodden with sweat that it looked as if they had been swimming. I insisted that they took salt tablets, but even so one or two men fainted from sheer exhaustion. They worked, literally, until they dropped.

Amazingly, they thrived: the men put on weight. Like machines which needed their fuel, they ate hugely. They got through two breakfasts, a huge lunch and a large supper every day. Twice a day each man consumed a heaped plate of rice measuring 18 inches across. If they did not have their masses of food, their pace of work slowed down. Ten hours a day, six days a week, they worked. Yet the atmosphere inside the boat shed was exhilarating. On a good day the carpenters actually ran from one job to the next; they laughed and joked, and their good humour was infectious. The noise they made was an index of their enthusiasm. The tap-tapping of the ropeworkers' mallets mingled with the sharper blows of the carpenters' hammers on their chisels to produce an unrelenting sound which could be heard a mile away across the sands. It was an urgent, irregular, pattering noise, a sound I had heard in the shipyards of Beypore where perhaps two dozen wooden ships were being built by three or four hundred men. Now at Sur the same sound was much more urgent and far louder, and it was just one single ship under construction by thirty men.

Each carpenter quickly established his own character and nickname, for their proper names were an impossible jumble of syllables in Malayalam, the tongue-twisting language of the Malabar coast. There was Big Foot, the largest carpenter, a big powerful man from the Beypore shipyards who inevitably teamed up with the smallest carpenter whom I instantly named Mighty Mite. He had the smallest body, the largest turban and the biggest grin of all the carpenters; and as he capered across the planks, dancing to amuse his friends, he reminded me of Rumpelstiltskin. Then there was the serious, quiet carpenter I thought of as the Yorkshireman. He always took a considered, deliberate look at his work before he began, seldom talked, and never put down his tools until the job was not only done, but done well. Even the youngest carpenter, who came as an apprentice, was a fully fledged craftsman by the time the hull was complete.

Our usual day began at five o'clock with the first glimmer of light and the dawn call to prayer from the little mosque beside the great house. In my room on the balcony I could hear the cocks crowing, and the scraping sounds of the town goats scavenging beneath my windows. The goats ate up the rubbish and kept the alleyways clear. The next sound was the rhythmic pumping of the cooks brewing up the kerosene stoves for first breakfast, and as I washed I could hear the low throb of engines as two motorized *sambuks* passed down channel on their way to the fishing grounds. The banging of a tin tray announced that first breakfast was ready to be served, a bowl of rice and lentils to each man. Then at 6 a.m. I would step out on to the balcony and blow a couple of blasts on a whistle for assembly. The greenshirts loved it: they would sally out of their dormitories, shrugging themselves into their green workshirts, gathering up their hand tools, calling out to hurry up the inevitable laggards. As befitted his rank, Mohamed the foreman would march out of his dormitory one minute later than the rest, and stroll with due deliberation across the courtyard to meet me at the foot of the stairs and discuss the day's work programme. Then I would ask if anyone was sick, though my total medical repertoire extended only to aspirin or a laxative. Anything more serious required a trip to the town dispensary later.

Now Mohamed would call out the day's work schedule and select the men he needed; then the greenshirts would set off, ducking out through the little postern door in the great double gate like the dwarves of Snow White, especially if they were led by Mighty Mite. They worked until 9.30 in the morning, when the two cooks appeared, walking across the sand towards the boat shed balancing cooking pots on their heads. The pots contained stacks of golden brown pancakes, three or four to a man, and yet more rice or beans. Second breakfast took half an hour, and then the work went forward until the lunchtime curry taken back at the house, followed by a short siesta to avoid the worst heat of the day. The enthusiastic banging of an iron rod on a 40-gallon oil drum awoke the afternoon sleepers at 2 o'clock, and work at the site continued until 5 o'clock when the men were free to stop. But very often they preferred to stay until six or seven in the evening before walking back to the house, dog tired, to wash and then sit cross-legged on the mats spread in the courtyard while they took a second massive dose of curry. By half past eight in the evening they were fast asleep. On Fridays the men would wash their clothes, write letters home, or go fishing in the shallows. They sought little entertainment. They were in Oman to earn hard cash for their families in India, and they carefully hoarded their pay against the day when they would return home.

The greenshirts had now been reinforced by a third batch of recruits. All the men in this third group were from Minicoy, the same island as Mohamed and Man in a Million. These were the jacks-of-all-trades: they could do a little carpentry or even a little ropework if asked to, but they were not nearly as skilled at either job as the professionals who had worked all their lives at these specialities. The Minicoy men were essentially seamen who were working on land, so they rigged the blocks and tackles to swing the heavy baulks of timber into position, repaired the work shed, built the staging alongside the ship, and so forth. Like most sailors they could turn their hands to almost any job, including operating the only machine tools we used in building the ship – the hand drills which bored out the stitch holes in the planks, and the routers that cut the grooves into which the stitches were recessed. The Minicoy sailors also operated the terrifying Indian-made bandsaw which was used to shape the rough outlines of the ribs. This bandsaw was a monstrous contraption, a perpetual menace to the men, its great spoked wheels spinning crazily, and its blade merely soldered together over a charcoal fire. I feared that one day the blade would come flying off and sever a limb. But, like the misplaced hammer blow of the carpenter, it never happened.

February was the worst month. A cruel wind blew out of the Wahiba sands, cut through the gap in the hills behind Sur, and swept across the building site. The thatched shed creaked and groaned in the gusts. Dust flew up into the men's eyes as they squinted at their work. A small fire started when embers were blown into the thatch: a hastily assembled chain of greenshirts threw buckets of water to quench the flames before they took hold, but it was a warning of just how easily the project might collapse. The worst effect of the wind was the damage it did to the planks of the ship. To produce the right curves we softened the timbers in a home-made steam box. After three or four hours of steaming we would knock open the box, seize the plank in hands wrapped in sacking, and rush it to a cradle in the ground. There the Minicoy men would clamp the plank between the jaws of levers shaped like great tuning forks, and crank on windlasses arranged to twist the plank into shape. The planks popped and creaked under the strain, and if a hand was placed on the pressure points you could actually feel the heat escaping from the tortured wood. But when the desert wind was blowing it dried the planks so fast that a number of them split with a rending crack that meant a whole morning's work lost. Alternatively we would bend the plank into shape, go off to lunch, and return to find that the devil wind had arisen, the humidity had dropped, and the plank had bent away from the shape we wanted. In these difficult days the men began to break out in boils, perhaps because their sweat dried so fast on their skins or possibly because their diet was wrong.

With memories of Captain Cook's remedies, I ordered them to eat fresh limes every day.

By now I had been joined by Bruce Foster, a professional photographer from New Zealand. His first responsibility was to photograph every step in the building of the ship. It was probably the last big sewn ship ever to be made, and I wanted to keep a complete record of the unique process. I had met Bruce when I was on a lecture tour in New Zealand, and he had volunteered to assist with the project. Whenever I had to leave Sur on a trip to Muscat Bruce would take over as my deputy and supervise the greenshirts. An inveterate traveller, Bruce had twice visited India, and he and I were both very used to our greenshirts. We knew that they were exceptional workers, but they could not resist a chance to test our gullibility.

It was a lesson which an old friend of mine, Trondur Patursson, had yet to learn. Trondur came to Sur to replace Bruce when he went on holiday to New Zealand. By profession an artist, Trondur lived in the Faeroe Islands, and he had been a member of the crew of *Brendan*.

'Good. It's good,' he said approvingly as he clambered up on the bow piece of the ship for the first time, and gazed its length, looking like some Norse sea god with his bushy beard and curly hair. 'You see, Tim, that shape is same shape as the whale, blue whale, when it swims under the sea.'

Trondur's wife Borgne was with him, as well as little Brandur, their two-year-old son. Together the family settled into the big house, at first a strange sight with their pale northern skins but soon acquiring a deep Oman tan. Very sensibly they took to wearing Omani dress to keep cool. The Suri women in the adjacent houses gave Borgne baggy pantaloons and an overshirt, and little Brandur scuttled about in a tiny *dishdasha* and turban, from under which protruded the bright red, sun-scorched tips of his ears. Trondur fell in love with the colours and shapes of the desert behind Sur, and on weekends he would depart, taking his sketch pad with him, to draw and paint the weird shapes of the sand dunes at dawn and dusk when the low rays of the sun turned the dunes purple and ochre in strange, contorted shadows.

I left him to supervise the boatbuilding at Sur while I made a trip to London, and within a couple of days the more wily of the greenshirts began to probe Trondur's defences. The greenshirts found that he was a gentle, reasonable man: he did not complain when they began leaving work early, and he accepted their excuses about lack of tools and materials. They even persuaded him that they should observe Indian national holidays, of which there were many, as well as the national holidays of Oman. With alarming speed the pace of work faltered: progress on the boat slowed to a crawl and dropped behind schedule. But the greenshirt ringleaders had not taken Borgne into account. She watched and waited until the situation was intolerable, then she exploded. Like an irate Viking virago she shouted at the Agatti men; she berated the cooks who had begun cheating her on the daily ration money; and she castigated Mohamed for not keeping the men up to the mark. All this Trondur told me with a slow, wondering grin, when I returned.

'Borgne, very very angry,' he confessed. 'Work now much better.'

So the sides of the hull grew upward and we began to get visitors. Sayyid Faisal came to look at progress. His Ministry were ideal sponsors: they left us alone to get on with the job, and Dharamsey Nensey supplied everything I asked for. Once a month Dharamsey sent down a supply lorry loaded with our basic provisions – sacks of rice and beans, bags of cardamom, sticky packets of coriander, and tins of coconut oil for cooking. He also sent an Indian clerk who sat cross-legged on the ground in the middle of the courtyard while the green-shirts lined up for pay, and the cash figures were neatly entered in red ink in a great ledger propped on a cushion.

Word had spread that a large sailing ship was taking shape on the beach at Sur, and dignitaries of the province began to arrive. In their cloaks and silver daggers, they were magnificent figures, escorted by ceremonial askaris carrying rifles and with dramatic-looking bandoliers criss-crossed over their chests, brass cartridges gleaming. The august visitors would clamber up on the staging, peer down into the bowels of the ship, and shake their heads approvingly.

'*Tamam. Wayid gawi* – very strong. *Mazboot* – correct,' they would announce approvingly, and pat the rock-hard coconut stitching. The new ship was gaining a reputation and the beginnings of their affection.

Among the visitors was a gaunt-faced, spritely old man of at least seventy. He walked with a very bad limp, but this did not stop him from clambering up the scaffolding, which was now 12 feet high, and prodding at the plank joints with his camel stick. Hoodaid, the head shipwright, told me that he was Saleh Khamees, a retired sea captain, perhaps the best in Sur, and that no one could tell me more about the old trading days. So I tracked down Saleh Khamees in his house in the middle of Sur and passed a delightful afternoon with him. He was the Omani equivalent of an old sea dog, as full of yarns and vigour and

Above On a Portuguese atlas of 1519 AD a squadron of three Arab vessels (centre picture) can be identified by their straight prows as *booms*, an Arab ship type which must have existed before the first European ships arrived in the region. *Below* The x-shaped marks on the hull of the stylized vessel shown in the *Maqamat of al-Hariri*, an Arab manuscript of 1237 AD, indicates that this was a sewn ship

'So I went to the Sultanate of Oman, a country on the south-eastern corner of the Arabian peninsula whose existence since earliest times has been intertwined with the sea.' *Top* On Oman's Batinah coast fishermen still use the *shasha*, one of the oldest boats known to man, made of a bundle of palm fronds tied together. *Above right* From a Batinah fishing community came four of the expedition's Omani crew members. Three others were from Sur, the country's most famous shipbuilding centre.

Above A Suri fisherman smears a traditional antifouling of lime and mutton fat on the hull of his boat

Left Saleh Khamees, retired sea captain of Sur, talks to Tim Severin about a lifetime's experience of sailing the Arabian Sea

Left 'My companions and I found the timber we were looking for in the hills behind Cochin. There, fine stands of *aini* were being felled for logs by Indian timber merchants.' 140 tons of *aini*, a wood very similar to teak, were cut for the replica ship.

Lower left Her masts and spars were selected from logs floating in the backwaters of the shipbuilding port of Beypore on the Malabar coast. Timber, coconut rope, 50,000 coconut husks, fish oil and tree gum were then shipped to Sur in Oman (*below*), where, on 4 February 1980, the first plank was sewn onto the 52-foot keel, cut from a single massive log.

Right A team of carpenters, affectionately known as the Greenshirts, built the 90-foot ship in just 165 days. 'The greenshirt carpenters worked with a frenzy that was difficult to imagine in the blazing heat. . . . The soft iron chisel was their tool, and with it they could work wonders. They could carve a plank into delicate curves, or shape the 60-foot spar into a taper as if it had been turned on a giant lathe'

A dozen specialist ropeworkers from Agatti Island in the Laccadives archipelago stitched the ship together with coconut cord in the traditional Arab manner.

Right First they pounded the coconut husks with wooden mallets to dislodge the loose dust, then made up sausage-like 'pythons' of wadding to lay behind the joints of the ship's planks. *Above* 'When Kasmikoya, the senior ropeworker, was ready, he divided his men into pairs, an inside man and an outside man. Each pair worked at passing a strand of the finest-quality coir cord out through a hole in the plank, back through the opposite hole in the keel, round the python and out again. There the outside man took a turn of the cord around his lever of stout wood, put his feet against the hull, leaned back, and hauled the string as tight as he could. On the inside, his partner tapped on the string to help it tighten. . . . Three times, stitch and overstitch, they lashed together plank, keel and python until finally the last stitches were plugged with little tufts of raw coconut fibre'

400 miles of coconut rope sewed the planks and ribs of the ship together, and the final task was to treat the ship with oil. *Above* 'The Agatti men climbed back inside the hull. Tins of vegetable oil were lowered down to them and, using mops and brushes, they swabbed oil on the stitching of the pythons. . . . The ropeworkers told me how important it was to keep the rope oiled if the ship were to survive. If the rope was treated with oil once every four or six months, they would guarantee that the ship would last sixty years, or even a century.'

Over Launch ceremony for the ship, named *Sohar* at the Sultan's request in honour of Oman's ancient port and reputed home of Sindbad the Sailor

Below and lower centre Tribesmen and women from the coastal villages and the interior joined with the people of Sur in celebrating the birth of the new ship with an exuberant display of singing, dancing and drumming. 'The noise was stupendous. The air thundered with the endless throbbing of drums, the high rasp of pipes, and the clap-clapping of the participants. The rhythmes were African, and most of the skin tones were black. Everywhere there were smiles and excitement. It was total jubilation.'

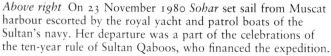

Above right On 23 November 1980 *Sohar* set sail from Muscat harbour escorted by the royal yacht and patrol boats of the Sultan's navy. Her departure was a part of the celebrations of the ten-year rule of Sultan Qaboos, who financed the expedition.

Far right 'A specially ornate copy of the Koran was handed to Khamees Navy with instructions that he was to carry it to the Moslems of China.' Tim Severin and crew member Lieutenant Khamees al Araimi, Sultan of Oman's navy, embark to join *Sohar* after the farewell ceremony at the start of the seven-and-a-half month voyage.

Over: Sohar

Left Sohar's mainsail, more than 2000 square
feet in area and bearing the crest of the
Sultanate, dwarfs Tom Vosmer, the ship's
American crew member. Each of the blocks was
hand-carved from a solid piece of timber, and
the traditional Arab rig of the ship weighed
more than four tons.

Above right Jumah, the veteran dhow sailor.
'He carried himself with a quiet dignity that was
very noticeable, and gave the impression of a
self-sufficient man who had seen much, and had
come to terms with all he had seen. . . . Jumah
was a treasure house of information about the
traditional ways of an Arab sailing ship.'

Centre right Abdullah – *Sohar*'s best helmsman.

Below Khamees Police. 'Over the next eight
months his fizzing enthusiasm never slackened.
From the very first day of sailing trials when we
tried out the ship, Khamees Police was always
leading the headlong rush down the deck,
leaping along like a jack-in-the-box with
whoops of delight, and hurling himself on a
loose rope or wrestling a flapping sail into
submission'

Left Peter Dobbs. 'Six feet three inches tall, Peter had recently served with the Parachute Regiment in the British Army, and had been trained in all sorts of exotic techniques of warfare. He came back from his visit to the armoury of the Sultan's land forces shaking his head in wonder. "They said I could borrow anything I wanted . . . pistols, rifles, machine guns, grenade launchers, anything." ' Warned of the risk of pirates in the South China Sea and Malacca Strait, *Sohar* carried automatic rifles and gas grenades, and the crew held regular arms drill.

Below Front row, left to right: Peter Dobbs, Musalam, Khamees Police, Ibrahim, Jumail, Abdullah (seated on deck), Saleh, Jumah, Tim Severin. Back row, left to right: Eid, Andrew Price, Tom Vosmer, Dick Dalley, Peter Hunnam, Khamees Navy, Nick Hollis, Tim Readman

gusto as a man half his age. He told me how he had taken command of his first ship, when he was only twelve years old, on the return passage from India when his father, the owner of the vessel, had died at sea. The twelve-year-old boy had brought the ship home, and for the next forty years had sailed regularly two or three times a year across to India. Saleh Khamees waved his arms excitedly, and his eyes gleamed as he spoke of storms and shipwrecks, of men rescued from the water, of record passages, and how eventually his own son, who took over his ship when Saleh was too old, ran her aground on the south Oman coast. She was a total loss. No other ship was built to replace her, because the trade was dead. But Saleh had kept his old charts and sextant as souvenirs, and he delved among the boxes and bundles in his room, and showed them to me proudly.

One story he told was of particular interest. Outward bound from Sur, he said, his ship had been caught in a fierce storm off Ras al Hadd. The sea had become so rough and the waves were running so high that his ship was in danger of foundering, so he had lightened her. He and his crew flung all the cargo overboard to make the vessel ride higher. But hadn't he been worried that the ship would capsize? I asked him. No, he replied, he kept 6000 kg of dates low in the bilges to hold her upright. I made a note. By simple arithmetic it told me roughly how much ballast I should put in the new ship.

Saleh Khamees also told me why the great houses of the waterfront, including my own house, were abandoned and empty. It was a result of a great catastrophe a generation earlier, he said. Almost the entire African fleet of Sur was returning home, fully laden, from Zanzibar when a storm had overtaken them just as they neared the coast of Oman. The captains had run for safety near the Kuria Muria Islands, and cast their anchors. But the storm was so fierce that the cables had snapped, and the entire fleet was driven ashore and wrecked. The loss of life had been horrendous. It was said that from the largest ship, a *ganja* that was the pride of Sur, more than two hundred souls had been drowned. Men, women and children, entire families, had been wiped out. Their fortunes smashed with their ships, the shipowning community of Sur had never recovered, and several families were ruined beyond hope of survival.

The Paturssons could only stay in Sur a couple of months, and I needed to find a new deputy. While I was in London a letter arrived, asking for a copy of the technical drawings for *Brendan*, from a modelmaker who was planning to make an exact scale model of the leather boat. His request was so detailed and professional that I invited him to meet me so that I could answer his question. He turned out to be an American, Tom Vosmer, a teddy bear-like figure with a bushy beard and a quiet manner which concealed a very staunch spirit. Tom was working his way around the world doing all manner of different jobs, and as I talked with him about the ship models he had built or repaired for clients, the thought occurred to me that here was just the man to help out with the new ship. There was no one alive who had any actual experience of building a medieval Arab ship. Yet here was someone who had built, in miniature, all manner of early vessels from eighteenth-century gunbrigs to Roman galleys. When I asked him if he would like to help make not a model, but a full-size replica, of a medieval *boom* Tom's eyes sparkled with delight behind his glasses. He jumped at the chance. Give him three weeks to clear up his affairs in London, he said, and he would be on his way to Oman.

Tom and his girlfriend, Wendy, duly arrived, and like the Paturssons had to withstand the probing of the greenshirts. One day a telegram arrived for one of the Agatti men. A few minutes later one of the Malabar carpenters came over to Tom to ask him what the English word 'deceased' meant.

'Dead. It means dead,' replied Tom automatically. Then, after a pause, he asked, 'Why do you want to know?'

'Because Kasmikoya has received a cable from home to say that a member of his family is "deceased".'

Tom, very distressed, went to look for Kasmikoya and found him apparently almost fainting from emotion, and surrounded by other islanders with doleful faces. He was shown the fateful telegram. It read, 'Come home. Daughter Jameela deceased.' Sympathetically, Tom brought Kasmikoya back to the house and arranged for the cook to give him cups of tea. Then he came hurrying up to see me.

'Kasmikoya's daughter has died,' he said despondently. 'He's just received a telegram. The men are most upset. I have given him the afternoon off.'

My suspicions were aroused. I knew my greenshirts, and looked at the calendar. Yes, we had just had pay day, and the conditions were favourable for a touch of chicanery. Kasmikoya had contracted to work on the ship until it was launched. If he was hoodwinking us into leaving early, then the other ropeworkers would follow suit and the ship would never be built.

'Here's the telegram,' said Tom, handing me the message.

I read it. The telegram had indeed been dispatched from Agatti. I sent for Kasmikoya to come and see me and he shuffled in, looking distinctly nervous.

'Kasmikoya,' I began, trying to sound as neutral as possible. 'I'm very sorry indeed to hear that you have received this telegram reporting the death of your daughter Jameela. Who you think sent it?'

'My cousin. It will have come from my cousin.'

'Do you want to go home?'

'Yes, I must go to look after my family. My wife is deceased also, and there is no one to look after my other children.'

'But this telegram may be a trick, from someone who wishes you to be sad. Before you leave, I will make inquiries to make sure of the details. It would be better to know exactly what has happened.'

Kasmikoya looked down at his feet.

'I will send a telegram to Agatti,' I went on. 'I will address the telegram to the Responsible Officer in Charge of Island Affairs, asking for details of your daughter's decease.'

Kasmikoya left the room. Half an hour later there was a timid knock at the door. It was a different Agatti man. 'Kasmikoya does not want you to send the telegram,' he said sheepishly. 'He will wait to help finish the boat.'

Next morning Kasmikoya did not even look a trifle ashamed, but was as merry as if he had never heard of the telegram. The other greenshirts, however, were gleeful. They enjoyed a battle of wits, and winked and sniggered as Kasmikoya appeared on morning parade. Tom, meanwhile, learnt never again to take anything on face value from the greenshirts.

By now it was May, and the heat was ferocious. The shade temperature rose to 118 degrees. By ten in the morning the glare reflected from the sand hurt one's eyes. All normal activity on the waterfront ceased. The dogs crept into the shade, and shared this minor refuge with the goats who already lay there, panting. But work on the ship did not slacken. Across the waves of heat, shimmering over the sand, continued the ceaseless clatter of hammers and mallets as the work progressed and the flanks of the ship crept steadily upward. It was impossible to work through the noonday heat; instead we got up in the dark, worked till noon, and then lay prostrate with heat on our cots until three in the afternoon. Then it was back to the ship as the air began to cool, and work went forward into the evening. At night the greenshirts slept on mattresses spread in the courtyard.

We now had another expert to help us, a genial giant of a shipwright, Robert Marten, who lived not far from my home in County Cork in Ireland. Robert was the one man the greenshirts never tried to dupe. He was too canny for them, and they knew it – he admitted with a wry grin that the greenshirts were only beginners in the art of hood-winking compared to some Irish shipwrights. But there was another reason why it was impossible for the greenshirts to pull the wool over Robert's eyes – he had the knack of being able to recognize the handiwork of each individual carpenter. To Robert's practised eye, each carpenter left a personal signature on every bit of work he did, so that Robert could walk around the ship at any time of the day and tell me exactly how much work each man was doing.

The last of the ribs of the ship were now being fitted. The ribs, too, were stitched into place so that they could flex and slide against the skin of the vessel. A great crossbeam was placed across the ship to take the weight of the mast; the deck was laid on its beams, and the Agatti men, finished with all the stitching, spent a week stuffing coconut fibre plugs into the stitch holes in the planking, a tedious but essential task. I estimated that we had drilled more than 20,000 holes in the planking, and if these holes were not pegged properly the ship would leak like a huge sieve. On the outside of the hull the holes were blocked up with a sticky putty made of molten tree gum mixed with pounded seashells, and rolled out on a board to the consistency of pastry. Finally the Agatti men climbed back inside the hull. Tins of vegetable oil were lowered down to them, and using mops and brushes they swabbed oil on to the stitching of the pythons. The coconut fibre soaked up the oil. The ropeworkers told me how important it was to keep the rope oiled if the ship were to survive. If the rope was treated with oil once every four or six months, they said, they would guarantee the ship to last sixty years, or even a century. I did not doubt them. I had seen the planks of a sixty-year-old sewn ship and inspected its stitching: between the planks the original coconut rope was as good as new.

In the final week before launch we applied a coat of anti-fouling to the outside of the hull to protect it from being attacked and eaten by shipworms. The anti-fouling was strictly traditional, a coating of lime mixed with mutton fat and smeared on by hand. We boiled up lumps of fat which we purchased in the *suq*, stirred in the lime powder and set to work. Time was so short that I telephoned the local training camp of the Sultan's navy. Could they send some extra help? Yes, of course. They had a class of trainee officers, and would send them along to do the job. Forty young Omanis, dressed in shorts and singlets, duly arrived in a couple of army trucks. To the shouted commands of their petty officers they set to work smearing on the evil-smelling sticky mutton fat: when it dried it gave the underside of the ship a smart white finish. Above the waterline the vegetable oil brought out the rich, dark brown tones of the *aini* wood. The Minicoy men began to dismantle the shed. As they pulled away the rolls of palm matting, the new ship emerged like a butterfly breaking out from its chrysalis. The vessel seemed immense, towering over the sand, a monument to the skill of the men who had built her, 140 tons of raw timber turned into a single, elegant artefact, every joint and stitch dedicated towards her sole function of harmonizing with the sea.

We strapped a cradle under the hull, knocked away the keel blocks, and shackled up a tractor to tow our creation to the water's edge. Under the skids of the cradle we laid the last of our timber from India, greased with mutton fat. The tractor's engines revved up, and took up the slack. With a loud twang, the steel towrope snapped. We tried again, and again the tow parted. We tried again and again, with heavier cable, with levers from astern, and with telegraph poles tucked under each side of the ship and fifteen greenshirts dangling from them like monkeys, in an attempt to unstick the hull. But the ship would not budge – she was immovable. There was consternation all round. We were due to launch the vessel the following morning, and the Ministry had arranged for an official ceremony. I felt like a pyramid builder who finds that he cannot shift the pinnacle stone into position. A helpful engineer appeared from the desert construction site with a theodolite. He took his measurements, and told us the bad news. The ship was poised at an angle on the platform. We were trying to drag her uphill.

There was only one choice – we had to cut away the gravel platform and remove enough earth to make a downhill slope for the vessel. It was a herculean task: everyone, including the cooks, laboured throughout the entire night with crowbars and shovels. We shifted ton upon ton of earth. We rigged up lights, and worked non-stop for eighteen hours. Inch by inch we dragged the ship forward. The greenshirts reached such a pitch of exhaustion that they slept where they dropped on the piles of gravel, only to be awakened after an hour's rest to return to the labour. By the time the sun rose we were all dazed with exhaustion, but we had hauled the ship on to the sand flats of low tide. She sat there waiting for her ceremony, and behind her the gravel work platform which had given her birth looked as if it had been churned up by the tracks of heavy battle tanks.

'Well, where's the party then? Where is everyone?' asked Robert, looking round the beach. There was not a soul in sight. The place was deserted. 'Haven't they been told that there's a launching ceremony today?'

Just then we heard a faint, strange sound. It was the distant braying of conch shells mixed with the throb of drums. The strange noise grew louder, and we could distinguish the rhythmic chant of singers and the clapping of hands. But it was odd. Where was the sound coming from? Not from the sand dunes behind us – there was still no one in sight. The noise seemed to be coming from the sea. Then we saw it. Racing up the estuary was a handsome fishing *sambuk*, going at full speed with throttles wide open. From the tip of her mast streamed a huge flag, and her sides were decorated with poles which carried gaily coloured bunting fluttering in the wind. The deck was jammed with men – at least fifty of them. They were all standing facing the shore, dancing, stamping and clapping to the rhythm of a group of drummers and pipers on the poop. It was a stirring sight. They were men from the coastal villages who had come to greet the birth of a new ship, and they roared out traditional songs to salute the new vessel as their boat swept past, circled and closed in to the land. Then the dancers leaped into the waist-deep water. Never stopping their music for a moment, the band was carried shoulder-high to the shallows, thumping away on their drums and the lead piper wailing away on his instrument. On the sand the coast men began a surging, whirling, stamping dance, all flying gowns and flinging arms, while the band's instruments pounded and brayed in a torrent of sound.

More music was heard. Emerging from the houses of Sur came three columns of men. At the head of each column were dancers and singers and a cluster of banners and standards, so that the columns looked like the battalions of a medieval army. A forest of camel sticks waved to the rhythm of the songs, and from time to time groups of men broke away to perform dances to the swing of their battle swords. The columns flowed around the ship, and soon the hull was lapped in a sea of chanting, singing and dancing men. The noise was stupendous. The air thundered with the endless throbbing of drums, the high rasp of pipes, and the clap-clapping of the participants. The rhythms were African, and most of the skin tones were black. Everywhere there were smiles and excitement. The atmosphere was one of total jubilation.

Some men pranced up and down waving portraits of Sultan Qaboos; others formed dancing snakes, one man behind the other, and went stamping and chanting through the crowds. Even the women joined in, resplendent in black silk robes blazing with silver filigree. Massive gold ornaments hung around their necks and from their ears, and chains of gold were looped across their cheeks, attached between earlobe and nostril. Bangles clashed at their ankles as they danced and turned and let out wild ululations which rose to an unearthly high pitch. I had never seen a launch party like it.

The rising tide finally brought an end to the celebrations by driving everyone off the beach, and we were left to the serious business of getting the ship afloat. At first I thought it would be easy enough: the ship floated momentarily on the peak of the tide and moved a few feet forward. But then the cradle struck a sand bank, the ship slewed slightly, and she stuck fast. The tide ebbed away and our vessel, as reluctant as ever to join her natural element, hung forlornly on the beach. For a second night we laboured. The tides were dropping, and we had just one day to dig a channel for her. The next day we were ready, with two anchors laid out into the stream to haul her off, a squad of navy men ready to pull from an anchored boat, and the greenshirts standing chest-deep in the water to give the cradle a push. The Minicoy men, who could swim like fish, were diving down to check for obstructions round the skids of the cradle.

At last the tide rose to its peak. Standing on the deck of the new ship I gave a signal to the navy men and they began to haul. The greenshirts roared out their work chant, and gave a tremendous heave. Looking astern, I saw the shore sway: the ship was moving. Gently and sweetly she eased out into the water. She was afloat. As she moved into the channel I heard whoops of triumph and there in the shallows were the greenshirts, capering and hallooing. They were ecstatic. Big Foot flung himself in a somersault through the air, to land with a huge splash; and Mighty Mite, who was aboard the ship but could not swim, threw himself over the rail in an incredible bellyflop of happiness, to be rescued and towed ashore by a grinning Minicoy man. We hauled the ship out to a mooring buoy in midstream, cleared away the cradle, and there was a wonderful moment as Mohamed and I stood at the top of the companionway, each inviting the other to be the first to go down below deck and inspect the hull. Together we checked the bilge. A trickle of water was coming in, a trickle that would stop as soon as the wood soaked and swelled.

'Congratulations, Mohamed,' I said. 'You've done a wonderful job. She's superb.'

He swelled with pleasure, and climbed back up the companionway to leave me alone in the empty hull. The whole sensation of the ship had changed. Now she eased and shifted gently in the flow of the current. I could hear the chuckle and gurgle of the tide running past the skin of the ship. I put my hand on the planking which had taken so much time and care from so many craftsmen. I could feel the whole ship quivering with the tug of the tide. My vessel was alive. To build her had taken, not three years, nor sixteen months as had been prophesied, but just 165 days.

From *The Arabian Nights' Entertainments,*
trans. Edward William Lane, 1877

—4—
Sailors of Oman

By command of the Sultan the ship had a name – *Sohar*. It was to honour the ancient trading port of Sohar on the Batinah coast, once the most prosperous city in Oman and the terminus for ships embarking or returning from voyages to the farthest Orient. A team of French archaeologists was even then excavating the great fortress of Sohar that had once commanded the roadstead where the foreign-going ships lay at anchor. Among the fort's foundations the archaeologists were finding buried fragments of medieval Chinese porcelain which must have been carried all the way from China, probably in Omani ships. Now, by an extraordinary coincidence, I was about to set out in the opposite direction to trace the same age-old trade route and with a similar ship. But this time I would be taking sailors from modern Oman.

I calculated that *Sohar* needed a crew of about twenty men. Eight of them, forming the core of the team, would be Omani sailors who would handle the vessel in traditional style. They would have to be prime seamen, accustomed to shiphandling, because they would have to teach the rest of the crew how to sail the vessel using the very special rig of an Arab *boom*. Throughout the voyage the main work of *Sohar*, the handling of the sails, the adjustment of the rigging and the general maintenance of the ship, would fall on the shoulders of the Omani sailors. To record the Omanis in their work, and to back them up, would be other volunteers, mostly Europeans, who had specific technical skills. Bruce Foster would take still photographs; Tom Vosmer would operate the ship's little amateur radio; and a cameraman and sound recordist would make a film of the voyage. We would also need a purser, a diver, and of course a ship's cook.

My first Omani volunteer was from the marine division of the Royal Oman Police. He was a corporal, very smart in his dove-grey uniform, a black police beret pulled jauntily down over his black curls, and his

73

boots, badges and buttons all glistening. With an athletic salute he came crashing to attention.

'Khamees Sbait, sir!' he barked. 'I want to sail to China.' His stiff expression broke into an engaging grin as he almost bounced up and down in the aftershock of his terrific salute.

Khamees, which means 'Thursday' in Arabic, had the physique of a welterweight boxing champion and such gusto for life that he almost quivered with enthusiasm. He was from Sur, he told me in halting English, and had been keenly following the building of the ship. As soon as the call had gone out for volunteer crew members he had dashed round to see his commanding officer for permission to join up. Why did he want to come on the Sindbad Voyage? I asked him. To see the world, he replied with another instant grin. Wasn't he worried or frightened about such a long voyage? Oh no, he said. He had no family except for a widowed mother. She would receive his police pay which would continue while he was at sea; and anything his forefathers had done, he too was ready to tackle. All would turn out well. It was a beautiful ship, and the voyage would be excellent. If, I thought to myself, I found such boundless enthusiasm in anyone else, my ship would almost propel itself.

Khamees Police, as his nickname became, was to live up to his first impression: over the next eight months his fizzing enthusiasm never slackened. From the very first day of sailing trials when we tried out the ship, Khamees Police always led the headlong rush down the deck, leaping along like a jack-in-the-box with whoops of delight, and hurling himself upon a loose rope or wrestling a flapping sail into submission. Never once did his good humour evaporate, and his disposition was so sunny that he cheered up the entire ship's company.

Young Eid, the other arrival from the Marine Police, was much quieter. At twenty-two he was the youngest of the volunteers. Also from Sur, his jet-black skin and African features were proof of the close links between Sur and the coast of Zanzibar. Indeed at first glance one would have thought him pure African, and I immediately recognized the relationship between him and the gentle master shipwright I had seen building a *sambuk* at Al Aija during my very first visit to Oman. Yes, he told me as we struggled to understand one another in broken Arabic, for he did not speak a word of English, the master shipwright was his cousin. Eid had been born in Al Aija. His family were boatbuilders and fishermen, and he himself had recently joined the Marine Police as a civilian trainee. Eid had an appealing naivety.

He was at a point in his life when he simply craved to leave the confines of his little town, to travel, to see how other people lived, to find his own destiny. He was completely unaware of what the Sindbad Voyage might involve, and he could not have had the least idea of what countries or seas lay on the road to China, or even how long the voyage might take. But it did not matter. To young Eid the Sindbad Voyage represented a chance for an adventure.

By contrast the stocky, terrier-like figure in dazzling white naval uniform who clambered up *Sohar's* side as the ship lay moored in Muscat Bay for fitting-out seemed a little over-qualified to be a candidate for an ordinary seaman's berth aboard the replica of a ninth-century Arab sailing ship. The spotless uniform told me that he was a junior officer in the Sultan's navy, and I wondered if he realized that his officer's rank could have no meaning aboard my ship. I need not have worried. Khamees Navy turned out to be the most highly motivated Omani member of the ship's crew: he volunteered to sail aboard *Sohar* because he wanted to do something for his country. He felt that if the Sindbad Voyage succeeded, it would bring credit to the flag of the Sultanate, and so he wanted to be involved at whatever cost. In the months to come this straightforward patriotism was to buoy up Khamees. One had to admire his sense of duty and his unflinching willingness, and I was to come to realize that among the other Omanis Khamees was something of a loner. He was set apart by reason of his family background, his education and his tastes. Khamees came from one of those Omani families who had been wealthy or well-connected enough to send their sons abroad to receive an education which was not available in Oman under the rule of the previous Sultan, so Khamees had been sent to Kuwait. There he had been to school, learned to speak good English, and was ready to return to Oman for officer's training when Sultan Qaboos took over the throne and decided to modernize his country.

Khamees Navy came from Bedu stock. That is, many of his tribe were semi-nomadic, not settled people of the towns or coast. His tribe, the Araimi, lived in the hinterland behind Sur in the eastern province of Oman, in a wild, bleak land of barren brown hills and scarps with occasional villages clustered round waterholes or in the wadis. Some of the Al Araimi were businessmen and traders, but the more traditional members of the tribe still moved with the seasons. In winter they filtered down to the coast where they scattered along the shore to fish during the season of the north-east monsoon. The slant of the coast gave them shelter from the winds, and they harvested a sea rich in shark, tuna, giant horse mackerel, and garopa. They lived on the coast until the wind swung round to the south-west, and began to blow great cresting breakers clear across from East Africa to crash in a welter of foam on the beaches of Oman, and shut the coast to all traffic. Then, as they had done from time out of mind, the Al Araimi Bedu would gather up their goat flocks and drive them into the interior, and reoccupy their houses near the date gardens until the fishing season came round again. Their part of the coast was notorious for the corsairs it had spawned until well into the nineteenth century. It was a true pirate coast, and Khamees Navy's ancestors would once have made their living by preying on passing ships, attacking them with fast, sleek pirate craft and seizing their cargoes. It was not hard to imagine Khamees Navy in a pirate's turban and loincloth aboard a marauding *bedan*, ready to snap up a passing merchant ship. His face was pure Arab, but not the gaunt, hawk-faced desert variety. Khamees's small, slightly hooked nose, his black eyes with their almost almond shape, his full lips on a small mouth, and his short black beard framing high cheekbones, gave him classic south Arabian features. It was a face whose profile can be found on the stone carvings of the Sabaean peoples of South Arabia, in whose lands had been located the fabled kingdom of Ophir and the realm of the great Queen of Sheba.

Musalam was the second volunteer from the Sultan's navy. A handsome, quiet man, he was a petty officer and came from the little town of Suwaiq on the Batinah coast. It was his uncle, whom I had met on my very first visit to Oman, who was the builder of *shasha* boats made from palm fronds. Musalam brought three civilians from Suwaiq who wanted to join *Sohar*'s crew. Had they any experience of the sea? I asked. Of course, he replied, they all came from fishing families and had grown up near the water. They had done a bit of fishing, and made several voyages. I thought it sounded rather vague, and asked him why these men wanted to join the Sindbad Voyage. Because they're out of work, he replied in a matter-of-fact way, and beckoned to three turbaned figures who had been hovering in the background. They came forward to be introduced, a curiously assorted trio. The strangest was a tall, languid man, almost as dark-skinned as young Eid, and with the same strongly African features. His sleepy-looking manner was accentuated by one eyelid which drooped permanently, making it look as though he was perpetually on the point of falling asleep. He wore a very grubby *dishdasha*. Paradoxically his name was Jumail, which means 'Beautiful'. The stocky, barrel-shaped man next to him was obviously a seaman, for he walked with a rolling gait and his massive, black-haired forearms looked as if they had been hauling at nets or pulling at oars all his life. He was Abdullah. The third member of the trio was the oldest. A trim, delicate-boned man, he had well-chiselled, almost aristocratic features, and was neatly and plainly dressed. What made him stand out was his manner: he carried himself with a quiet dignity that was very noticeable, and gave the impression of a self-sufficient man who had seen much, and come to terms with all he had seen. His name was Jumah, Musalam explained, and he was a professional sailor. It was an apt description. Jumah had been a blue water dhow sailor all his life. He knew no other trade, and when I asked him why he had first gone to sea he replied quite simply that there had been no other choice. He had been born to a poor family in a coastal village, and the only opportunity open to him was to work aboard ship. Without that prospect, he said, he would not even have been able to think of earning enough money to marry a wife. So he had shipped out, with no more than the hope that at the end of a successful voyage his captain would pay him a wage. There was never any contract, no official salary, no conditions of work. One simply placed one's trust in Allah, and sailed.

Jumah was a treasure, a storehouse of information about the traditional ways of the Arab sailing ship. He very rarely offered an opinion unless he was asked, but he could give sensible advice based on a wealth of experience. He could advise on how to rig and sail *Sohar*, and I was to learn that he knew exactly what to do in a crisis aboard ship, what rope to cast off, which way to turn the vessel. He had been so long at sea that he had lost track of all the voyages he had made. In his lifetime he had made half a dozen voyages to East Africa, as many to India, and countless trips up into the Arabian Gulf. He did not even know his own age, for he had been born at a time when no civil records were kept in Oman. He claimed to be between forty and fifty years old, but he must have been at least ten years older than that. Yet he was as fit and active as a man of twenty-five, and he had a quiet sense of mischief that was to show itself in practical jokes aboard ship and left a puckish gleam in Jumah's eye so that he looked like a mischievous elf. His reason for coming on the trip was perhaps the ultimate statement of his life as a sailor. All the traditional ships had disappeared, he told me. For the last fifteen years he had been ashore, living quietly at home, seeing his family grow up, talking with the neighbours, thinking of the past. Now he had heard about *Sohar*, and that we planned a voyage to far China where he had never been. There was nothing to hold him back. His family had grown up, he was satiated with life on shore, and he wanted to make one more trip, one more voyage, and return to his old lifestyle. It was the clearest expression I had ever heard of a phenomenon known as 'the call of the sea'.

The arrival of Jumah, Abdullah, Jumail and Musalam meant that *Sohar* now had four Omani crew members from the Batinah coast, and these four exactly balanced the four men from the eastern province behind Sur, because Eid and the two Khamees, Navy and Police, had been joined by Saleh. I was never quite sure exactly when Saleh first showed up. I simply noticed him on board one day during sailing trials, a rather wild-looking figure in a mauve turban and flapping *wuzar*, the kilt-like loincloth. Someone told me that Saleh had been a professional fisherman, the first mate aboard a fishing boat out of Kuwait, and that he had also served as a deck hand in the Abu Dhabi navy. But there was no doubt from the way that Saleh moved about *Sohar* that he knew how to sail. So I had found my eight Omani crew members, and they in turn would teach the rest of the crew how to sail a *boom*.

First we fitted out *Sohar* in one of the most spectacular harbours in the world, Muscat. On one side, high above her, loomed the walls of Fort Mirani, a soaring fortress originally built by the Portuguese to protect the Bay of Muscat against intruders. Now the claret-coloured standard of the Royal Guard fluttered from the flagpole in the light easterly breeze, as the fort was the barracks of the Sultan's bodyguard. Every morning on the way to work we drove past army lorries brimming with heavily armed guardsmen in berets, battledress and suede desert boots. On the Sultan's birthday the soldiers wheeled out a line of artillery guns, their brass and paintwork polished to a sparkling brilliance, and banged off a twenty-one-gun salute whose roar echoed off the hills around the bay. Aboard *Sohar* we got the full blast, holding our hands over our ears, for the guns were pointed directly at us and we could see the belch of flame from the muzzles and watch the flaming wads spit out. The object of the salute was the Sultan's Flag Palace, an extraordinary creation of pale, umbrella-topped marble columns and huge glass windows, fringed by an immaculate emerald lawn that came down to the water's edge at the back of the bay. With its fountains and enormous lanterns hanging over the arcades, the Flag Palace looked what it was – a modern version of the palaces which the great Indian princes and maharajas had commissioned as their official residences. To the left of the Palace one could just make out from *Sohar*'s deck the flags of the American and British Embassies, which occupied fine old Omani houses in Muscat town. Further to the left and completing the panorama was the crenellated bulk of Fort Jalali, the twin guardian of the bay, and then the whale back of the famous hill on whose flanks are painted the names of ships that have moored in Muscat Bay over the past two centuries. The most recent names were fresh and clear with new paint, and commemorate destroyers and troop ships and merchantmen. But other, more faded names stretch back well into the nineteenth century when, it is said, Nelson himself was in the shore party which painted his ship's name. Surrounded by such an extraordinary mixture of history and pomp, it did not seem odd to be fitting out a medieval dhow, erecting the solid 61-foot main mast with its characteristic forward rake, stringing up the coconut rope rigging, and hoisting the great spars. The silhouettes of sailors scrambling up *Sohar*'s rigging, or inching their way out along the mainyard, looked utterly natural against the backdrop of the fortress bay.

It was romantic to the eye, but the nose gave quite a different impression. *Sohar* stank. The smell was not noticeable when approaching the ship in a small boat or even when standing on the deck, unless one was near the open hatches when an occasional whiff came up from below. But the moment one climbed down inside the hull of the ship, the stink was frightful. It was the smell of rotten eggs, the classic stench of a schoolboy's stink bomb, and even without scientific analysis to confirm it I recognized the smell of hydrogen sulphide gas. The smell itself did not worry me: it was objectionable, but one could live with it. The problem was that the gas which made the smell also attacked metal objects. A silver bracelet left below decks, for example, would start to tarnish in a matter of an hour or so. A day later the bracelet would be black. I shuddered to imagine what would happen to the metal circuitry of a radio set that would have to stay below decks for half a year. Even with the hatches open, the gas was noticeable, and if we left the hatches covered overnight a great blast of rank gas welled up when the hatch covers were rolled back in the morning.

The smell came from the bilges. When one pulled up a floorboard the wave of gas was enough to make one gag. Yet there seemed to be no way of curing the problem. We flushed out the bilges with fresh sea water, but it did not make any appreciable difference. Next morning the stink was as bad as before. With immense labour we changed the entire ballast of the ship, dumping overboard 15 tons of sandbags, and in the blazing sun we reloaded 15 tons of freshly washed sand in new sandbags. Even before we had finished this backbreaking chore the appalling smell was seeping back at us. I consulted water scientists for advice. They took samples and confirmed that the bilge water was giving off hydrogen sulphide. Gloomily they warned me that if the gas was too strong it could kill us, but they neither came up with a suggestion for getting rid of the smell, nor identified the source. I suspected that the gas had something to do with the interaction of sea water and the vegetable oil which had been spread on to the stitching of the ship to preserve the coconut cords. But I did not dare clean out the bilge with a powerful detergent for fear that it would dissolve away all the protective oil or, worse still, attack the stitching itself. If that happened, and the stitching was eaten away by the chemicals in the detergent, the whole ship would fall apart.

Mohammed Ismail, my head shipwright, was not worried by the smell of rotten eggs. He just shrugged, and said that the bilges of wooden trading ships always smelled like that. I tried to console myself with the fact that I had once read that wooden warships in the eighteenth century had smelled so powerfully below decks that a junior midshipman would be sent to walk the length of the lower decks carrying a silver spoon. When he reappeared on deck he gave the spoon to the captain for inspection; if the spoon had tarnished, it was judged to be time to scour the hull. It seemed to me that *Sohar* and an eighteenth-century warship had at least one feature in common – the stench. And yet I continued to worry. It was, after all, the unmistakable smell of rot, and I could imagine the vital cords which held the ship together slowly disintegrating until the day when they would fail. Then *Sohar*'s seams would burst apart like a swollen seed pod. Every day, without making it too obvious to the crew, I quietly levered up a floorboard and, holding my breath, wriggled into *Sohar*'s bilge and stabbed away at the coconut stitching with a marlin spike, trying to detect if it was growing soft and spongy.

Sohar was now the focus of frenetic activity. The two rubber dinghies which we would use as tenders on the voyage shuttled constantly back and forth carrying carpenters and stores, volunteer sailors and casual visitors. The ship rapidly began to fill up with the hundreds of items necessary for a sea voyage that would last seven or eight months. The forepeak was stuffed with bosun's stores – coil upon coil of rope of every size, from bundles of light lashing twine to 8-inch-thick spare halyards. There were dozens of extra blocks, each one lovingly carved out of a single chunk of wood and with their wooden wheels revolving on wooden pins. They were works of art, and the greenshirt ship-wrights were justifiably proud of them. There were spare sacks of lime for the day when we careened ship in a foreign port and smeared on a new coat of the traditional anti-fouling. There were tins of mutton fat, rank and nauseating, to mix with the lime or to grease the running ropes and tackles. There were marlin spikes and mallets, chests of carpenter's tools, odd lengths of spare timber, bolts of spare sailcloth, lengths of extra chain, and, remembering the experience of the leather boat *Brendan*, I took along several pieces of spare ox-hide, and the needles and thread to sew chafing patches and heavy leather straps. There were no fewer than four anchors, one of them a traditional Arab grapnel anchor with its four curved claws, which navy divers had salvaged from the bottom of Muscat Bay. Catted up against *Sohar's* bow, it looked exactly like the illustrations in medieval manuscripts.

Modern equipment was also loaded, including a small generator to charge the batteries for the radio and navigation lights. I was rather doubtful that the generator would survive the long journey, and so I made sure that we had plenty of hand torches and hurricane lamps. Then there was the ship's safety equipment; liferafts, lifejackets and flares, emergency rations, and a good supply of fire extinguishers, for I was very aware that we would be sailing in a wooden ship, soaked with oil and dried out under a tropical sun. All the safety equipment took up valuable space, but I did not consider that any expedition, however true to its ancient predecessors, should risk human life un-necessarily. If I had made a mistake in my research or in the construc-tion, if we were run down one black night in the Malacca Strait by a tanker, or capsized in a typhoon in the South China Sea, then I wanted the crew to have the very best chance of survival.

The food had to be chosen, packed and loaded. With a crew of twenty hard-working, hungry men there was not enough room to store all the provisions for the entire journey. I calculated that we would carry a basic store of rations, and supplement our supplies with pur-chases made at countries along the route. Also there was the problem of whether we should have Arab-style food for the Omani crew, or western-style food for the Europeans. As it turned out, we purchased every possible ingredient in Muscat and mixed them together as the need arose. We had boxes of nuts and dried fruit, hundreds of eggs preserved in grease and wrapped in sawdust, sacks of onions, dried peas, rice and packets of spice. For variety there was a selection of tinned foods and sauces. Our cooking would be done on deck over a simple charcoal fire burning in a tray of sand. The thought of fresh-caught fish, grilled over charcoal, was mouth-watering, but we would have to wait and see if we would have any fisherman's luck. One food item, however, I was determined to take aboard in good supply – dates. Omani dates are famous in the Arab world for their flavour and sweetness. In the days of Sindbad dates were the main item of cargo, as well as an essential source of food for the sailors: in fact, so important were dates as cargo that the Arabs calculated the capacity of their ships by the number of sacks of dates they could carry. As I watched a ton of dates being manhandled aboard *Sohar* in sacks, I thought what a satisfactory ballast they must have made in the old days. Each sack dropped on deck with a satisfying thud, and together they made a compact stack. We were particularly fortunate: the dates for *Sohar* were supplied directly by the royal victualler, my old friend Dharamsey Nensey, and the dates were the same type that went to the royal kitchens.

The list of necessities was unending. Half a ton of charcoal for the cook box; two magnificent Omani trays and a traditional Omani coffee pot for when we had to entertain visitors in foreign ports; inoculations for the crew against smallpox, cholera, typhoid and tetanus. Bruce Foster proved to be a genius at ferreting out strange but vital items from the twisting alleyways of the *suq*. And two or three times a week he would roar off to the airport in a small truck to collect vital ship's equipment which had been airfreighted to us. In another, typically generous offer of help for the project, Gulf Air, the airline jointly owned by Oman, Bahrain, Qatar and the United Arab Emirates, had offered to carry all our equipment and passengers free of charge.

'Your Sindbad Voyage is important to all the Gulf countries,' Yusif Shirawi, the airline's chairman, had said to me. 'All the Gulf countries share a sense of history of the sea, and if you succeed in your venture, it will remind us of our past. I know that this is a project sponsored by Oman, but I think that all the member countries who own the airline would approve if we offered you free travel facilities – and I mean not only for you yourself, but also for your crew and your air cargo.' Once again it was an offer which made it seem that the Arabian Nights still existed, and I was able to understand this generosity better when I learned that Yusif Shirawi's father had been a sea captain, and how the spirit of the modern, oil-rich Gulf States is still mingled with salt water. In the Klondyke world of the Arabian Gulf, with its brand-new cities bursting upward in concrete, multi-million-dollar business deals, air-conditioned limousines and the rest, there is an underlying sense of nostalgia for the traditional way of life before the oil boom. Grateful as they are for the benefits of the wealth created by oil, many of the older generation believe that something of value is being submerged in the rising tide of modernization and prosperity. Many of the most successful men in the Gulf States, the new merchant princes and dynamic ministers, come from families who for generations have flourished as shipowners and shipmasters. Their memories are inextricably bound up with the old Arab trading vessels, and they would speak with happy pleasure of their recollections of the ships and the voyages of their youth. It was a phenomenon that touched me deeply, and I wondered if aboard *Sohar* my mixed crew of Omanis and Europeans would be able to do justice to such memories.

Scientific stores began to arrive. In planning the voyage it had seemed to me that *Sohar* would make a handy observation platform for marine research. The ship would be moving slowly along a 6000-mile traverse of the ocean, often in areas far from the shipping lanes. I contacted various universities and marine research institutes. Was there any useful marine research that the ship could do? I was put in touch with several marine scientists, and we worked out a scientific programme. I would allocate three places aboard *Sohar* for scientists, and they would come and go as they wished, joining the ship at agreed landfalls so that they could come on the particular legs of the voyage that interested them.

As the scientists' crates began to heap up on the dockside, the outline of the scientific programme began to emerge. There was a huge, hollow torpedo: that must be from the marine biologist who wanted to study barnacles. He proposed to tow the torpedo behind the ship all the way to China, and see what barnacles stuck to it. I feared that the barnacles would die of old age, for the torpedo was so massive that it would slow the ship down atrociously. So I sent the big torpedo back and accepted a little torpedo in its place. Next there was a sledge, a small one luckily, with some absorbent pads that looked like baby's nappies: that had to be something to do with the pollution programme, for collecting oil floating on the sea's surface. A refrigerated packet of snakebite serum obviously belonged to the man who was hoping to collect sea snakes *en route*. There seemed to be an endless supply of plastic jars, drogues, dipnets and other scientific paraphernalia. I thought wrily of the start of Captain Cook's third voyage, when his scientific team had demanded so much space aboard ship for their equipment that it was seriously suggested that an extra deck should be built on top of the hull to provide sufficient accommodation. Knowing that it would make his vessel unwieldy and dangerous, Captain Cook had refused; and most of the scientists had left in a huff. I hoped that *Sohar*'s scientists would be more flexible.

The three scientists for the first leg of the voyage duly arrived in Muscat, and I could begin to match them to their kit. Andrew Price was the person interested in sea snakes and plankton. John Harwood from Cambridge University came only with a whale identification book and binoculars, so he had to be the man from the Sea Mammal Research Unit who would be counting whales *en route* as far as India. The owner of the torpedo would not join the ship until Sri Lanka, and he sent a note asking for *Sohar* to tow the torpedo until he got there. The third of the scientists for the first leg of the voyage was Robert Moore, as archetypal a marine scientist as ever stepped aboard a ship. He came clutching an ingenious folding box of his own design, stuffed with gleaming test tubes and flasks and mysterious jars of chemicals. He had a precise, donnish manner, solemn brown eyes behind thick spectacles, and a goatee beard. He also sported the most splendidly stick-like legs beneath his flapping shorts. Given a butterfly net, he would have been the very essence of a Victorian scientist-explorer.

'I'm afraid we can only ship aboard about half of that stuff,' I told the three scientists, gesturing at their piles of equipment. 'Your first job is to select what equipment is not essential, and leave it behind, or send it back home to your universities. Afterwards, we will find room for what is left and stow it aboard. As soon as that is done I want you to help out with the general loading and rigging of the ship.'

'But we've come as scientists . . .' began Andrew.

'Not on *Sohar*, I'm afraid,' I broke in firmly. 'Everyone is first and foremost a sailor, or the ship can't operate. I want all of you to handle ropes and rigging, and to stand watches. Sailors first, scientists second.'

Three pairs of scientific eyes regarded me dubiously.

Our sailing date was announced. It was to be 23 November, at the conclusion of the celebrations for ten years of Sultan Qaboos's rule. All Oman was in a great state of excitement, getting ready for the anniversary. Triumphal arches were erected over the roadways, while portraits of the Sultan appeared on street lamps and hoardings and hung from balconies of private houses. Squads of workmen clambered over the façades of every office block and ministerial building, stringing up lines of coloured bulbs which turned the capital into a fairyland at night. Experts arrived to prepare the great firework display. Technicians erected four enormous tableaux showing scenes of Omani life. One was a map of the Indian Ocean, and superimposed upon it was a little model of *Sohar*. Lines radiating from Muscat showed the ancient seaways of Oman, and at night little beads of coloured light ran twinkling along the line that led to China. I hoped that it was not too optimistic.

Sohar herself had to look smart for National Day, so we painted around the hull a band of red, white and green, the Omani national colours, and rigged light bulbs on the two great slanting spars so that on firework night in Muscat Bay, when Fort Jalali thundered and smoked with a tremendous firework display, *Sohar* took her place among the assembled fleet of gunboats and patrol craft, dressed overall in lights. *Sohar*'s only problem was that her tiny generator was far too small to light up all the bulbs on the spars, so the power came from an extra generator chugging away in a rubber boat tied alongside. Firework night was an ideal occasion to give the greenshirts a farewell party. In their smartest clothes they clambered on board to gaze in awe at the fireworks bursting overhead, and to consume a last, vast chicken curry topped off with slices of sticky cake under a layer of lurid icing. The next night the officers of the naval base entertained *Sohar*'s crew to dinner, and the evening culminated in some violent mess games which left a satisfactory number of bandaged heads and limping figures next morning.

Fresh fruit came aboard – a sure sign that *Sohar* was nearly ready to sail – and also our weapons, which were being provided by the Sultan's armed forces. It was ironic that pirates were once again active in the Malacca Strait and the South China Sea, just as in Sindbad's day, and so *Sohar* was equipped to give them a nasty surprise if she was attacked. She carried tear gas and side arms, and three wicked-looking Kalashnikov automatic rifles, picked out by *Sohar*'s chief diver and effectively her master-at-arms, Peter Dobbs. Six foot three inches tall, Peter had recently served with the Parachute Regiment in the British Army, and had been trained in all sorts of exotic techniques of warfare. He came back from his visit to the armoury of the Sultan's land forces shaking his head in wonder.

'They said I could borrow anything I wanted,' he told me, 'pistols, rifles, machine guns, grenade launchers, anything. I could make *Sohar* a warship if you want. We've already got enough sandbags in the bilges to build strong points all round the deck. In the end I chose the Kalashnikovs. There were plenty of them available, all captured from the rebels in Dhofar. I've brought back a Russian-made one, a Chinese-made one, and a Czech-made one. I was told not to return them. When we've finished with them, we're to dump them overboard in the ocean.'

Sohar was ready. Victualled and armed, she was poised for her great adventure. On 23 November the dignitaries began to assemble at the naval base. Two missile gunboats, two police guard boats, and the white royal yacht were there to see her off. Speeches were made by Sayyid Faisal and a Chinese envoy who had specially flown in from Peking to see us set out. We received a blessing from a religious leader, and a specially ornate copy of the Koran in a red velvet box was handed to Kahmees Navy with instructions that he was to carry it to the Moslems of China. Then an old sea captain from Sur, a rumbustious figure with a beard hennaed to a bright red-orange, declaimed a poem he had written on the prowess of Oman's ancient sailors and the prospects of the voyage. Sayyid Faisal shook hands and said goodbye to me, and the Chinese envoy said he hoped to be there to greet us in Canton. The Royal Oman Police band struck up the National Anthem and, as always, the Omanis stage-managed the departure with tremendous flourish.

On the stroke of 11 a.m. a signal gun fired with a single sharp crack that echoed round the cliffs. On the instant we broke out the special pennant for the voyage, a scarlet-forked pennant with a golden phoenix flying along its length, and over it the rubric *'Bismillah et Rahman et Rahim'* – in the name of Allah the Compassionate and All Merciful. There was a rumbling roar as the escort boats started their engines and began moving into an arrowhead formation around *Sohar*. Khamees Police slipped the cable to the mooring buoy, and a naval picket boat towed us in a wide, slow circle so that we could wave up to the dignitaries lining the balcony of the naval base headquarters. Then *Sohar* was moving out to sea. We passed between the headlands, and five minutes later dropped the tow.

'Course south-east, until we clear the land.'

'Make sail!'

The Omanis laid hold of the mainsheet, a stout 6-inch rope which led up to the sail, now lashed neatly to the main spar 50 feet above our heads. *'Ah! Yallah! Ah! Yallah!'* called Khamees Police, and they heaved down the rope. Above them, the light cords brailing the sail to the spar popped apart, as intended. First the corner, and then the whole expanse of the vast sail began to open out like a window blind. There was a satisfying rippling, popping sound as the light cords broke all along the length of the spar, and even as the great sail came down it flapped and filled with the breeze until it blossomed out into a workmanlike curve.

'*Yallah! yallah! Allah 'l-mueen!* – Go! Go! Allah will help!' chanted the crew as they hauled in the mainsheet to set the sail to best advantage, and *Sohar* was sailing. Over the radio I could hear the laconic commands of the British captain of the royal yacht which was the senior ship in our escort. Moments later we were sailing past the *Youth of Oman*, the Sultanate's own sail training ship. Her cadets in their yellow shirts dressed the cross yards and cheered *Sohar* as she glided past. From somewhere Jumah produced a conch shell, and leaping up on to the gunnel he blew long, resonant blasts in answer. Then the warships were tearing past us, full speed in line ahead. We heard yet another band playing merrily away, bagpipes this time, aboard the royal yacht. There was the sound of Verey pistols being fired, and the flares, red and white, came arching over our heads and falling so close that I put a couple of men on standby with fire extinguishers in case we collected a blazing flare on our dry wooden deck.

Then the escort turned for home, and raced back to Muscat leaving their churning white wakes in straight furrows behind them. The old motor dhow which had been chugging along beside us, at my special request carrying the greenshirts, also turned to go.

'Goodbye, goodbye, greenshirts!' I called across the widening gap. 'Thank you for building a lovely boat. Thank you.'

Looking through my binoculars I could see them. Every man had tears streaming down his face. I turned back to my crew.

'Let's get the ship tidied up, and everything in its place. We're on our way.'

The eight Omanis busied themselves coiling up ropes and making everything shipshape. They were helped by the other, more experienced, crew members: Mahomed Ismail, the head shipwright who wanted to come as far as India to see how the ship he had built performed: Trondur Patursson, who had come back for the first leg of the voyage because he could not resist the chance to sail an Arab *boom*; and Tom Vosmer, modelmaker turned shipwright and now appointed radio operator.

'I hope nothing goes wrong with the radio,' Tom muttered to me, 'I haven't any idea how to repair it.'

'Don't worry,' I replied. 'There'll be plenty of time to learn. Just don't lose the handbook.'

We would all have plenty of time to learn, I thought to myself. In the wake of Sindbad the Sailor and the early Arab navigators, we were setting out to cross the Seven Seas on the route to China known to the Arab merchant adventurers a thousand years earlier.

From *The Arabian Nights' Entertainments,*
trans. Edward William Lane, 1877

—5—
The Sea of Arabia

It is a general rule that the first few days of a venture like the Sindbad Voyage are among the most frustrating. This is the time when new ropes snap, poorly tied knots come undone or jam hopelessly tight, sails rip, fittings break off, and hours are wasted in searching for items that have been buried in the last-minute rush of packing and loading. Also the crew is at a low ebb. The surge of excitement at the departure has faded, and a reaction sets in. Men who have not yet found their sea legs lurch and slip. The unlucky few retch and vomit over the rail as the ship begins to move with the waves and swell. Surreptitiously the crew members study one another, fully aware of the months that lie ahead which will be spent cooped up together in a confined little wooden world.

Sohar's voyage began with an accident. On the second morning I was writing up the log in my cabin in the stern of the ship, when I heard the clanking sound of the little diesel generator being started in order to charge the batteries. The engine burst into life, but almost immediately there came an alarming banging, and simultaneously a series of heavy blows shook the deck above my head. Then there was a scream of pain. I dashed up the companionway and on to deck to find the generator toppled over on its side, dripping oil and fuel. A raw, jagged edge of metal showed where the front end of the generator was smashed. Peter Dobbs was collapsed on deck, his face twisted in agony as he clutched his foot. Blood was pumping up between his fingers, and there were splashes of blood everywhere. Some of the crew were standing around Peter, themselves in a state of shock. They pulled themselves together, and three men lifted Peter on to a deck box and made him comfortable. Bruce raced below for the first aid kit, and with Khamees Navy to help me I staunched the blood pouring from Peter's foot and took a look at the wound. A deep, ugly gash had cut through to the bone.

'What happened?' I asked.

'I was starting up the generator,' Peter explained, his face white with shock and pain. 'The starting handle jammed just as the motor fired, and began spinning round. Then the whole generator fell over. The handle hit the deck, snapped, and the whole front end of the generator burst open. A chunk of flying metal hit my foot.'

In effect, the damage was a shrapnel wound, a deep puncture that needed attention. *Sohar* did not have a doctor on board, and I was worried that the wound might turn septic if it was not treated properly. So I cleaned it as best I could, hoping to have got out all the metal fragments, and Bruce put on a bandage. The bleeding continued.

Over the radio I called up Neil Edwards, a radio amateur in Muscat who was organizing a group of radio amateurs in Oman to listen out for our signals.

'This is *Sohar* calling. We have had an accident on board, and a man is injured. Please could you arrange for medical assistance to be sent out.' Neil promised to do whatever was possible, and an hour later he called back to say that the Sultan's navy was sending a doctor. A patrol boat would leave Muscat in two hours' time. What was *Sohar*'s position? I gave our estimated position and calculated that with luck the patrol boat might reach us in eight hours. Meanwhile Peter was obviously in great pain, and it seemed fortunate that *Sohar* was crossing the shipping lane used by oil tankers coming and going to the Arabian Gulf through the Straits of Hormuz. At that very moment we had three large oil tankers in sight, and perhaps we could get temporary help from them.

'Tom! Get on the VHF radio and see if you can contact one of the tankers. Tell them we need a visit from a doctor if they've got one on board. Tell them we have an injured sailor.' Tom switched on his radio, and began putting out a call. There was no reply. For three hours he called, repeating the message time and time again, but there was never any reply. We checked that the radio was transmitting properly. It was working perfectly. The tankers were simply not keeping a radio watch.

That afternoon two tankers actually passed *Sohar* less than a mile away. It was a perfect day – bright sunshine, crystal-clear visibility – and our ship was easing along in a light breeze with her huge white sails set. No one could overlook us. I ordered red distress flares to be lit, hoping to attract the attention of the tanker crews. The flares hissed and sparked and set out a lurid red light which must have been visible for miles. The tankers ploughed on, ignoring us.

It was an object lesson in the helplessness of an emergency at sea under sail. We had every modern safety device on board – flares, radio, signal mirror – and we were within sight of large, modern ships. Yet without proper watch-keeping on board these ships, and without an engine on *Sohar* which we could switch on so as to manoeuvre across their course, we were helpless. We might just as well have been in the most desolate wastelands of the Antarctic.

Even the rendezvous with the navy patrol boat was a sobering experience. The patrol boat was able to travel at better than 20 knots, was equipped with radar, and manned by a crew trained in intercepting vessels at sea. Yet for over fourteen hours the navy boat had to hunt for us. *Sohar* presented a feeble radar target, and I could not give the patrol vessel an accurate position to locate us until the first stars came out that evening and I was able to take a star sight. Finally, at 10 a.m. the next day, the patrol boat found us, not by radar but by a glimpse of *Sohar*'s white sails low down on the horizon. The navy doctor was put aboard by rubber boat and examined Peter's injured foot: he pronounced the wound to be clean, and sewed up the damage. Peter wanted very much to continue on *Sohar*, so I asked the doctor if he would recommend it. There was a risk, the doctor replied, that the foot might become infected, and once we were well out into the Arabian Sea there was no way we could get further help. On the other hand, if Peter could rest the foot, keep it clean, and the gash healed properly, he would be fit in three weeks' time. I talked it over with Peter, and we decided that he should stay on board. It was a good decision. Peter, powerful, disciplined and an expert diver, was to be a key member of the crew in the difficult times that lay ahead.

The navigation of *Sohar* was an essential element in the whole Sindbad Voyage. One of the objectives of the project was to find out how the early Arab navigators had succeeded in finding their way to China. It was a stupendous achievement: they had sailed nearly a quarter of the way round the world at a time when the average European ship was having navigational problems in crossing the English Channel, and the Arabs had steered their routes, not by luck, but by careful calculation. The earliest Arab texts gave a few hints as to how they had managed this feat. They stressed that they used the stars, not the sun, to fix their position; and there were a number of vague references to charts and pilot books which seem to have been carried on board, and which had been compiled from the experience of senior navigators. But no early Arab sea charts have survived, and not until the fifteenth century did a book appear which began to lift the edges of the veil of mystery which surrounded Arab navigation. Suitably, the book was written by an Omani. He was a master navigator from Sur, by the name of Ahmed Ibn Majid, and he was one of the most renowned seafarers of his time. Fortunately his writings had been translated and painstakingly annotated by an English scholar, Gerald Tibbetts. I had taken a copy of Tibbetts's edition of Ibn Majid's book with me aboard *Sohar*, and now it became my manual in trying to test out the methods of early Arab navigation.

It was a difficult manual to follow, not least because Ibn Majid had written it in verse. Often he was more interested in poetic elegance than in giving practical advice. The book was one of a series of writings by Ibn Majid, in which he claimed to be summing up all the methods of the early Arab navigators. He certainly offered a great deal of astronomical theory, explaining how the stars moved in the heavens at different times of the year and how to identify different constellations, and so forth. But what interested me were the practical details. Just how did an early Arab navigator measure his position? How did he lay off his course? The instrument he used was no more than a wooden tablet about 3 inches wide with a hole in the middle of it; through this hole ran a piece of string with a knot in it. The navigator placed the knot between his teeth, stretched out the string until it was taut, and closing one eye held the tablet so that one edge of it touched the horizon. He then checked the height of the Pole Star against the side or the upper edge of the tablet. It seemed devastatingly simple.

I cut a sample tablet out of a piece of cardboard, pierced a central hole, rigged the knotted string, and went on deck to try out Ibn Majid's instructions. He had advised the navigator to wash his eyes with cold water before taking an observation, to adopt a firm stance, and to avoid looking upwind if possible so as not to make the eyes water. The best time to take an observation, he said, was when there was a clear horizon. The moonlit night was perfect, and after a few moments of waving the tablet unsteadily I got the knack and found I could measure the height of the Pole Star. Then I took a star sight with a modern sextant, worked out *Sohar*'s position, and made a note of the result. The following night I repeated the experiment, and saw how the position of the Pole Star had altered against the side of the cardboard tablet. I consulted my copy of Ibn Majid's manual, and compared his data with a set of modern navigation tables. The relationship was obvious, though Ibn Majid did not use degrees and minutes for his measurements, but calculated the height of the Pole Star in finger widths, which he called *isba*. By the third night I was able to judge the height of the Pole Star accurately enough to plot the ship's latitude position to within a variance of 30 miles, using only a bit of cardboard and a string with a knot in it! I was only a beginner, yet already I could have navigated *Sohar* to any selected point on the Indian coast a good 500 miles away from *Sohar*'s present position. All I needed to know was the height of the Pole Star in finger breadths at that location, sail south until I counted the same number of finger breadths aboard *Sohar*, turn east and keep the Pole Star at the same height until I made my landfall.

It is a technique now known as 'latitude sailing', but what made Ibn Majid's achievement much more impressive was that he claimed to know how to calculate his latitude not just by the Pole Star, but by a whole series of other stars which he used when the Pole Star was invisible. He produced lists of stars whose altitude, if measured at the right time, could be substituted for Pole Star altitudes. Some of these stars were easy enough – he used the stars in the Southern Cross, for example – but others had to be measured in pairs, when they were in a particular relation to one another, and in a certain lunar month. Thus Ibn Majid's knowledge of the constellations and their movement had to be encyclopedic. He also explained how to allow for variations in the height of the Pole Star, how to set a course to take account of wind drift, what signs to look out for when approaching land after an ocean passage, and so forth. He did not know how to calculate the longitude of a place, that is its east–west position, but that did not matter. On the voyage to China the coasts mostly lie north and south across the track of the ship, and to know one's latitude position would have been enough.

Ahmed Ibn Majid also knew what to look for when he made his landfalls. He knew the distinctive outlines of particular hills and headlands, and he gave a whole list of the *isba* positions of the most important ports. Little wonder that Ibn Majid had been considered a *mu'allim*, the highest grade of navigator. Among the Arabs the lowest grade of navigator was a man who knew his coastlines and could sail along them safely, avoiding reefs and dangers. The second grade of navigator was knowledgeable enough to make open water passages out of sight of land by travelling on a direct course from his point of departure until he made his landfall. The third and highest grade, the *mu'allim*, had to be able to navigate his ship at all times out of sight of land, from any port to any port, using only the stars and his fund of experience, and never losing his way even if buffeted by storms or carried off his track by the current. Ahmed Ibn Majid was a *mu'allim*. It was formerly claimed that he was the same Arab pilot who had shown Vasco da Gama the route from Africa to India. Having rounded the Cape of Good Hope and sailed up the East African coast, Vasco da Gama hired this pilot to lead his Portuguese ships to Calicut on the Malabar coast of India, because the Arab and Indian *mu'allims* had been making the same ocean passage for centuries. Thus what was a voyage of discovery to the Portuguese was a regular routine for Arab *mu'allims*.

The star-reading tablet and string, known usually as a *kamal*, worked for me, but would it work for other members of the crew? Several of them tried holding the piece of cardboard at the end of the string and measuring the Pole Star. We found that the piece of cardboard worked best for someone of my own size. Other people produced different readings. I consulted Ibn Majid's writings and he had an answer for that problem too. In the constellation of Capella are two distinct stars. The distance between the two stars is exactly four *isba*. So if a man made his own *kamal*, he should check it against the two stars of Capella, and that way he would know whether his *kamal* was correct. But had the early Arab navigators also used the compass to guide them? Certainly by Ibn Majid's time in the fifteenth century the compass was in widespread use, but earlier texts make no mention of it. Once again, the answer must have been to use the stars. When I asked Saleh, who had skippered an Arab fishing boat, to tell me the Arabic names for the compass points, his answers were revealing. Most of his compass points were not as westerners use them, but were the names of stars. It was a relic of the day when Arab navigators steered by the direction in which the stars rise and set during the night. Through *Sohar*'s night watches the skilled Omani sailors steered by the stars in the night sky. By day they were content to keep a correct general direction by watching the sun, and keeping the steady monsoon winds at the same angle to *Sohar*'s sails.

To check our progress I needed to know how fast *Sohar* was moving through the water, and so I gave this problem to the scientists aboard. The three of them spent an enjoyable hour with their calculators, stopwatches and a dozen oranges. First they measured the exact distance along the length of the ship. Then Robert Moore, even more like an eccentric professor in a turban which he managed to wrap round his head so that it looked like an untidy tea cosy, perched himself in the bows.

'Now!' he shouted, dropping a piece of orange peel into the water, and John Harwood started the stopwatch. The orange peel bobbed back down the length of the ship.

'Now!' called Andrew as the orange peel floated past him where he was perched on the rudder head. John stopped the watch, and copied down the figures. Several more pieces of orange peel made their little journey back alongside *Sohar*. John tapped away on his calculator.

'Skipper, we are travelling at 4.38396 knots, give or take a few minor errors.'

'Anyone want an orange to eat?' muttered Robert. 'I've got several ready peeled.'

The sounds aboard a medieval Arab sailing ship are unique. The groaning and creaking of timber and rope, the constant background to our lives, had begun to assume special characteristics. There was the high-pitched creak of the coconut fibre ropes holding the mast, a sound unlike that made by any other type of rope, and which varied with the degree and rhythm of the rolling of the ship. Then there was the soft, regular thump of the tiller nudging against the tiller lines with each wave that passed under the ship, followed by an occasional gentle clatter of the blocks as the steersman adjusted the tiller. From high above came a soft, rubbing sound as the great spars nuzzled the masts, each spar bandaged against chafe with a great wad of coconut husk stitched into a canvas jacket. Dozens of wooden joints talked gently in every part of the hull, as the ship shouldered her way through the waves. The large planks of the lower deck crept up and down against one another in sympathy with the slight flexing of the hull, and in my cabin even a slight change in the wind direction or speed could be detected without even going up on *Sohar*'s deck. The whisper of water along the side of the hull told the speed of the ship, and *Sohar*'s angle of heel was marked by little beads of moisture which seeped through the un-caulked planks at the water level outside.

During the first few days of the voyage boxes, cartons, ropes, sacks, saucepans and bits of clothing were scattered higgledy pig-gledy all over *Sohar*'s deck until it seemed there was hardly a clear space to stand on. Arab dhows are notorious for their chaos on deck, but *Sohar*'s clutter seemed to be setting a record. Towels flapped from the rigging to dry. Spools of fishing line became tangled round one's feet. Nets of fruit swayed over the hatches. Only gradu-ally did the chaos diminish as the fresh fruit was eaten and the personal effects began to disappear below to each man's berth. Every crew member had been allotted two ammunition boxes in which to keep his clothes and personal possessions. These boxes were stowed under the canvas bunks which lined each side of the hull below decks. To keep the interior of the ship as cool as possible there were no bulkheads, just a single long hold running the length of the ship from the bosun's store in the forepeak to the canvas wall which divided off the captain's cabin in the stern. Here in the main hold the entire crew lived – scientists, Omanis, everybody. Only I, as captain, was lucky enough to have my own accommodation. Along-side the massive trunk of the main mast where it came down through the deck were the lockers for tinned foods and sauces. Farther aft, on the centre line of the ship, were lashed two large chests, one for the scientific equipment, the other for the photographic gear. Both chests served also as desks and work benches. Farther aft again was the main food store, a pile of sacks and barrels kept down by a cargo net, and next to it the radio desk. On the aft side of the canvas dividing wall, in the very stern of the ship, lay my own cabin, with two more bunks, some planks laid across the stern to make a desk, and a fine curved antique Omani chest as a bench. Seated on the chest, I had only to glance up to see the bare feet of the helmsman standing on the grating of the aft hatch directly over my head.

Our clothes suited the conditions. Except by night, the Omanis discarded their *dishdashas*, and wore only light shirts and *wuzaras*, their long loincloths. The rest of us quickly followed their example, abandoning trousers in favour of *wuzaras*, and going barefoot, which was far more comfortable and practical. Our day began at dawn with the morning prayer of the Omanis, followed by a break-fast of bread or fried pancakes. The crew was divided into three watches, which worked four hours on and eight hours off, so there

Above left Food was the Arab sailor's diet of rice, fish and dates, supplemented with tinned stores, and cooked on a charcoal fire.
Above right Washing in one of the two 'opera box' lavatories slung over the ship's stern. At night 'you could throw down a bucket on a rope and scoop up the water to take a shower, and wonder in amazement as the sea water ran off your skin in ghostly rivulets. . . .'
Below Evening prayer.
Over Sunset at sea

Above Repairing the rudder. The rope and leather lashings holding the rudder often stretched and frayed. *Sohar* put into the remote coral island of Chetlat so that the divers could make repairs. Two men tightened the lashings, while a third mounted guard against curious sharks.

Right Few Chetlat islanders had ever seen a stranger, and their women and girls 'looked like clusters of tropical flowers scattered at random among the trunks of the coconut palms. . . .'

Opposite The crew spent Christmas at Beypore in India where the sails were carried ashore for mending. The beach became a sail loft and *(over)* Indian fishermen were trained as sailmakers. In less than a week they sewed a complete new set of sails

Above Beaching their ship at Beypore, the crew scraped down her hull to check that the timber had not been attacked by shipworm. Untreated panels of wood were so badly infested they could be snapped with bare hands, 'like wafers'.
Below In Sindbad's time the Arabs came to the Malabar coast to trade for spices. In Calicut Indian women still sort areca nut for export

was plenty of time for leisure. The daily chores were few: sails had to be tended and adjusted to the best angle, the tiller manned, the fresh water in the deck barrel topped up, the rigging kept taut. Every morning a foot of evil-smelling yellow bilge water was pumped overboard, leaving a dirty streak in our wake, but there was very little other work to be done. The off watch read, wrote letters to be posted at the next port of call, or dozed in the sun. The foredeck was the favourite spot. Here the huge curve of the mainsail spilled a gentle breeze which was pleasantly cool, and if the sun was high the sail also provided a welcome patch of shade.

The crew was beginning to take on individual characteristics. Burly Abdullah with his great forearms and rolling gait had revealed himself as by far the best helmsman on board. He had a knack for steering *Sohar*: he would perch himself on the windward gunnel, gather the tiller lines in his massive fists, and sit there, totally relaxed. Very occasionally he would give the tiller line a small tug, or make a minor adjustment without even looking down at the tiller itself. Always the ship obeyed him, running a steady, easy course, and drawing a clean, straight wake behind her. No one could match Abdullah at the helm. To a greater or lesser extent all the rest of the crew were reduced to fiddling with tiller lines, adjusting and readjusting the rudder or resetting the angle of the sails, and leaving a curving trail behind the ship.

Young Eid proved to be the best climber in the crew. He was extremely fit and well co-ordinated, and though at first he did not have a head for heights and climbing the rigging made him giddy, he had the courage to go aloft whenever he was asked. He would catch hold of the great main halyard where it slanted up from the deck, and clamber up it hand over hand, hanging upside down like a lemur until he reached the masthead 50 feet above the deck. Then with a kick and a wriggle he would swing himself up on top of the mainspar, and carry on upwards, clinging to the timber with arms and legs. At first I made Eid wear a safety harness in case he fell, which would surely have crippled, if not killed him. But within ten days Eid was so confident that he was up and gone aloft long before there was time to find his harness, and he would be perched high up on the masthead, his jet-black face grinning down at me, topped by a bright orange turban.

Night was a good time aboard *Sohar*. Occasionally we had a blood-red moonrise as the moon rose slowly through the layers of desert dust that lay behind us towards Arabia. As the light faded, the colours of the night became silver and black. The rigging took on a perfect geometry against the sky. The crimson emblem of the Sultanate on the sail turned to the colour of dried blood in the moonlight, and the curves of the sails arranged themselves into graceful patterns and intricate relationships. The helmsman became a silhouette, and the sleeping crew, curled up on deck to avoid the bilge gas that left sore throats in the morning if one stayed below all night, merged into darker shadows among the other shadows of the deck. Often there was phosphorescence in the sea, and *Sohar* drew a luminescent trail behind her. At such times if you climbed into one of the traditional Arab lavatories, which were slung over the stern of the ship like theatre boxes, and gazed down into the water, you could see darting flashes, like lightning flickering beneath the sea, where the larger fishes were turning and twisting in the turbulence of *Sohar*'s passage. Or you could throw down a bucket on a rope and scoop up the water to take a shower, and wonder in amazement as the sea water ran off your skin in ghostly rivulets, and left flecks of light where the luminescent plankton lay stranded on your body like ghostly fireflies.

Dawn was marked by the slow slapping sound of Shanby, the ship's cook, kneading the dough for the crew's breakfast chapattis. Shanby's breakfast chapattis were palatable, but the rest of his cooking was a total failure. It was my fault. Shanby had shown up at the dockside on the very last day before we sailed from Muscat. A man of uncertain background and indeterminate age, he cut a strangely familiar figure in his worn grey *dishdasha* and a grubby skullcap of imitation lace perched on top of a crinkled, nut-brown face that had a strong resemblance to a friendly chimpanzee. After a moment's reflection I knew what it was – Shanby's crumpled smile and wary brown eyes were the look of a born survivor, a man who was picking his way carefully through life, watching and waiting, trusting to his instinct for self-preservation, never stepping too far into the limelight. He was the old soldier who serves thirty years in the army with no particular taste for advancement or distinction, but with a well-developed sense of how to be comfortable. On that first day Shanby had spoken to me in a language I did not understand, so I turned helplessly to Musalam who was standing beside me on the dock.

'What is he saying?' I asked.

'I don't know,' replied Musalam. 'He's speaking Baluchi – he must be a Baluch.'

From that remark I gathered that Shanby came from Baluchistan on the Pakistan–Iran border. The Baluch coast had once belonged to

Oman, and quite a number of Baluch had settled in the Sultanate. Luckily a bystander understood a little of the language.

'He says he wants to come on your ship. He says he wants to volunteer. He says he has experience on ships.'

'But what can he do aboard ship?'

'He says he can cook. He is an experienced cook.'

I did need a cook, someone who could cope with producing food for twenty men on an open charcoal hearth on deck. Shanby was the only volunteer for the job, which I had begun to fear would have to be taken in turns by the crew if no one showed up who actually claimed to be a cook.

'All right, then. Tell him that he's to go aboard at once, and cook lunch for us. If his lunch is acceptable, then I will hire him as the ship's cook.'

Shanby hitched up his *dishdasha*, and scrambled on board. The meal he cooked was passable, but only just. It was a tasteless curry of vegetables and gluey rice, so I gave him the benefit of the doubt. After all, I reasoned, he was new to the ship and unused to the charcoal hearth, and he probably lacked the pots and pans he liked to use. Furthermore, he had not selected the ingredients for himself. I should have been more honest with myself, and confessed that *Sohar* had to have a cook and quickly, since there was less than twenty-four hours to go before we set sail. So I told Shanby that he was hired, that he was to go at once to the *suq* to buy whatever he needed in the way of cooking gear and spices, and that he was to report back aboard next morning. Shanby reappeared an hour before we sailed. That night there was no need to cook because the deck was so cluttered and we were still settling in, so we ate a supper of apples and bread. Next day Shanby produced lunch. It was exactly the same lacklustre curry of vegetables and tepid rice as his trial meal. For supper we were offered the cold leftover curry. Next day lunch was identical – the same curry, with perhaps a very slight variation of vegetables. It dawned on me that Shanby knew how to cook just one dish – that same grisly curry. We were condemned to eat it from one side of the Sea of Arabia to the other.

Shanby was the cross we had to bear for the next three weeks. We all suffered: nothing is worse on a ship than a thoroughly bad cook, and Shanby was appalling. At breakfast he was agonizingly slow. It took him two hours to make the chapattis, and latecomers were ravenous by the time they were fed. At lunchtime Shanby was slipshod:

he peeled the vegetables so inadequately that he left rotting lumps in the food, and he never drained the rice properly, so that it bonded together into a soggy mess. At suppertime he was lazy: he either offered the remains of the curry – not surprisingly there was usually plenty left – or he opened a few tins in desultory fashion and served them up lukewarm.

It was no use helping Shanby – he merely took advantage of the kindness. Terry Hardy, the sound recordist on *Sohar*'s crew, enjoyed good food and tried to give Shanby a hand. Shanby seized the chance to disappear off into his bunk, and reappeared only to take his place at the head of the queue for supper. Nor did shouting at him have any effect – he had a skin like a rhinoceros. One day Eid came near to hitting Shanby, since he was so angry to see him washing his feet in the cooking bowl. The next day I observed Shanby's grubby feet back in the bowl, but out of sight of the Omanis.

Shanby was such an unprincipled rogue that he actually achieved a certain charm. He could lurk around the deck, apparently able to look in all directions at once in order to avoid being called upon to do any work. If seen, he adopted a stance that seemed to indicate a readiness to help, yet at the same time gave the impression that he was already occupied. His usual dress was a pair of very grubby and extremely baggy pantaloons, an expensive English check shirt which had been accidentally left on board by a visitor in Muscat harbour and promptly disappeared into Shanby's wardrobe, and his sordid lace skullcap. The latter was sometimes replaced by a bright yellow duster tied round his head, which made him look like a cross between a cleaning woman in a stage comedy and a yellow-scarfed US cavalry colonel in a western. Squatting on his heels in this bizarre attire, his false teeth soaking in a bowl of water by his side, and desultorily stirring his abominable curry while the ash from his cigarette dropped into the food, I knew at last the origin of the insult: 'Son of a sea cook!'

The scientists had settled into their programme of research. Andrew collected plankton samples every day by streaming a fine mesh drogue from *Sohar*'s side, and bottling the results. Also twice every twenty-four hours he lowered the oil-collecting sledge into the water, and it skipped along beside the ship skimming the water and picking up any surface oil and other pollution. Pleasingly, it seemed that although *Sohar* was crossing an area used by oil tankers, there was little pollution. And for an hour every morning Andrew hunted the ocean's humble surface creatures, scooping up little colonies of crabs and insects which inhabited the drifting rafts of seaweed and other flotsam that floated gently past *Sohar*'s hull. Sitting on the gunnel with his long-handled fishnet, Andrew in his straw hat and swimsuit looked like an Edwardian child taken for a treat to catch shrimps at the seaside.

Robert Moore, his scientific colleague, was busy studying the concentration of trace metals in the sea water. These trace metals are vital for life in the ocean, and *Sohar* was uniquely adapted for Robert's work. Because the hull of the ship was made only of wood and string, it did not give off minute quantities of metal as would have been the case with a ship made of steel or nailed together, which meant that Robert's samples of sea water were less liable to be contaminated aboard *Sohar* than on most other types of ship. Robert spent hours in the bowels of *Sohar*, hunched over his conjuror's box of scientific equipment, looking like a modern necromancer in his untidy turban as he swirled test tubes full of bubbling water, and bottled mysterious concoctions of sea water essence which he would be taking back to his university to study.

The third scientist, John Harwood, passed much of his time at the opposite end of the ship – dangling high up near the masthead in a bosun's chair hoisted by a jib halyard. With notebook and binoculars, John was on watch for sea mammals – whales, dolphins and the like – and also keeping a log of all the birds we sighted. But whales, even small ones, were few and far between; and as John ruefully observed, the most important thing he learnt was that when it came to spotting whales the experienced sailors on *Sohar* were far more adept than the scientists. Trondur and Mohammed in particular could see from the deck the spout of a whale long before John at the masthead. And it became a standing joke with the crew to call up, 'John! John! Wake up! Didn't you see that whale?' John would look down, grin sheepishly, and swing his binoculars around to peer in the right direction.

When it came to identifying birds John was an ace, and he greatly added to our enjoyment as he identified the birds which flew round the ship. Most of the birds were familiar – gannets, shearwaters and the tropic birds which wheeled on long, narrow wings – but there were also some surprises. He saw two skuas which were not supposed to be found in those waters, and a nightjar which is certainly a land bird but apparently quite happy to be far out at sea. The nightjar made no effort to return to the mainland, and circled the ship for hours at a time. Like most mariners, early Arab sailors had used birds as navigation marks, following their flight paths and knowing when they were near land by the change of species. Rather charmingly they believed that the little petrels, which look so fragile and delicate and yet survive through fair weather and foul, never came to land at all, but lived for ever on the sea, and hatched from the sea foam.

On 29 November our trailing lines caught our first fish, a small bonito and another fish similar to a mackerel. The fish were too small to feed a hungry crew of twenty men, so we cut them up and hung them to dry into shark bait. Already there was a 6-foot-long shark cruising daily in our wake, a sinister dark shadow waiting for scraps.

Sohar's progress was good, but not spectacular. We were advancing at about 70 or 80 miles a day, depending on the wind. When the breeze was behind us, the ship rolled abominably, slopping back and forth with a great groan of the spars against the mast, and a clatter of wooden blocks as the shrouds first sagged, then tightened with the uproll. When the wind drew ahead *Sohar* ploughed forward gamely, but was hampered by the cut of her sails. They were sorry-looking specimens, as baggy as flour sacks. They had been sewn in India by a village sailmaker who still turned out sails for Indian country craft, and once again I was learning the lesson that when building a replica medieval ship every single detail must be supervised personally, whether the selection of each tree for the planks or the number of stitches to the inch in the seams of the vessel's sails. The sailmaker had skimped on his work and already, before sailing from Muscat, we had tried to improve the workmanship, turning the parade ground of the naval base into a sail loft covered with sails being re-stitched, much to the annoyance of the executive officer who had been obliged to cancel morning parades until we cleared out. But now at sea it was evident that the original sailmaker had also used very poor-quality canvas. The cotton canvas was hand made in order to be authentic, and with the first tug of the wind the loosely woven cloth had stretched until the sails bulged ineffectively. At our next port of call, I realized ruefully, we would have to organize a new set of sails or *Sohar* stood little chance of reaching China before the typhoon season in the South China Sea made navigation very hazardous.

My other main worry was the rudder, which was wagging loosely back and forth and threatening to fall off entirely. The rope lashings which held it to the sternpost had stretched. Two of the lashings were below the water line and had worn through completely – their frayed ends waved forlornly like a seaweed beard. There was nothing for it but to make a temporary repair. On the next calm day Mohamed and Trondur lowered themselves over the stern and put on new lashings above water. But I decided to leave the underwater fastenings alone, as the rudder was heaving and groaning in the swell and there was a danger that someone's hand would be crushed between the massive rudder blade and the sternpost. Besides, the shark was still there, nosing hungrily around the ship.

Tropic bird

—6—

The Coconut Rope Islands

On 4 December we received our first gale warning: a tropical depression had formed in the Bay of Bengal and was moving across the Indian peninsula in our direction. We prepared the ship for possible squalls, cleared up the clutter on the deck, and hurried to finish sewing the canvas hatch covers. *Sohar*'s main hatch measured 12 feet by 6 feet, and was normally covered by an open grating to allow air to get into the fetid hold. I did not relish the prospect of covering up the hatch in a gale and trapping the gas in the bilges, but in bad weather we would have no choice. The tropical depression petered out before it reached us, but I noted how the crew cheered up when there was work to be done.

Indeed, it was evident that the Europeans aboard were finding it difficult to adapt to the long hours with little to do, the cramped conditions, Shanby's dreadful food and the strange surroundings. They were fit, active young men, and the limitations of the ship confined them. The Omanis, by contrast, were less troubled. Their needs were simpler, and they had a far greater capacity to relax and pass the idle hours. The foredeck was frequently decorated with the recumbent forms of the Omani sailors, fast asleep on the planks, turbans unwound and draped over their faces to give them shade. But any impression of idleness was superficial. When there was work to be done the Omanis laid into it with a zest. They loved to work as a team, and to sing as they worked. Whether hauling in the mainsheet or sewing a hatch cover, they preferred to work in a group. One of them – usually Eid or Abdullah – would start up the work chant, the others would respond with the refrain, and then the lead singer would reply. Then, phrase and counterphrase, they sang their way through their work. If the job was a heavy one like hauling up the mainyard, then the singing introduction would be very deliberate and measured. The team would assemble by the halyard. Eid, standing where they could all see him, would call out the first line and the others would respond. Back and forth went the song, slowly picking up the rhythm and increasing in volume until all the men were in the same mood. Then Eid would give a thundering stamp of his bare foot on the deck, a great ringing clap of his hands, and the entire team would burst into action, laying hold and hauling away like Trojans as the spars soared aloft. It was a workstyle that was so efficient and so attractive that within a fortnight the Europeans were joining in, and I happily observed the first signs of the crew welding itself into a unit.

Tidying up the ship had improved morale, and so did the news from Tom's amateur radio that Musalam's wife back in Oman had given birth to a baby girl. That night the foredeck rang with the happy songs of the Omanis holding an impromptu concert to celebrate the birth.

Halfway to the Indian coast and with 600 miles of sailing behind us we held a safety drill. The danger of a ship as large and as stately as *Sohar* was that, if someone fell overboard by accident, it would be a considerable time before we could hope to pick him up. Without a motor to turn on we would have to heave to, inflate and lower a rubber dinghy as a lifeboat, and send it back to pick up the man overboard. In a strong wind or a heavy sea *Sohar* could well be a mile away by the time the dinghy was ready to go. A safety line trailed from *Sohar*'s stern at all times, with a loop in the end of it. If someone did go overboard by accident, then he had a chance to grab hold and hang on. But if he missed the rope, his life depended on the speed with which we launched the lifeboat dinghy to go back and get him.

The lifeboat drill was a sobering experience. I divided the crew into two competing teams to see which was faster in recovering a cardboard box dropped overboard as *Sohar* sailed along. The first team performed adequately. The cardboard box splashed into the water with a cry of 'Man overboard!' The team dragged out the rubber dinghy, inflated it with a bottle of compressed air from our diving equipment, lowered the dinghy into the water, fitted the outboard engine and roared off. Already the box was half a mile away and out of sight between the swells, and the boat crew admitted that they were lucky to find it. But the second team's efforts nearly turned into a real emergency. In their haste they failed to fit the dinghy's floorboards properly, and as the dinghy was manhandled over the gunnel it flipped over and its floorboards tumbled out and began to float away.

'Quick!' I yelled. 'Go after them!' The floorboards stiffened the rubber dinghy, and without them it would not work properly with an outboard engine so that our 'lifeboat' would be next to useless. Mohamed and Peter scrambled into the dinghy, grabbed the paddles, and began frantically paddling back towards the floorboards. I had deliberately chosen a choppy, breezy day for the drill, and now the crew watched thoughtfully as they had a first-hand view of the risks of falling overboard. Caught by the breeze on her hull and spars, *Sohar* was drifting fast downwind, though Trondur at the helm had stalled the ship so that the sails flapped freely. The gap between the dinghy and the ship widened quickly. Mohamed and Peter paddled flat out towards the floating floorboards, but the hastily inflated dinghy was soggy and slow – it was designed for an engine, not for two paddles. Then Peter's paddle snapped off in his hands. Another lesson learned – ordinary paddles were not strong enough. He began paddling with the broken blade, and very gradually the dinghy caught up with the floorboards. From a distance we saw Peter plunge overboard to retrieve the floorboards and get them back to Mohamed, then he scrambled back into the dinghy.

All this time we had been feeding out a long line, nearly half a mile of ropes joined together, which was attached to the dinghy like an umbilical cord. It took twelve men of *Sohar*'s crew pulling steadily to bring the dinghy back to *Sohar* and safety. All of us could imagine what might happen if a true emergency had taken place at night or in a gale – the chances of recovering a man overboard from *Sohar* were obviously very thin. And now John Harwood, who had watched the whole episode from his observation point at the masthead, drew our attention to one other interesting fact.

'It was the strangest thing,' he said, 'but when Mohamed and Peter were thrashing off in the rubber dinghy, two sharks suddenly appeared beneath and beside the rubber boat. And the two sharks stayed all the time they were in the rubber boat. It was as though the sharks had sensed the commotion. One was nearly 3 metres long.'

There were also comic interludes to cheer us up. Andrew had finally succeeded in picking up ten barnacles for study. They had attached themselves not to the specially designed barnacle torpedo which we had been trailing behind *Sohar*, but to the safety line. Andrew was pleased, for it showed that the young barnacles did not attach themselves to ships only when in harbour, as one theory suggested, but swam in the open ocean and could attach themselves to ships at sea. He began studying his specimens, each day carefully taking their measurements with a set of calipers to see how fast they were growing. Hauling out the safety rope one day, he let out a yell of rage.

'The swine! The absolute pig!'

We looked round to see what was the matter. Andrew was holding the dripping rope and hitting it with a belaying pin. Dislodged by the attack, a handsome green crab dropped to the deck and scuttled for shelter.

'He's eaten half my barnacle specimens!' Andrew cried in outrage. 'The greedy swine, I'll fix him.'

There followed a hilarious hunt round the deck, with the crab pursued by several members of the crew armed with belaying pins, sheath knives, cooking ladles and whatever weapons they could lay their hands on. Finally the offender was cornered.

'Got you!' exulted Andrew as his hand shot out and seized the crab. 'For punishment you can serve the cause of science,' and he popped the animal into a waiting jar of formalin.

The crab, which had been living comfortably in a crevice near the keel and sallying forth to breakfast on Andrew's barnacles and other scraps, was not the only hitchhiking nuisance we had aboard *Sohar*. The dark cavities under the gunnels housed a thriving colony of stowaways, a large family of crickets which were driving Terry the sound recordist mad.

'No one will ever believe that the sound track of our film was really made at sea, if all they hear is crickets chirping in the background,' he lamented, and he planned lengthy campaigns of attack. At night when Terry was on watch there was the flickering light of a torch, and the sound of stealthy footsteps followed by thumps and curses as he endlessly hunted down his tormentors. But the crickets bred faster than Terry could dispatch them, and the soft sea nights were filled with the incongruous sound of their buzzings and chirpings.

At the end of the first week in December we detected signs of land. The scientists trawled up an extra amount of plankton in their nets, and the Omanis soon afterwards caught our first decent haul of fish. A dozen splendid tuna struck at their lures. Khamees Police threatened Shanby with physical violence if he dared touch the fish, and half an hour later they were grilling over the charcoal. As our most skilled fisherman, Khamees Police selected the fattest of the tuna and carefully grilled it. Then, cutting off the best portion, he brought the dish to me to eat.

'You are the captain,' he said. 'You must be the first to eat any fish. No one else should eat until you have taken food.'

The increase in plankton and the presence of shoals of fish indicated that *Sohar* had passed out of the deep ocean of the Arabian Sea and must now be over the Bassas de Pedro Reef, some 250 miles off the coast of southern India. Now we would have to navigate very carefully, for *Sohar* was entering dangerous waters. If my calculations were correct a chain of coral islands, the Laccadives, should lie across our path. These tiny islands, many of them no more than a mile or so long, rise only just above the surface of the sea. The tallest things on them are the coconut palms, and the islands are guarded on their eastern side, the side from which *Sohar* was approaching, by coral reefs which could tear her bottom out. There would be no warning of these reefs, no gentle shelving of the sea floor to alert us. The islands rise sheer out of 100 fathoms of water. If we ran on them in the night, we would be lost.

I checked and rechecked *Sohar*'s position, and on the night of 9 December we glimpsed the distant loom of the lighthouse which marks the northerly point of the Laccadives. I ordered a change to our course, six points to the west, and reduced sail so that *Sohar* was just creeping through the black night. At dawn, as the light suffused the horizon and a pale sea fret dispersed, we saw land. There, directly ahead of our bowsprit, was a barely discernible, olive green distortion of the horizon, a mere smudge of something that was not the same sharp blue sea we had been seeing for the last few weeks. It was the tiny island of Chetlat, the most northerly island in the Laccadives, and the first in the chain of stepping stones which had led the early Arab navigators to China, and in turn provided the raw material for the stories of Sindbad the Sailor.

'To these islands,' wrote the Arab geographer Idrisi in the twelfth century, 'come the ships of Oman to gather coconuts and cut wood and build their vessels. They stay on the islands building their ships, and then sail home in them.' Though the Laccadives are mere fly specks in the vastness of the Arabian Sea, it was easy to see why the Arab sailors had come across them, for they lie directly in the track of ships sailing from the south of the Arabian peninsula to the west coast of India. The island's groves of coconut trees would have provided excellent boatbuilding rope for the Arabs – indeed *Sohar* herself was fastened together with Laccadive coir; and the Agatti men who had stitched her together were Laccadive islanders. The historic Arab connection now means that over 90 per cent of the islanders are Moslems, and they claim that Islam was carried to them during Mohammed's lifetime by a Moslem saint wrecked on the Laccadives.

Politically the Laccadives now belong to India, and when the British governed India the islands were declared a Protected Area; and the islanders were regarded as a people whose culture had to be defended from outside damage. By all accounts the Laccadive culture was well worth protecting. The islanders lived in an almost idyllic society, each tiny island effectively a commune governed by a council of all the menfolk who met to arrange the running of island life. The council had no power except that of public opinion, and the islanders obeyed the council simply because that was what the community wanted. Serious crime was unknown. In the colonial records there was not a single instance of murder or even physical assault. The only misdeed ever to appear, and even that was rare, was the theft of coconuts from another man's trees. If restitution was not made the culprit was asked to sit in a corner, facing the wall, like a naughty child. In this guileless society such ostracism was enough. The other crime was failure to partake in a rat hunt, the regular drives organized against tree rats which ravaged the coconut crop. The young men climbed the trees and shook the branches until the rats fell down, where the waiting crowd dispatched them with sticks. Failure to show up for a communal rat hunt was frowned upon, and the council sent a warning to the absentee. But they gave him a chance: if he could produce five dead rats within the next few days he was excused, even from sitting in the corner.

Coconuts and fish were the only products of the islands – even their rice had to be imported from the mainland. Society was usually divided into four grades according to one's occupation; there were landowners, boatbuilders, fishermen and coconut tree climbers. Separated from India by up to 200 miles of open water, the Laccadives were geographically and politically insulated from change for centuries. After Independence the government of India retained the special status of the islands, and declared them to be a Union Territory: the Laccadives were to be administered directly from New Delhi, and with one or two exceptions the islands stayed off-limits to foreigners.

Gazing at the low green outline of Chetlat, as *Sohar* crept closer under full sail, it seemed that indeed we had sailed into a dream. The island appeared to fit every notion of a tropical paradise. A line of dazzling white sand became a beach which sloped up gently into the palm plantations. Among the trees we could make out the red-tiled roofs and palm thatch of native houses. To the south of the island a bright aquamarine expanse of water indicated the presence of a coral shelf, and there a lazy swell creamed over the coral and spent itself into a light blue lagoon. Two native boats, cockleshell dugouts, were fishing in the lee of the island and edged over timidly to watch our approach. I wondered what they made of *Sohar*, a picture out of history, with the great white sails and crimson crest of the Sultanate.

I had to concentrate, though. This was the first time I had ever taken a fully rigged sailing ship, without an engine, into an anchorage, let alone without any notion of the currents or the state of the tide. There was one moment of alarm when a line of cresting breakers appeared near the spot at which I had chosen to anchor, but a glance through the binoculars showed that the breakers lay on the far side of the anchorage. *Sohar* slid gently through the dark blue water. It was a classic coral island. Half a mile from shore, the leadsman still found no bottom at 200 feet. Then suddenly the water changed from darkest blue to a jade green, and we were gliding over the coral ledge.

'Down mizzen!' I called to Mohamed, and the aft sail was brailed up and lashed, and the Omanis lowered the mizzen spar to the deck. *Sohar* was now within 80 yards of the chosen spot. 'Down jib!' I called.

'Down jib! Down jib!' echoed Mohamed. The Omanis and Europeans were equally competent in ship commands in both Arabic and English, and the jib, the foremost sail of the ship, vanished like a trick handkerchief in the hands of a conjuror.

All those men who were not handling the sails were now lining the rails and gazing at the island, spellbound by its beauty. *Sohar* was almost on her mark now.

'Let go mainsheet. Helm hard over, Khamees,' and the tiller block squealed as Khamees Police, ducking his head to look under the sail, pushed the tiller out to the lee side and brought *Sohar*'s head to wind. Tom eased out the mainsheet, and the mainsail spilled the wind.

'Let go the anchor.' Trondur on the foredeck cast a glance behind him to make sure that all was clear, gestured to a man to watch out for the flying chain as it rattled overboard, and with one slash of his knife cut loose the best bower anchor to send it plunging into 30 feet of beautiful, clear water mottled with coral patches. *Sohar* came gently to a stop. She turned her head upwind, and then lay quietly back to her anchor cable.

Our arrival had been noted – out through a gap in the reef chugged two small motor launches. The welcoming committee did not look very inviting. The launches were loaded down with armed policemen, dressed in khaki and carrying rifles. This discouraging sight was relieved, on closer inspection, by the fact that the armed police were either gaping in amazement or grinning with delight. *Sohar* in all her exotic rig might as well have been a spaceship from another planet. As the leading launch pulled alongside *Sohar*, I identified the officer in charge, a gentle-looking man in a British Army captain's uniform of about 1940 vintage. His men were rather bizarrely dressed in jungle slouch hats with bright red linings that could be seen whenever they took off their hats to mop their brows, which they did frequently in the heat. They had well-pressed bush shirts with 'LP' for Laccadive Police on the metal shoulder tabs, and the most remarkable shorts we had ever seen. Starched to an extraordinary rigidity, these shorts stood fore-and-aft 8 inches clear of the wearers' thighs like the gaping mouths of church bells. The cooling updraught must have been very welcome for the wearer, but the visual impression was decidedly comic. This strange rig was completed, lower down the leg of each policeman, by tightly wound khaki puttees ending in the top section of khaki socks. The foot of each sock had been cut off to allow bare ankles to emerge, and feet clad in tennis shoes.

It was clear that this detachment of Laccadive Police had dressed themselves up for the special occasion, so we watched politely as they attempted to negotiate the steep climb from the motor boat up *Sohar*'s side. It was equally evident that they had arrived to arrest the ship; and the officer's face was a study in mingled embarrassment and a self-conscious attempt to look stern. The effect of his first firm footstep on deck was ruined by the fact that what he thought was a boarding step was a carton of eggs. There was an unmistakable crunch, and he toppled gently forward into Trondur's arms. His troops, encumbered by their World War II rifles, jostled around in the launches trying to get up the side until Peter Dobbs leaned down and offered to hold their rifles for them. With obvious relief, they handed over their weapons.

'What are you doing here?' asked the officer, after he had disentangled himself from Trondur's embrace. He spoke excellent English. 'This is a forbidden area. I must ask you to leave.'

'I have an official letter from the Ministry of Foreign Affairs, Government of India,' I replied. 'It states that the Ministry has no objection for my ship to visit the Laccadives.' The officer looked mildly relieved.

It was evident that he hated chasing us away from Chetlat. Visitors were extremely rare.

'Then I will contact my headquarters, and inform them of the situation. Meanwhile your men are not allowed on the shore. Please come with me to the police station to enter the necessary documents.'

Ten minutes later, escorted by the gendarmerie, I was aboard the motor boat heading through a gap in the reef. Chetlat was so beautiful that it was still difficult to believe the island was not a fantasy. As the launch wallowed through the channel and into the pale turquoise lagoon, I could see the palm-fringed crescent of the western beach. The sand was dazzling, a few houses were visible, and there was a small rickety jetty and some curious-looking thatched longhouses, end-on to the beach. The launch came alongside the jetty, lines were thrown up and made fast and, accompanied by the police captain, I walked up the wooden staging.

A crowd was waiting at the foot of the jetty, men and children staring at me silently. The men wore long, straight sarongs reaching to their ankles; a few of them wore shirts, and the older men wore a distinctive head scarf, a piece of plain cloth placed on top of the head and pulled over the ears so the ends hung down like a wimple. Some distance behind the men I could see small groups of women, wearing bodices and skirts of vivid colours. Their glossy black hair was shoulder length, held back by brightly coloured head scarves. They looked like clusters of tropical flowers scattered at random among the trunks of the coconut palms that formed a complete canopy over the little island. Everyone, men, women and children, was staring at me with timid curiosity.

'They are frightened,' said the police captain. 'Most of them have never seen a non-Indian before. Your white skin frightens them.'

In an age of radio and television, illustrated magazines and world-wide travel, it seemed extraordinary that most of the present generation of Chetlat islanders had never seen a stranger who was not an Indian citizen. Only those men who had crossed to the mainland had any notion of the outside world. Before Independence the island would have been visited once a year by the district commissioner or his assistant on tour. But since Independence no white man, so I was told, had ever been on Chetlat. As I walked with the captain to his office, up the sandy path that meandered between the palm trees, some of the men walked backwards ahead of us, never taking their eyes off me. A covey of children scurried from tree to tree on each side, peeping out from safety. Those men who had travelled showed their sophistication by forming up in a squad behind us, and marching self-importantly in escort.

The police captain's office boasted a radio transmitter, the island's only official link with the outside world apart from a government ferry which was supposed to anchor off the reef once a fortnight, and stay a few hours to unload cargo into native boats. During the south-west monsoon this ferry service was suspended due to the heavy swell and breakers, and even at the best of times it was very erratic. When *Sohar* arrived, Chetlat had been waiting three weeks for the overdue ferry, and some islanders hopefully came out to *Sohar* to beg for cigarettes. While the police radio operator tapped away on his morse key, I glanced around the police office. Its only furniture comprised a desk, four chairs, and a broken box which served as a waste paper basket. Lowering himself into one of the chairs, the captain carefully searched a drawer until he lifted out an ancient government form, the paper grey-brown and beginning to crumble with age. Turning it over so he could write on the back, he looked appealingly at his sergeant. Without a word the sergeant reached into his pocket, and handed over the single office ballpoint pen.

Official business took a pleasantly long time. Green coconuts were brought in to provide us with a drink. The police escort went off to change out of uniform and reappeared more comfortably in sarongs and loose shirts. There was an interval for fish curry.

'We get full rest here,' admitted the sergeant, who kept peering over his officer's shoulder to check what he was writing.

I read the labels on the shelves behind the captain's head – 'Chetlat Station; Crime Reports' and 'Chetlat Station; Files Pending'. The labels were old and curling. The few documents above them had the air of not being disturbed in a long, long time.

'How many armed policemen do you have under your command?' I asked the captain. He was about to reply, when the sergeant glared at him. Obviously the sergeant thought I was a spy, and this was important intelligence information.

'There are enough,' replied the captain lamely.

'When was the last crime on the island?'

He thought for a moment. 'Last year we had a case of alleged theft.'

'And what happened?'

'The man was acquitted.'

I had counted at least a dozen armed gendarmes, in addition to the captain, sergeant and radio operator – it seemed excessive for such a peaceful place.

'How long has there been a police station established on the island?'

'Ever since the government of India decided to help the Laccadives, and make the islands modern.'

'But I have read that in the old days there was no crime on the island. Why do you need so many policemen?'

'Ah, that has changed. Now the islands are modern. So there must be crime.'

And that, I found, was the sad story of Chetlat. The gentle paradise described forty years ago in the official reports of the district commissioners was being ruined by the bureaucracy sent by the government of India, which was claiming to be the guardian of the Laccadives. The idea of protecting the islands and sending special help was a poisoned chalice. On the one hand the liberty of the islanders was severely curtailed under the pretext that they had to be preserved from outside influences. The police were required to compile reports about the islanders. One official notice threatened the islanders with jail if they made signals to foreign ships. To travel off the islands, the Laccadive people needed special permission. Their coconut rope, which was their main cash crop, could only be sold through government-appointed agents and this was an ideal pressure point for extortion by unscrupulous dealers. Rice and sugar was doled out by official quota. In short, the islanders were half-citizens, and their lives were made miserable by the possibility of blackmail by petty officials. Conversely, the notion of protecting the island culture by sealing it off from the outside world was made a farce by the number of government functionaries who actually flooded in from outside. There were policemen, agricultural advisers, fishery advisers, men from the Board of Works, medical assistants – the list was endless. Chetlat had a population of about 1600 souls, and there must have been at least fifty civil servants living there, all bringing in the morals and attitudes the island was supposed to escape.

The futility of these government functionaries was near-total. The police had no real crime to deal with, and were reduced to being little more than spies. The fishery experts could teach little to the islanders, who had been fishermen for generations. Besides, even if the fish catch was improved, there was no way of preserving the catch for export: it would simply rot. The men from the Board of Works were unemployed. There were no roads to build, as Chetlat had no motor cars;

no bridges, as there were no rivers; and the only worthwhile project, a new jetty in the lagoon, had been halted for the last two years for lack of materials. The iron pilings were rusting away in the warm salt water, and the islanders still used the original shaky jetty built of wood. The agricultural advisers had been sent to teach the islanders to grow new crops, but when I tried to buy fresh produce for *Sohar* the only offering was some miserable-looking pawpaws, a handful of peppers and some limes. Everything else had failed, and the islanders were still basically eating coconuts and fish. Even their health was being neglected. The influx of petty government officials had brought new illnesses with it. The medical attendants were pitifully short of medicines. Chetlat was suffering from a minor flu epidemic, and it was *Sohar*'s medicine chest which supplied the only aspirins available.

Only nature's gifts to Chetlat remained unspoiled. The sole eyesore was the ugly complex of government sheds by the jetty, complete with a tatty notice announcing: 'Office of the District Sub-Inspectorate of Engineering, Chetlat Island'. For the rest, the island was a pleasant landscape of coconut groves and immaculate coral sand. The footpaths wandered from house to house among the treetrunks. Chickens clucked and scratched for food. A solitary goat nibbled at some leaves, and the only sound was the distant rumble of the sea on the coral reef and the constant rustling of the trade wind in the palm fronds. The soft sand muffled all footfalls, and the islanders themselves walked so languidly that it seemed that the pathways were ankle deep. Down by the jetty the captain kindly took me into one of the thatched longhouses. Inside, protected from the sun, was one of the unique island boats, an *odam*, a graceful 30-foot upswept hull sewn together with coconut rope like *Sohar*. On the Malabar coast I had seen an *odam* afloat, riding the sea as elegantly as a gull. Twenty years earlier the *odams* had still made their regular trips to the mainland, carrying coconut rope for sale and navigating, I was told, with the Arab tablet and string. Now there was not a single navigator on Chetlat who knew how to use one, and the *odams* rarely sailed. The few passengers who came to the island preferred to wait for the government ferry, however erratic, and the price of the coconut rope under the government monopoly was too low to make the trip worthwhile.

Nature's most generous bounty lay hidden under the sea around Chetlat. Dave Tattle, *Sohar*'s specialist collector-diver, made an exploratory dive as soon as I returned to the ship in the later afternoon. Dave had dived professionally all over the Pacific Ocean, and even under the ice of the Antarctic, collecting specimens for marine bio-logists. Now he went down with a spear gun to look for our supper. He was underwater for less than three minutes when his head popped out alongside *Sohar* and he wrenched away his mouthpiece to call out excitedly: 'You should see the reef down there! It's incredible! There are so many fish that you can only see fish wherever you look. There are walls of fish, and they are not in the least bit spooked. . . .'

In a cloud of bubbles he disappeared back underwater, and was still very excited when he reappeared five minutes later with half a dozen nice fish, 6–8 lb each, for our supper. 'I've never seen anything like it,' he said. 'That first dive as I dropped down through the water, I literally found myself falling on top of a large garopa. The fish must have been about 50 to 60 lb in weight. I've seen garopa about that size before, but not often. They are usually solitary fish living alone, and then I saw something I've never even read about. There was not just one giant garopa underneath me, there were twelve of them. All large fish, they were all moving very slowly among the rocks, and not in the least frightened of me. They looked like a herd of cows at pasture.'

The richness of Chetlat's underwater life was a treat for *Sohar*'s marine biologists. For four days they dived and collected with an excitement that rekindled every time they moved from one diving site to the next. Andrew was in raptures over the starfish and sea slugs that were his particular study. 'Look at this!' he would exclaim, holding up some particularly revolting specimen of a sea slug for us to admire. It was a fat, oozing bladder. 'Marvellous! I've never seen such fine specimens,' and he would drop the creature back with a soggy splash to nose round one of the many buckets which now made the deck look like an aquarium with its population of starfish, crabs and knobbly lumps of coral inhabited by clusters of hermit creatures. The pride of his collection were one massive starfish, a buff-coloured monster the size and shape of a very large cottage loaf, and another which had long thin arms that measured 2 feet across.

The numbers of large fish exceeded anything the divers had experi-enced. The fish were seldom afraid of humans, and it was obvious that there had been no previous diving off Chetlat. Hunting for the pot, Dave Tattle discovered his problem was to find fish *small* enough for him to tackle, fish that would not break his line or tow him too far away from the ship. The shoals were so dense that once or twice, as he shot a fish with his spear gun, the spear shaft passed clean through his prey and went into a fish on the other side, so he collected two fish at one shot. Other divers reported seeing giant wrass up to 100 lb in weight, and frequently they encountered species which normally would have been found only in deeper water. On the coral itself swarmed a full range of the coral-dwelling species, and large schools of parrot fish grazed over the surface of the coral, leaving a milky cloud of white dust hanging in the water behind them. The divers could hear the scrabbling sound of their teeth as they cracked upon the tips of the coral outcrops.

The expression on the face of the police captain was even more embarrassed four days later when he gave me the expected news. The Home Affairs Ministry in New Delhi, which was responsible for the administration of the Protected Territories, had gone back on the permission given by the Indian Foreign Office. *Sohar* was ordered to leave the Laccadives.

The early Arab navigators had regarded the Laccadives as forming part of a vast archipelago, the Dibajat Islands, which lay sprinkled across their sea routes between India and the Arabian peninsula. Arab geographers sometimes distinguished between the coconut rope-producing islands in the north, the Laccadives, and the islands in the south which produced cowrie shells, the modern Maldives. These cowrie shells were used as a form of money in some African and Indian communities, and so Arab ships called at the Maldives to pick up cargoes of them, as well as to trade for the shells of the turtles which came ashore in thousands to lay their eggs. The Arab geographers believed that the Dibajat Islands were ruled by a woman, a queen who lived in great splendour; and there was a sailors' yarn about one island which was populated entirely by females. This was the notorious Island of Women, where according to the collection of sailors' tales known as the *Marvels of India*, an Arab crew came ashore by accident. They had lost their way at sea, and thought themselves saved, but they were seized by a huge crowd of women, more than a thousand of them, who took them off into the hills and used them so demandingly that the men died of exhaustion. The only survivor was an old sailor, a Moslem from Cadiz, who was hidden by an old woman and managed to make himself a canoe. In this he escaped with his saviour, and lived to tell the tale.

One source of the story of the Island of Women may have been the island of Minicoy which lies halfway between the Maldives and the Laccadives, and visiting Arab sailors may have brought back information about the traditional culture of Minicoy which placed the women in charge. The man's only duty was to provide food, whether fish or coconut, and once he had delivered the day's ration his duty ended. All major household decisions were taken by his wife. She owned the house; property passed down through the female line; and when a man married he went to live at his wife's home, and the man took his wife's name. Also it was very likely that, then as now, the women of Minicoy were in a majority, because the men of Minicoy were seamen who were often away from home. Superimposed on this idea of a matriarchy was probably the fact that the Laccadive Islands, which also formed part of the Dibajat, did actually belong to a female ruler. They were fief to the kingdom of Cannanore on the mainland of India, to which they had to send an annual tribute of coconut rope. The ruling dynasty of Cannanore recognized the female right of accession to the throne, and the ruler of Cannanore was often a woman, essentially a queen, known as the Arrakal Bibi.

This notion of the Island of Women seems to have been mixed up with the Indian practice of *suttee*, or widow suicide, to produce the Adventure of the Burial Cave in the stories of Sindbad the Sailor. On his travels Sindbad finds himself in a country where he becomes a great favourite of the ruler. The ruler would like Sindbad to stay in his land, so he arranges for Sindbad to marry a local woman of good family. Sindbad lives happily and prosperously with his wife, until the day she falls sick and dies. To his horror Sindbad learns that he must be buried alive with her. The local custom is that the husband of a dead woman is lowered on a rope down into a charnel cave with his wife's corpse and a small quantity of food and water. The entrance to the cave is then blocked up by the mourners, and the man left to perish. Sindbad does not take his fate lightly, but his companions insist. They lay hold of him, and lower him into the charnel cave. When Sindbad refuses to untie himself from the rope, they drop the loose end on top of him and depart. There, surrounded by bones, Sindbad survives in a gruesome manner by killing the other widowers who are lowered down to him, and stealing their food. Eventually he is startled by a wild animal scuffling about in the cave, and follows it along a narrow passageway to find himself on the beach; there to his intense joy, he sees an Arab merchant ship sailing by. He manages to attract its attention, and is rescued, so to continue with his adventures.

Only 170 miles of the Sea of Larwi, the medieval Arab name for the Arabian Sea, separated us from India when *Sohar* sailed from Chetlat on 13 December. And on this leg of the journey John Harwood had his first whale sightings. On the morning of 14 December we drifted up to a herd of about seven or eight whales, probably false killer whales. They were directly in our track, surfacing regularly to breathe and completely relaxed. Occasionally they threw themselves clear out of the water and fell back with a resounding splash. At other times they poked their heads up, like watchful guard dogs, to keep an eye on *Sohar* edging towards them. Soon afterwards, a group of nine grampus cruised past the ship about 150 yards distant. They too were not in the least hurried or perturbed, and they stayed on the surface with their grey-green fins cutting through the water beside us. Fifteen minutes later a second school of six grampus appeared, this time on the opposite side of the ship, and when the wind got up and *Sohar* began to move more briskly through the water, a pair of bottle-nosed dolphins took up their station and played around her bow, twisting and diving in the disturbed wake. To make John's notebook complete, yet another small whale passed close astern of us in the evening.

The abundance of marine life was witnessed by the flocks of sea birds, mostly sooty terns, which wheeled and swooped over flurries of white splashes in the water. Fish of about 1 lb in size were driving small fry to the surface. The fry hurled themselves into the air to escape their tormentors, and the sea birds screamed and stabbed at them with their beaks. In turn the predators fell victim to larger fish, dashing into the attack from below, and the surface of the sea burst open like a cannon shot as a heavy predator went thrashing into the attack.

'Shark! Shark!' shouted Khamees Police, pointing over the side. There, firmly hooked on our fishing line, was a small shark. Swiftly it was hauled aboard by Peter, stabbed with a fish trident by Trondur, and banged over the head with a belaying pin by Mohamed. Khamees Police carried it off with a grin of triumph. This truly international effort produced an excellent supper of shark meat, and I made a note of the Omani recipe. The shark was cleaned and boned, and the flesh was boiled in sea water until tender. Then it was drained and the flesh wrapped in a towel and squeezed firmly until all the juice was out. Then the meat was crumbled into small pieces and added to onions frying over the charcoal fire. Chillies and tinned tomatoes were put in to taste, together with tamarind, pounded garlic and crushed cardamom. The whole dish was then reheated and served: it was delicious.

Shanby had now reached the absolute nadir of his cooking career. He was refusing to cook chapattis for the evening meal, and had taken to hanging round the cook box waiting for someone else to do the cooking – then he would swoop in to take the first plateful. To crown it all, he was caught stealing food from the ship's stores. He scuttled away to his bunk where he crouched over a tin of peaches, trying to stuff them into his mouth before he was noticed. He was, I concluded, exactly like a beagle – appealing to the eye, always sniffing out food, and unteachable.

A hundred miles off the coast we saw undeniable evidence of mainland India – great swathes of pollution lying floating in windrows on the sea. There were pieces of timber, bits of plastic, scraps of fishing net, decaying vegetation, an occasional old bottle, clots of oil, bundles of seaweed, and general trash. Despite its unappetizing appearance the scientists became quite excited, and scooped up samples of the rubbish. Oil clots were netted and bottled for analysis. Lumps of seaweed were hauled aboard to be examined for resident animals. Small, rather repulsive-looking worms were found; tiny crabs, barnacles and larvae. To compensate for this revolting group, the dipnet also brought up some beautiful, tiny fish of many colours, which had been living around the rubbish, feeding on its organisms. Once again *Sohar*'s deck looked like a travelling aquarium as the vivid fish finned their way round and round the buckets of sea water while waiting to be photographed and identified. The next afternoon *Sohar* passed through another brand of pollution, which we thought at first were the petals of flowers or the leaves of trees blown out to sea. On closer inspection the petals turned out to be the wings and bodies of millions upon millions of moths, which for some unknown reason had committed mass suicide.

A baby sperm whale appeared. It was 16–18 feet long, and all alone: John guessed that it must have become separated from its parents, and was lost. Perhaps the baby thought *Sohar* could foster it, because the animal showed great curiosity. It swam up astern until only 30 yards away, and then turned and wallowed along on our quarter, inspecting the ship for some time. Then it puffed slowly off, still on the surface, and regularly shooting out the characteristic forward-sloping spout of a sperm whale until finally it sounded with a flip of its flukes. John commented that in the 1860s there had been enough whales in the Laccadive Sea to attract whaling ships. Now, so it seemed, the whale population was almost gone. The whole of the Indian Ocean had recently been declared a whale sanctuary, but perhaps it was too late.

Saleh, who was at the tiller, now told us how 'Haut', the great whale, was capable of rubbing up against a ship's side and overturning it. To frighten the 'Haut' away, he said, one should bang two pieces of metal together and make a loud noise. His ideas were interesting, for his story was almost a word-for-word repetition of the early Arab tales, and I noted how once again the whale has dominated so many tales of the sea. In the fifth century St Brendan was said to have landed on the back of a whale, which its crew mistook for an island; and Sindbad, too, had almost exactly the same adventure. Sindbad's whale island had rocks and soil on its back, and trees growing, and a stream of fresh water where Sindbad's companions had gone to wash their clothes. When the whale dived and the rest of the passengers rushed back to the ship, Sindbad saved himself by climbing into a large wooden wash tub, which he paddled with his arms and legs, 'the fish nibbling at his feet', until he came to real land.

A bright yellow and green sea snake, about 4 feet long, was *Sohar*'s next sign of land. The learned *mu'allim* Ahmed Ibn Majid had predicted that the presence of sea snakes was a sure indication that one was approaching land, and Andrew confirmed that all the known species of sea snakes except one live in shallow waters, so Ibn Majid was, zoologically speaking, correct. Andrew, however, was not enthusiastic about catching our yellow and green visitor to add to his collection. According to his textbook on sea snakes they are lethargic and slow-moving animals, and not at all vicious. But this one must have been an exception or in a very bad mood. When it saw *Sohar*, the snake swam very fast at the ship, turned aside at the last moment, and wriggled past the side as far as the trailing safety rope. When the rope brushed the snake, the animal promptly swung round and struck at the rope with its fangs. Since sea snakes are many times more venomous than the most poisonous land snakes, Andrew looked distinctly thoughtful.

That night we ran into an unmistakable land squall, and took a sharp buffeting from a line of black clouds, lightning, and heavy rain that sent the Omanis scurrying to the sheets to keep the ship from being taken aback and dismasted. At dawn the sun illuminated the high green hills of the western Ghats of India, and we caught sight of distant sails. They were Indian country craft, the last major survivors of the days of trade under sail. They were magnificent ships. The largest of these country craft were bigger than *Sohar*, and had black, barge-like hulls that were rather inelegant. But there were other smaller, more graceful craft with curved bows and splendid galleon sterns. All of them boasted the most amazing assemblies of sails. Whereas *Sohar* wore only plain ocean-going sails, the Indian craft were rigged for coasting passages in light airs, so they set great clouds of canvas to catch the breeze. Triangle upon triangle, sail upon sail, they boasted every conceivable arrangement. There were mainsails and mizzens, spankers and jibs, sky sails, staysails and topsails. One barque carried no less than four jibs, and a tiny forecourse no bigger than a large bedsheet, set on a bamboo pole down by her cutwater. As *Sohar* passed her, going on the other tack, it was a scene to be remembered – two tall sailing ships, strangers passing in silence while the two crews watched one another intently.

'Hell's teeth!' exclaimed Dave Tattle. 'Would you look at that.' He was peering at the beach through binoculars, as *Sohar* sailed parallel to the coast about half a mile offshore. 'The people! There must be thousands and thousands of them. They're like ants. What on earth are they all doing?'

I borrowed the binoculars. Yes, one area of the beach was black with people, but it was nothing extraordinary. Villagers were buying fish from the flotilla of dugout canoes returning with the day's catch. But Dave had never seen anything like it before. He came from New Zealand, and it was his first sight of the seething crowds of humanity which make the Malabar coast of India one of the most densely populated strips of land on earth. Dave kept staring at the scurrying figures, and muttering under his breath in astonishment as *Sohar* made her way quietly towards a motor dhow, anchored in the roadstead off the town of Calicut. He was still staring when the anchor plunged overboard, and *Sohar* came to a halt.

'My God,' he kept on muttering, 'so many people. Where do they all come from? What can they do? There are always people coming and going. What on earth for?'

Next morning, after we had spent a miserable night rolling and pitching in the swell of the exposed anchorage, and drenched by another land squall, there was still no sign of customs or police coming out to clear the ship, so I decided to go ashore to find the authorities for myself. As the rubber dinghy approached the shore, riding on the backs of the waves, yet another crowd began to assemble. This time it gaped with bovine interest at the rubber dinghy. At the last minute someone in the crowd shouted and pointed behind us; I turned my head just in time to see a large breaker curling up behind the rubber boat. It seized the dinghy, slewed it sideways and flipped it upside down in a crash of water. Pitched ignominiously on to the sand, my nose told me the answer to Dave's question about what the inhabitants did on the beach. They used it as a public lavatory.

Brown booby

—7—
Christmas in Calicut

'You have not had my permission to come ashore,' screamed the deputy collector of customs in a frenzy. His eyes were bulging with rage, and the feeling that his authority had been flouted. 'You have no right to land without permission from me. What do you mean by it! You should wait until I send a boarding party to inspect your vessel. It is the regulation. I can forbid you to land!' He drew himself up in his chair, and glared. The effect was totally spoiled by a scavenging black crow which flapped down on to the ledge of the open window behind him, and uttered a harsh, derisive caw. The collector gestured angrily at an underling to chase the bird away. The underling, a retired customs sergeant with the demeanour of a sycophant of many years' service, made shooing gestures at the crow which launched itself back into the air. The deputy collector was almost apoplectic with anger. The retired sergeant had just told him that, after being capsized on the filthy beach, I had gone to the local hotel to wash and change before I came to the customs office of Calicut.

I looked around the office. It was a picture of decrepitude and neglect. Once it must have been a fine building, airy and elegant, with high ceilings and open eaves to let in the breeze. The tall windows gave a magnificent view of the sea, and the roof was constructed of pleasant red tiles, but now the place was down-at-heel and scruffy. It might have been last painted twenty years ago, and spots of green mould disfigured the peeling whitewash on the walls. The deputy collector's office was on the upper floor, and when I had put my hand on the banister to walk upstairs, the rail had wobbled alarmingly, its supports eaten through by insects. To arrive at the collector's office door you had to skirt around sagging patches in the floor where the building was collapsing on itself. Outside the window I could see the skeletal remains of the customs jetty; it too had largely collapsed, and the broken iron pillars would have impaled any boat that was foolishly brought alongside. There was no customs or police launch in sight. In fact it was evident that no such vessel even existed. Any ship which had waited at anchor offshore for a visit by Calicut customs would wait for all eternity.

The passport office, downstairs in the same decaying building, was even barer. There were the usual school desk, two hard chairs, and a cupboard with warped doors. The passports of the ship's crew were impounded by an elderly plainclothes sergeant of the Special Branch, who was clearly terrified of losing his pension. While he laboriously wrote out a receipt, I glanced at his log book. In the past twelve months only five foreign vessels had called at Calicut, all of them small motor dhows. Yet already I had counted seven policemen, and at least a dozen constables of the customs service. In another upstairs room were a port officer and an assistant port officer, together with an indeterminate number of clerks and orderlies, all idle, shabby, and with nothing to do. With a sinking heart, I realized that the dead hand of Indian bureaucracy was everywhere.

A tug was promised at an exorbitant charge, which would tow *Sohar* into the river mouth at Beypore, 10 miles south of Calicut. Beypore was the harbour for Calicut, and it would have been much easier for *Sohar* to have arrived directly at Beypore, but customs regulations forbade that logical course. Calicut was the official port of entry, so ships had first to clear formalities there. The tug, grandly described as the 'Property of the Port Authority', broke down before it even left port. For another day and a half we rolled and wallowed in discomfort on the Calicut anchorage before the tug finally put in an appearance and *Sohar* was moved.

Beypore produced an extraordinary sensation, as though we had been transported back into a seaport of the eighteenth century. It had all the smells, clamour, activity, squalor and moments of transcendent beauty of, say, Genoa or Hull in the days when sailing ships docked in the worst stews of European ports. At night, when a miasmic vapour curled up off the Beypore river, shrouded the black shadows of the wharf and lapped around the hulls of the sailing ships so that only their spars stood above the river mist like lances, one half expected to hear a muffled cry, and then the splash of a murdered corpse being tossed in the stream. The blackness was full of soft, sucking sounds as the turgid river flowed past *Sohar*'s hull. Occasionally a dugout canoe on some unknown errand would glide past in silhouette, or hover suspiciously near the anchor cable of the ship, merging into the hull's shadow. The stranger was probably just curious to have a look at the foreign ship, but *Sohar*'s deck watch had orders to keep a sharp lookout for thieves. Beypore smelled of villainy.

The first glimmer of dawn brought the magic. Beypore's waterfront began to take shape and substance as the light fell on palm-thatched boatbuilding sheds, great hangar-like structures which lined the northern bank of the river. Under these sheds stood the skeletons of perhaps forty or fifty wooden ships under repair or construction. Beypore is probably the largest wooden shipbuilding centre left in the world. Her yards are still busy after a thousand years, building everything from dhows for the Arabs to warships for the Royal Navy. A Beypore-built ship of the line had fought at Trafalgar. In the foul waters of the foreshore lay half-sunk logs, like monstrous reptiles, which would be hauled ashore and cut into planks and beams for the shipwrights. A quarter of a mile upriver one could glimpse the town wharf and, on a knoll above, the verandah of yet another decaying customs house. The broad expanse of the river extended inland, now a gunmetal grey in the first light but turning soon to the colour of *café au lait* as the light strengthened. The opposite bank was a wall of coconut plantations broken only by the mouths of backwaters, and the occasional pathway leading southward along the coast. Scattered about the river anchorage was the most remarkable collection of sailing craft, vessels of every size, shape and description, *dhangies, patmars, thonis*, some of them swinging at anchor, others moored in rows, yet others lying tilted over on the beach where they were being cleaned. As the sun rose higher and the light strengthened there came the unmistakable sounds of a new day at Beypore – the raucous cries of thousands upon thousands of Indian crows which had their nests in the coconut groves. Soon the crows began taking to the air, rising like black flakes of ash, flapping their way towards the waiting town where they would scavenge for their existence.

Aboard *Sohar* the morning invasion of the crows was a daily torment. The birds settled on the mast and spars, and scuffled and uttered their harsh cries. Their droppings spattered down on the deck, and if one's back was turned there would be an impudent scrambling flap of wings and claws as the crows swooped in to steal. They ate anything – scraps of food, old bits of fruit skin, even the rancid tallow we used for greasing the blocks. Everywhere, at all times, we were watched by the beady eyes of hungry crows, perched in rows above us on the spars or at a safe distance on the gunnels. The natives of Beypore gave us much the same feeling. They were everywhere – in canoes alongside, clustered in crowds standing for hours on the wharf, hanging about aboard country craft moored nearby. And always they stared at us with the same fixed glaze as the crows, and with almost the same hunger too. When Saleh cut clear some worn-out sail lashings, miserable shredded scraps of coconut rope which had served their purpose, and tossed the scraps overboard, an emaciated old man in a dugout canoe at once put out from the shore, picked up the old rope from the putrid water, and paddled off with it.

The oppressive atmosphere of Beypore weighed down on the European crew members. The ever-present poverty and squalor combined with the damp heat of the river to produce a wearisome lethargy aboard *Sohar*. There was vital work to be done – we had to make better sails, lighten the spars, careen the ship, and construct deck boxes to contain the loose items on deck. If *Sohar* had been a new car, she was now due for her all-important 1000-mile servicing. But the sheer inertia of Beypore was sapping. It took hour after hour of pleading and cajoling to get wharf space cleared for us to go alongside, to find timber for the spars, to locate a blockmaker to make spare blocks for the rigging. Meanwhile *Sohar* had to lie at anchor in the noxious river, swinging with the tide, stared at and idle. Within twenty-four hours the first crew members began to fall sick, debilitated by the damp, muggy heat, stomach disorders, the constant attack of mosquitos, the nightly rain showers which soaked through the deck, and food which it was impossible to wash and clean properly. The river itself was indescribably filthy, a vast open sewer. The only available fresh water came from a well on shore, and one day the Omanis found worms wriggling in it. The sickness, the stench, the general air of decay and cafard reminded me strongly of descriptions of the trading ships which sailed to West Africa two centuries earlier and lay idly in the river mouth, waiting for their cargo while the ships rotted and the crews succumbed to fever. Within three days half of *Sohar*'s European crew were suffering from aches and pains, and the Omanis had begun to shiver with heavy colds. This was how the expedition spent Christmas Day 1980.

Hard work and sheer physical effort were the only way to prevent the expedition from disintegrating. As soon as space was available at the wharf, *Sohar* was warped alongside, and with a concerted effort of self-discipline the entire crew mustered for the labour of emptying out the ship. It was a daunting task. In the muggy tropical heat we began shifting by hand every item we could set ashore from *Sohar*: ropes, bosun's stores, chain, spare anchors, all our food, fuel cans, every item to make the hull rise higher in the water. Then we turned our attention to the ballast. We pulled up the floorboards and began hauling out the sandbags, hundreds upon hundreds of them tightly packed into the bilges in Muscat; now they had to be landed. The conditions were atrocious, scorching on deck and on the quayside, and like an oven in the hull where the constant smell of the bilge gas caught in our throats. And yet, interestingly, under these appalling conditions a note of complete teamwork appeared amongst *Sohar*'s international crew. The men formed a human chain and tossed the sandbags along the line, up from the bilge, out through the hatch, across the deck, and into a neat pile on the wharf.

Someone, probably Eid, struck up the work chant. The Omanis began to sing. One by one the Europeans joined in; and suddenly the entire crew had forgotten its aches and pains and was roaring and stamping away with gusto. Sandbags were hurtling through the air. Grins and smiles appeared. Khamees Police looked like a prize fighter, glistening with sweat, as he tossed a steady arc of sandbags up through the hatch. Peter, his injured foot now almost healed, stood massively on the gunnel, all 6 feet 3 inches of him, lobbing sandbags ashore like tennis balls. Even sleepy-looking Jumail was tearing into his work, burrowing like an excited terrier after a rat into the bilges to drag out the sandbags, his bare feet sticking out and kicking like two strange animals, and his head occasionally surfacing for a breath of air. For some reason he had decided to shave his skull completely bald, and now it appeared from the bilges like some disembodied oddity, glittering with sweat like a shiny black football. In just two and a half hours we shifted 15 tons of sand by hand.

Jumail's shaven pate was explained to me that evening when Musalam accompanied me into Calicut. Jumail, he told me, was in disguise: by shaving his head he hoped not to be recognized in Calicut. It was the old story. Jumail had married a girl in Calicut when he was there on a previous voyage. He had left her behind and failed to send money for her support, as Islamic custom demanded. Now he was fearful that he should be spotted by the girl's family, and obliged to pay up the arrears.

I chuckled at the story. Indeed I had noticed that Jumail had been staying close to the ship, and not going off into Calicut in the evenings

Above Handing inboard the great mainsail as the mainspar is lowered for a sail change.
Below Ida Severin, the author's ten-year-old daughter, sailed from India to Sri Lanka.
'Attached to the bosun's chair by a safety harness, she was lowered into the sea. . . . A
crew member kept a sharp watch for sharks. When a menacing shadow appeared, Ida was
whisked up into the air by two strong men, and swung inboard like a parcel'

Above Hoisting a new jib off the coast of India as the ship meets the first strong winds of the voyage. *Below* 'When the mainspar hung vertical, its butt swept back and forth across the deck with the rolling of the ship like a lethal scythe . . . split second timing was called for.' *Opposite* Hauling in the mainspar, the crew gets ready to swing the great mainsail around the mast and set a new course

Above Adam's Peak in Sri Lanka, th‹
landfall for medieval Arab sailors.
Pilgrim lamps mark the path to the
spot where it is said Adam's foot fir‹
touched earth after he was cast dow‹
from Paradise.

Left A Sri Lankan gem miner
searches alluvial gravel for gem
stones. Sindbad twice visited the
island, then known as the Kingdom
of Serendeeb, and its mines of
precious stones probably gave rise to
his tale of the adventure in the Valle‹
of Diamonds. Sindbad also describe‹
the great wealth of the King of
Serendeeb, and Arab geographers
wrote of the dazzling royal
processions through the streets of th‹
capital.

Opposite In Colombo, Sri Lanka's
capital, a mummer dressed in prince'‹
finery continues the tradition during
one of the monthly *perehera*
processions.

Over The Doldrums. Swimming off
the ship to obtain this photograph,
photographer Richard Greenhill was
nearly left behind when a sudden gu‹
of wind blew *Sohar* on her way

Left Shark frenzy in the Indian Ocean. His bare feet dangerous[ly] close to the animal's jaws, Abdullah clubs a shark with a belaying pin. 'There were thrashing, snapping sharks slithering everywhere. They wer[e] incredibly difficult to dispatch. They twisted and flapped despit[e] a tremendous battering from bludgeons and knives.'

Below left Eid salts down the flesh of seventeen sharks, setting out the slabs of shark flesh to d[ry] in the sun

Above right Tim Severin shows Khamees Navy how to use a *kamal*, the medieval Arab navigation instrument. The *kam[al,]* a wooden tablet held out at the end of a string, measured the height of a selected star. With v[ery] little practice it was possible to obtain a latitude position accura[te] to within 30 miles

Below right Baffled by head win[ds] and then becalmed in the Doldrums, *Sohar* made no progress in the Indian Ocean for [a] month. Drinking water ran worryingly short and was strictl[y] rationed. Finally the south-west monsoon brought badly needed rain, and the crew were able to replenish the water tanks and at last wash in fresh water

Left 'The great 81-foot mainspar had snapped in two. It now hung like a broken wing.' Halfway across the Indian Ocean, *Sohar* was crippled when the mainspar broke during the night. One man was injured.

Below 'It was essential to bring down the damaged mainspar to the deck as fast as possible without smashing any more of the rigging or causing any further injuries. "Peter! Dick! Terry! want you three to control the aft end of the spar as she comes down!" I shouted. . . .' By the light of a torch Tim Severin directs damage control as *Sohar*'s crew tackles the crisis.

Right Next day the bosun's stores were ransacked to provide the ropes repair and re-rig the vessel

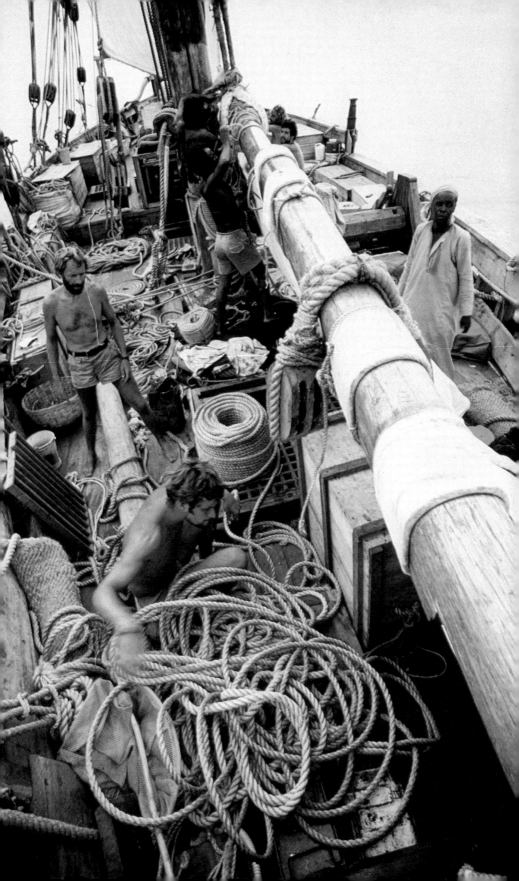

Above In the cold light of dawn the crew examines the jagged stump of the broken mainspar. 'Peter Dobbs and Tim Readman set to work with saw and chisel to round off the fractured end of the spar. When it was ready, the Omanis spent half an hour carefully balancing it to their liking. Then the spare mizzen sail was lashed on. Stays and halyards were disentangled and set up in their proper places, and *(right)* with our special hauling song, the entire crew hoisted the jury-rigged mainspar to the masthead.'

Opposite Sohar heads for Sumatra. 'Despite the queer combination of a jib and two mizzen sails, *Sohar*'s rig looked neat and trim. The sails filled out pleasingly, and although her speed was reduced by about a third, *Sohar* was moving briskly through the water'

Above Sailing down the Malacca Strait.

Left At Sabang in northern Sumatra Moslem townsfolk are intrigued to meet the first Arab sailors to have visited their harbour in living memory. Retracing the old Arab sea-route to the East, the expedition found Moslem communities flourishing in every port they visited.

Right Buying fish from Sumatran fishermen

Over

Above Ancient and modern: *Sohar* passes an oil rig in the waters off Singapore.

Below A Sindbad of the twentieth century, Shamees Navy at a Singaporean hamburger stand

like the rest of the Omani sailors. He was scared of meeting his irate in-laws.

But I was totally unprepared for what came next. Musalam cleared his throat nervously, and mentioned that he had found an Indian family in the town where he could stay, renting a room for 150 rupees a week, breakfast included. It was a Moslem family, of course, and Musalam asked if he could sleep on shore. Of course, I told him. His next words floored me.

'I want to marry a girl from the family, captain. But the crew agree that I must have your permission before I can marry.'

I was jerked into full attention, and noted how very smartly Musalam was dressed in new trousers, a green and white patterned shirt, and with his hair and moustache neatly groomed. Of course, he was courting. But how had he managed it? The ship had been only a few days in Beypore, and we had been working on her from dawn to dusk. Yet already Musalam had found a girl to marry.

'Tell me about the girl's family,' I asked, trying to gather my wits and assess the situation.

'I met her family one evening when I was in the town,' Musalam replied. 'They invited me to their house. I have eaten with them in the evenings. The family are very good Moslems. They are poor, but the family has met many Omanis. Sailors often stay at their house.'

'Why do you ask for my permission if you want to marry their daughter?'

'Because that is the custom,' Musalam replied simply. 'The captain must give his permission before one of his sailors can marry.' Then he paused. 'To marry her, I must give her family a present of money,' he continued. 'Captain, please, can you lend me the money for my wife?'

Now I really was floundering.

'How much money do you need?'

Musalam gave a gentle shrug. 'As you wish,' he replied humbly.

I was in a quandary. How on earth did I fix the price of a bride? It was not exactly the sort of valuation one is faced with every day. Besides, I remembered, Musalam had a wife back in Oman and a new baby daughter. 'What about your wife back home? Won't she be sad if you marry a girl in Calicut? You have your family in Oman to think of.'

Musalam had a ready answer. 'I can make my Omani wife happy, perhaps with a present when I get home. And if I am allowed to bring my Calicut wife back to Oman after the voyage, she can look after the house. She can cook, clean everything, and make life easy. Then my Omani wife can spend all her time with her children. When she is old, my new wife can look after everything.'

'How old is this girl you want to marry?'

'Fifteen.'

'But if you bring your new wife to Oman, will she live in the same house or another house?'

'The same house,' Musalam answered proudly. 'I have a new house with four rooms. Two are sitting-rooms, and there are two bathrooms. When I get home, I want to put in air conditioning. Soon I will have electricity.'

The conversation seemed to be taking a sidetrack. Musalam apparently had his mind firmly set on his Calicut marriage, and there was little I could do to change it. I made one last attempt. 'But Musalam, you know as well as I do that it is very difficult to bring an Indian bride back to Oman to live. You must have special permission, and enough money in the bank to look after her.'

For a moment Musalam looked doubtful. 'I think you must have 20,000 rials in the bank before you can bring a wife from India into Oman,' he told me.

'And if you do not have the money?'

'Then I will send money to her in Calicut.'

'How much money?'

'Not much. A hundred and fifty rupees a month. Ten rials, maybe, it is enough. A wife in India is not expensive.'

'And if you can't manage to send the money, what will happen then?'

'After three years the girl is free to marry again. Until then, she will wait.'

I knew that Musalam was perfectly genuine in his request to get married. The medieval Arab geographers had written how Arab sailors used to marry local girls when they arrived in the Maldive Islands; Sindbad himself seemed to find a wife in nearly every port; and from my own experience I knew that Jumail and Hoodaid, the shipwright of Sur, had acquired Calicut wives. It was a custom as old as the history of Arab trade to Malabar, and it was clear that Calicut's Moslem community thrived on it. For them there was no stigma if a daughter married a visiting sailor who might never return. Rather, the Calicut Moslem families were pleased to be allied by marriage to someone who came from Arabia, the homeland of their religion. Such a marriage was a status symbol. If the Arab seaman sailed away and was never heard from again, then social custom was organized so that the woman could find a new husband. Musalam and the other Islamic sailors were of course free to have up to four wives apiece, provided that they treated them fairly and equally, and I was sure that Musalam, one of the most decent men I had ever met, was not taking advantage of the situation.

As matters turned out, Musalam accepted my bewildered silence as tacit permission for him to get married. And that evening he, the girl and her family went before the local *qadi*, the Islamic judge, and were married. Next morning he appeared on board with his new bride and a brand-new brother-in-law in attendance. At least fifteen other members of the bride's family clustered on the quayside behind them. The girl was a delight. She was a slender, demure beauty named Zubaida, with huge, dark brown eyes and a timid smile. Musalam was a mixture of pride and protectiveness. He apologized profusely that the girl's clothes were so plain. She was ashamed, he said, but the family could afford very little. The brother-in-law promptly explained that he was the only son. His father was dead, and there had been six unmarried daughters. Now there were only five, and the money that Musalam gave would provide dowries for two more of the girls who wanted to get married. Only when marrying an Arab sailor did the man give money, he said. In other cases it was the girl who had to provide a cash gift, according to her means. I took the hint, and drew Musalam on one side. He could have 1000 rupees from ship's funds for his bride price, a sum worth between £50 and £60. Musalam seemed happy with the amount. To me it was a bargain, although the original budget for the voyage had not allowed for paying money from ship's funds to sponsor wives for my Omani sailors. I could not help thinking of the five remaining unmarried sisters, and the fact that there were another seven Omani sailors on my ship.

My premonition was correct. Over the next few days all but one of the Omani sailors got married in Calicut. The exception was Khamees Navy. The others all came to see me, one by one, for their loan of 1000 rupees. I had announced there would be no favouritism, and each man would have to make do with the same amount. Jumail tried, unsuccessfully, to get a special loan. It seemed that he too wanted to marry, but he first had to settle matters with the family of his previous Calicut wife whom he had abandoned. The lady in question had since managed to find another husband, so the indemnity Jumail paid was small, but it led to some hard bargaining with his former in-laws. All the sailors pronounced themselves delighted with their wives, except Saleh. For several days he hesitated, too shy and too uncertain to propose to his chosen lady. He kept on asking his companions if she was the right girl or not, until finally they egged him on, managed to get him dressed up in best *dishdasha* and turban, and marched him off to meet the girl's family and go before the *qadi*. Next morning they all came back aboard, almost helpless with glee, except poor Saleh who was hanging his head in embarrassment. He had married the girl all right, and spent just one night with her. Next morning she had run away, taking the 1000 rupees with her. For the remainder of our stay in Calicut Saleh remained on board glumly, and there was much nudging of ribs and chuckling whenever the other Omanis teased him about his marital experience.

Sohar was now light enough to be careened. Leaving a guard on the pile of stores on the quayside, we towed her across to a sandbar on the opposite bank of the river. At high tide we put her ashore, rigged block and tackle to her masthead, and on the falling tide laid her over on one side so we could clean the hull. It was a grisly task. The sewage in the water was so thick that, for the first and only time in the voyage, Peter Dobbs hesitated before going into the water. But there was no choice. We had to scrape off the weed and slime and barnacles, and apply a fresh coat of mutton fat and lime to protect the timber from teredo worm. Once again Beypore river echoed to an Arab work chant as *Sohar*'s sailors, Europeans and Omanis, cleaned down the hull. The muck came off easily, because the old lime and fat coat peeled away and took the fouling with it. The timber underneath seemed sound. But the panels of unprotected wood, which we had attached to the hull as an experiment, were honeycombed with wormholes as thick as a large knitting needle, for they had been ravaged by shipworm in the two months since they had been put in place. The worst panels, slabs of wood 2½ inches thick, could be snapped with one's bare hands like wafers. It was a sharp lesson in the importance of protecting *Sohar*'s hull from teredo.

While the ship was being careened Trondur had been drawing a new sail plan for *Sohar*, and I had dispatched a Gujerati merchant to Madras to buy new canvas to replace the sad, baggy material of *Sohar*'s original sails. By a judicious distribution of bribes the Gujerati managed to bring back 2½ tons of canvas as hand luggage aboard a passenger train, while the train guard pocketed money and looked the other way, and a stream of porters carried the bolts of canvas into a passenger compartment, filling it up entirely. The sailcloth was excellent, still made to the original specifications and marked with a red or blue line down the selvage to denote its weight and strength. India was one of the few countries in the world where I could have found such magnificent sailcloth, and only in India could I then have attempted the next step: to make *Sohar* a complete new suit of sails in less than a week. In Europe or North America it would have taken four months.

The first step was to select a firm, level stretch of clean, sandy beach near where the fishermen landed their dugout canoes. With pegs and string Trondur and I laid down the outlines of the new sails on the sand, and I appointed a reliable Indian foreman. He hired a dozen fishermen as they came ashore, and brought them to us. We showed the fishermen how to stitch the yard-wide strips of canvas together, distributed the needles and thread, and set the fishermen to work. They were delighted. The pay was in cash, and they had been promised a bonus. When the fishermen had worked for eight hours I checked how many square yards of sail they had finished and made a calculation. Then I asked the foreman to hire twelve more men. It took him half an hour to find them, and the labour force was doubled. In the end we had the remarkable sight of no less than thirty newly trained sailmakers sitting cross-legged on the huge sails spread out across the beach, and stitching away for all they were worth. In the heat of the day they slept or went fishing, and returned in the cool of the evening to pick up their needles again and work in pairs far into the night by the light of hurricane lamps placed on the ground between them. Five days later we had a creamy white set of new sails, nearly 3000 square feet of them, all ready to be loaded; and every one of *Sohar*'s old sails had been stretched out and reshaped with new ropes along the edges to remove the worst of the wrinkles.

Disposing of one unwanted 'cook' was far more difficult than sewing an entire set of new sails. In Beypore Shanby had excelled himself. He stole ship's stores, and slipped ashore to barter them for cigarettes, so I confined him to the ship and forbade him to have any contact with the locals. Meanwhile I tried to arrange his passage home. He was, as it turned out, a Pakistani citizen. He had never been granted Omani nationality, and this led to endless difficulties because India does not welcome discharged Pakistani seamen. And so for eight days I shuttled endlessly from government office to government office in Calicut, trying to get rid of Shanby. No one, understandably, wanted to have him. I grew hoarse explaining the situation to petty officials. They asked for bribes and I paid them, but it didn't do any good. A Special Branch sergeant even had the impudence to come back next day, and ask me to replace one of the bank notes that had vanished so swiftly into his pocket. The note was torn, he complained, and the bank would not accept it. A glimpse inside Calicut's Central Police Station was awe-inspiring. In the main office twenty desks faced one another in two lines. Every desk was piled high with disintegrating files and ageing slips of paper so that, for want of space, each clerk was obliged to balance an old-fashioned ink blotting pad on his knees to write on. But no writing was being done. Half the desks were unmanned, and those staff who had come to work either sat motionless or had tipped back their chairs against the walls and were gazing into space with massive indifference. Not a single file was moving, and yet by a strange act of common agreement every man was still balancing his empty blotter on his knees.

Finally, and with growing desperation to get rid of Shanby and his appalling cooking, I worked my way up the chain of command until I located the bungalow of the senior Special Branch officer in the district. As I walked into his living-room I saw he was reading a paperback copy of an English novel, *The Magus* by John Fowles. My spirits rose. Here at last was someone who would understand. Aboard *Sohar* I had another John Fowles novel, *The French Lieutenant's Woman*. Had the superintendent read it? He had not. Was he enjoying *The Magus*? Yes, indeed. It was a very fine novel. Then I could certainly recommend that he should also read Fowles's other books. Twenty-four hours later *The French Lieutenant's Woman* was in the hands of the superintendent and Shanby, his ticket and a month's wages in a grubby hand, was on a bus headed for Bombay Airport and ultimately Pakistan. As I watched him go, I knew in my heart of hearts that Shanby would be all right. He would always be a born survivor.

Ibrahim replaced Shanby as cook. He was a Minicoy islander whom I had known since my early days of hunting for timber in Malabar. By trade a clerk, he was heartily sick of being a civil servant with no prospects, and he said he could turn his hand to cooking. Anything would have been an improvement on Shanby's cuisine, but Ibrahim turned out to be a very fine cook in his own right. His crisp chapattis and tasty curries were to be another step on *Sohar*'s road to improved morale.

Robert Moore, John Harwood and Dave Tattle of the scientific crew had to get back to their universities, and so signed off from *Sohar* at Beypore. So too did Trondur, who had to leave in order to prepare an important exhibition of his drawings and sculptures in Scandinavia; and Mohamed Ismail, the shipwright, also rejoined his family, who lived not far from Calicut and were glad to see him home after an absence of nearly a year. To replace them came Peter Hunnam, another marine biologist who specialized in marine conservation work, and my nine-year-old daughter Ida. She had been allowed off school for a few weeks in order to join the ship on the next leg of the Sindbad Voyage, and came to Calicut with Peter Hunnam, a four-day journey from London, by plane, train and the inevitable moribund taxi.

Ida was round-eyed with wonder at the sights of Beypore. The daily scenes in the narrow lanes and back alleys leading up from the waterfront must have seemed like moving illustrations from her story books. Fish porters staggered past at a bent-kneed trot with dripping baskets of sardines and small fry balanced on their heads, yelling out to the tally men who counted the porterage from a little hut by the landing. In the opposite direction flowed a constant stream of foot passengers for the green-painted dugout canoes which operated a ferry service across the river – men pushing bicycles, women in saris, schoolchildren with their satchels, more women carrying their market shopping, office workers in white dhotis and black umbrellas. Every back street had its stallholders offering fruit, cold drinks, cloth, vegetables, hanks of coconut twine, soap and haberdashery. Here was a tailor pressing a new shirt with an iron heated with glowing charcoal; there a copra worker was spreading coconut meat out on the ground to dry so that the pedestrians had to step round his stock in trade. Women were endlessly washing and sweeping, feeding goats, pounding cassava with mortar and pestle, and combing out with their fingers the long black tresses of their tiny daughters who stood motionless. Some women formed in groups to spin coconut yarn, ready for the men to roll it up into great balls, like grandmother's knitting wool, but 4 feet in circumference. These enormous balls of coir were carried away on the heads of porters, a surrealistic sight bobbing above the heads of the crowd. Coolies pushed two-wheeled wooden carts through lanes too narrow for cars or trucks. White-turbaned overseers from the boatyard advanced with ponderous dignity; a Hindu shipwright returned from his pilgrimage to the local shrine, dressed in a black *lungi*, an ash purification mark on his forehead and a marigold tucked behind his ear. One entire section of this town rang with the beat of metal upon metal, and peering inside the dark sheds one saw blacksmiths squatting down in pairs beside their anvils. An assistant wielded tongs to pluck a glowing metal strip from the charcoal burner and place it in position. Then the two squatting smiths struck away like automatons beating on a clock as they hammered out the 10-inch ship nails of soft iron.

It was easy to appreciate why the land of Al Hind, as the early Arab geographers called India, had seemed a country of wealth and wonder. They wrote of it as an enormous country divided into no fewer than thirty kingdoms, ranging from the great realm of the 'King of Kings', the Ballahara, to the tiny coastal state of Tekin. Each realm had its own characteristics. The women of Tekin were the most fair-skinned and from them the Ballahara himself chose his wife. Gujerat was said to be so well ruled that a lump of gold left in the middle of the road would not be touched. The Indian penchant for religion and philosophy was noted, and Indian merchants and Indian ships competed or co-operated with Arab traders on all the sea routes of the Indian Ocean. Indeed Indians appear several times as travelling merchants in the stories of Sindbad's adventures. The spices, cloth and markets of India were the lodestone for the Arabs – the best Indian cottons were reputed to be so fine that they could be drawn through a signet ring. From the Arabs the Indians wanted to buy horses and dates, neither of which thrived in India, and the Arabs exchanged these trade goods for fine cloth, timber and spices. The green hills of Malabar formed the Pepper Coast, where pungent green pepper seeds ripened like miniature grapes on their vines before being picked and dried in the sun. Indian spice was a compact, high-value cargo, and Arab ships carried the pepper, areca nut, ginger, cardamom, cinnamon and cloves of the Malabar coast both onward to the Orient and westward to Arabia and the Gulf. Calicut and Kulam Mali near Cochin were the great entrepôts for this trade, and when Vasco da Gama made his first landfall in the fabled Orient looking for spices his pilot, whether Arab or Indian, brought him directly 4000 miles across open ocean from East Africa straight to the waiting mart of Calicut.

Spice and cloth are still produced in Calicut. In courtyards and sheds men and women packed chests, bags and sacks with the exotic products of the region as if nothing had changed since Sindbad's time. Malabar remained a cornucopia. New crops – rubber, coffee and tea – had been added to the traditional spices, and in the evening one still saw Arab merchants, mostly timber buyers but also general traders, sipping cups of tea and sitting on the verandahs with their Indian agents, watching the sun sink into the western sea.

Sohar was almost ready, careened and freshly anti-fouled. We moved her back to the wharf, put back her ballast, and loaded her new suits of sails. She had a fine new bowsprit, and her mainyard had been shaved down to reduce weight aloft. A brass bell from Calicut's bazaar gleamed near the tiller to summon the watches, and six new deck boxes had swallowed up the worst of the deck clutter. The deck boxes had been made by six of the original greenshirts. They had heard that *Sohar* was in Beypore, and travelled down from their homes to visit her, grinning with delight as they saw the ship they had built. It was good to see them, but also a little sad to note how their condition had changed. Working in Oman, the greenshirts had been so confident and happy; now they seemed furtive and worried. Whenever an official, whether from the customs or the harbour authority, came near our ship I noticed that the greenshirts vanished. They had slipped overboard or ducked below deck. Were they working illegally? I asked. Oh no, they replied, but if a government employee saw them working for a foreigner it could make their lives difficult unless they handed over a portion of their wages.

I knew that officialdom could make *Sohar*'s departure equally difficult, on much the same principle. So I began to grease the machinery well in advance. Four Special Branch men and seven junior customs officials received small 'presents', and I received back the ship's papers, the crew's passports, and a sailing permit. There was one ugly moment when an ingenious policeman thought up the idea of forbidding my daughter to sail on the ship as she had arrived in India by air and not by sea. But the look on my face changed his mind. Everything seemed to be going smoothly, and then the trap was sprung. The final consignment of *Sohar*'s stores, bags of charcoal and coils of spare rope, were impounded by the customs at Beypore. The timing and financial calculation of the trap were immaculate. The value of the goods was almost exactly equal to the sum it would cost to bribe the entire customs detachment of Beypore. Also I had to admire the intricacy of the arrangement. The goods had only been impounded after the ship had received emigration clearance, so officially my crew could no longer come back ashore. If I chose to argue about the impounding of the consignment I would either have to obtain new immigration clearance, which would take several days, or leave my crew aboard *Sohar* eating up the fresh stores intended for the next leg of the voyage. Naturally the impounding of the goods was a mere pretext. The customs officials claimed that one of the merchants who had supplied the rope might not have paid state tax on the goods; the matter would take some time to investigate. Meanwhile the goods would remain under lock and key in a shed just by the landing beach near *Sohar*.

The scenario was clear. I sent word that I would be at the shed that evening after dark, and prepared my briefcase. Squelching ashore with the case, I stumbled round the back of the shed. In the moonlight I found a neat line of customs men and police officers, drawn up almost as if they were on parade. Mysteriously, the door of the warehouse was now unlocked and standing open. Like smugglers, *Sohar*'s crew appeared from the gloom in the rubber dinghies, and began carrying off bales of rope and sacks of charcoal down the beach. Meanwhile I was doling out the required sums. It was almost laughable. The recipients were placed in strict order of seniority, by rank and age; every man had his agreed price, ranging from a few rupees for the lowly peons to several hundred for a full inspector. The entire transaction was performed with complete friendliness. Like a general saying farewell to his troops, I chatted with each man, shook hands and gave him his bribe.

At the very end of the line, beyond two inspectors, I found the original police informer, the very same man who had first spied on our wet and dirty landing on Calicut beach. He bobbed his head discreetly. The deputy collector had come to say goodbye, he said; he was waiting round the corner in a taxi. The deputy collector would much appreciate a bottle of genuine Scotch whisky. That, too, did not surprise me. Genuine Scotch whisky was either unobtainable or astronomically expensive in Malabar — after all, it was the deputy collector's job to collect a massive import duty on it. As befitted an Arab Islamic vessel, no alcohol was served aboard *Sohar*, but there was a case of whisky tucked away in the bilges against such a moment, and from my briefcase I produced the necessary bottle and walked over to the lurking taxi. The bottle disappeared through the open window, and the same odious little man who had begun by screaming at me three weeks before suggested that perhaps I would like to pay for his taxi fare too.

At one o'clock in the morning *Sohar* dropped downriver on the ebb tide. There were no farewells, no tug, no ceremony. Just a silent, ghostly departure in the darkness, slipping past the faint outlines of the country craft, their crews all asleep. An opium runner taking 'foreign mud' to China must have felt exactly like this, I thought to myself as I watched the channel lights I had arranged. They were two hurricane lamps, held aloft by men in a pair of dugout canoes. The canoes paddled ahead of *Sohar*, fanning out on each side to mark the edges of the twisting channel that led seaward. We came to the bar, felt the ship heave and swoop in the foreshortened swell, and then we were in the open sea. The two fireflies of the hurricane lamps drew back to us, and the fishermen lay under *Sohar*'s stern. I leaned over the gunnel, handed down a last fistful of rupees, and the two dugouts dropped back out of sight in the gloom. *Sohar* made sail and left India.

Sea snake

—8—

The Kingdom of Serendeeb

Ida, my daughter, joined the Omani band as a cymbal player. In Calicut the Omanis had bought themselves a pair of drums, and now they showed up on the foredeck every evening for a cheerful singsong, drumming, clapping, singing and dancing. Ida would pick up the rhythm, and tinkle happily away on a small pair of Indian brass cymbals. The whole feel of the ship had changed. *Sohar* was a more relaxed, more confident vessel; it was as though the ship's company had emerged from the worries of our apprentice passage across the Arabian Sea from Muscat. Now everything seemed lighter and full of zest. The air was cleaner, the sea more blue, and the ship's wake crisper. *Sohar*'s new sails drove her faster through the water, and with an enlarged sail plan the ship balanced better to the helm. She felt easier and swifter. The green hills of Malabar slipped away on the port-hand side, and Ibrahim's food was a delight after the nightmare of Shanby's sole curry. The Omanis did not seem the least distressed that they were leaving their Calicut wives behind them. On the contrary, they were in high good humour, and bantered with one another, obviously looking forward to the next stage of the journey.

Ida settled in remarkably smoothly. She had one early mishap when she fell down the stern hatchway and tumbled 8 feet straight into the aft cabin which she shared with me. But she choked back the sobs, and her fine array of bruises soon faded under a new tan. She gazed enviously at the water, and longed for a swim, so when the ship was moving slowly we rigged a bosun's chair to a line rove to the upper end of the mizzen spar, and dangled her outboard. Attached to the bosun's chair by a safety harness she was lowered into the sea, and dunked up and down like a ducking stool while a crew member kept a sharp watch for sharks. When a menacing shadow appeared, Ida was whisked up into the air by two strong men and swung inboard like a parcel.

The scientists intrigued her. She sat with Andrew on the gunnel, pointing out targets for his dipnet, pouncing on whatever he brought up. She examined the plankton samples which were trawled up, and at night she swirled the buckets of sea water samples to make the phosphorescence glow, and exclaimed in delight at the display. She found a vacant deck space to claim as her own territory, a patch right under the sweep of the tiller, too small for anyone else. There she made her nest, a pillow and a blanket, safe from the stampeding rush of bare feet and the confused thrashings of heavy ropes whenever the crew rushed to work the ship. Only the heavy night rain drove her down into our cabin.

'Daddy, the roof's leaking,' she announced in a puzzled voice as the water cascaded in through the sun-dried seams of the deck and splashed on her bunk. I pulled a piece of canvas over the top of her and she fell asleep contentedly.

The weather was reasonably kind. By noon every day there was usually a north-east breeze to push the ship along at 4 to 5 knots, and often the wind held well after nightfall when it either died away into a calm, or backed suddenly into one of the night-time squalls off the land. Whenever the squalls swept down on us there was furious activity. The duty watch would call below for assistance, and the Omanis would come pelting up, pulling on their oilskins and dashing to the ropes. Already the watch would have hauled up the mizzen sail out of harm's way and cleared the deck for action. Usually it was Abdullah, our best helmsman, who took the tiller. He squinted upwind into the darkness, seeking to identify the leading edge of the squall, a sinister black shadow under roiling clouds, with flickers of white crests beneath it where the wind was whipping up the surface of the sea. Three or four men ran to the mainsheet, the rope controlling the mainsail, threw off the locking turns around the quarter posts so that the 6-inch rope would not jam, and stood by ready to ease out, or haul in, for all their worth. On the foredeck two more men stood by the jib sheet in case the ship's head was over-pressed. Then the squall would hit. The first sharp gust of wind made the rigging suddenly creak as it took up the strain, and then came the heavier blow as the main weight of the squall bore down on the vessel. Abdullah adjusted the helm as the ship heeled to the pressure, and began to swing her nose upwind. A nod to the mainsheet crew, and they let out 2 feet of rope. The sheet inched out around the quarter post with a massive squeaking sound, tightening its coils so fiercely that the water squeezed from the fibres to the surface like drops of sweat.

'*Lesim shwai. Lesim shwai* – Let go a little, let go a little,' and another foot of mainsheet slid out. '*Bus!* Enough!' The ship was steady now, on her true course and tearing into the blackness of the night.

Rain came, pelting down with tropical fury, running in sheets across the deck, hissing into the embers of the cookbox, swirling to make a pool in the waist of the main deck where the run-off backed up against the coamings of the main hatch and gushed out of the lee drain holes. Flashes of lightning lit up orange-red oilskins and faces, white or black, tense with effort. A few men hunched protectively inside their oilskin hoods, but most stood with bare heads, wet hair plastered to their scalps. Abruptly the wind was easing. 'Pull! Pull!' It was time to recover the 2 feet of mainsheet, so grudgingly given away to the demands of the squall. A dozen men ran to their positions, bare feet slipping and stumbling on the wet deck, grabbed hold of the rope, and lay back almost horizontal to the deck, feet braced against coaming or gunnel for purchase. Abdullah eased over the helm for a fraction, the pressure came off the mainsheet for an instant, and 'Aeeaeh! Yaah – Allah!' Men heaved back, clawing for the advantage. The coils around the quarter post crept in, helped by the hand of a man stationed to see that the rope came smoothly. 'Yaaah ... Allah!' Another grunting heave, and the job was almost done. '*Mawal!* Make fast!' A single sharp command, and the mainsheet was made fast. The squall was over.

Sometimes the wind changed direction with the passage of a squall so that *Sohar* began to run in dangerously towards the coast. Then I rang the brass bell which summoned all hands on deck. Up they came, rubbing the sleep from their eyes, and stumbling to their regular positions. '*Khai-or!* Wear ship!' The manoeuvre of wearing ship meant shifting the mainsail with its huge mainspar from one side of the mast to the other by swinging the whole mass of sail and timber, more than a ton of it, around the foreside of the mast. If the ropes and canvas got in a tangle which checked the smooth swing of the mainspar, the sail would be ripped to shreds, or we could snap the mainspar. It was a difficult and dangerous operation by day, and at night it required real care. Every man had his allotted position on deck so that he knew exactly where to lay his hands on the right rope in the dark, and when to dodge safely out of the way of the lethal sweep of the butt of the mainspar as it swung across the ship. When everyone was in their right place, the helmsman turned *Sohar* to run downwind. The foredeck crew dragged in the lower end of the diagonal mainspar so that its peak rose vertical, and it hung above the deck like an enormous lance, dangling from the masthead sheaves, the tip fully 80 feet above the deck.

Next, Saleh's madcap figure scrambled around the outside of the ship, skipping along the top of the rail, round the foredeck, and back down the opposite side of the vessel. He carried the heavy rope which controlled the mainsail, and which had to be transferred from one side of the ship to the other. As soon as this rope was in position and made secure, the helmsman began to swing *Sohar* on her new course. A quick, probing flash of a powerful torch beam aloft checked that the ropes and rigging were not tangled, and the maindeck crew cautiously began to ease out the ropes controlling the angle of the mainspar so that it began to tilt back to a diagonal, this time on the opposite side of the mainmast. When the spar had reached its correct angle, half the crew quickly laid hold of the mainsheet and hauled in so that the sail set correctly. The remainder moved about the deck, resetting the rigging, tightening up and making fast ropes, wearing round the smaller mizzen sail, rehoisting the jib, and finally the job was done. It usually took half an hour of hard work before the off-duty watch could turn in below to catch up on their sleep ... until the next time that the fickle wind changed direction, and the anxious voice of the watchleader called softly to me ... 'Captain ... wear ship?'

Sailing a traditional Arab ship could be very dangerous. *Sohar*'s tackle was so massive that it could easily injure a man. The double blocks, for example, weighed 10 lb apiece, and each one was suspended from the masthead on its rope so that if the block swung free by accident it whizzed across the ship like a deadly pendulum and could strike down a man like a fragile skittle. And every time we wore ship, when the mainspar hung vertical, its butt swept back and forth across the deck with the rolling of the ship, like a lethal scythe. At that moment, if a man slipped on the unstable deck or, worse still, was trapped between butt and the gunnel as the spar swung, he was certain to be hurt. The duty of the maindeck crew was to control the butt, to lasso it with rope to control its swing. Split-second timing was called for, and the courage to dash into the danger zone at the right moment to do one's work. This in turn meant that a man had to have complete trust in the actions of his team-mates. If they made a mistake, he could be injured. Under these circumstances it was scarcely surprising that *Sohar*'s crew soon welded itself into a highly co-ordinated team.

Except in a flat calm there was never a moment when the hidden power of the ship was not lying in wait, ready to strike down the unwary. Even a comparatively slender rope could unleash shocking force. *Sohar*'s jib looked tiny, a mere pocket handkerchief compared to her huge fair-weather mainsail. Yet whenever *Sohar*'s bow came too far into the wind and the jib gave a warning flap, this little flap sent a snaking curve racing down the jib sheet to strike the gunnel with the crack of a high-velocity rifle shot. Once, when the jibsheet was left loose, it snapped off its cleat with contemptuous ease, sheared through 1½-inch pins of iron-hard mangrove wood as though they were matchsticks, and flicked the cleat, 16 inches long by 4 inches thick, across the deck like barshot.

Thankfully, we had only one injury caused by sail handling. One day Jumail's left leg was trapped between the gunnel and the butt of the mainspar, and his thigh was badly bruised. He dropped to the deck, his face twisted with pain. We finished setting the mainsail, and then the other Omanis tended to him. They heated up a mash of pounded dates and salt, wrapped the hot mash in a cloth, and kneaded the bruised muscle with it. Then they tied the date and salt mixture to his thigh as a sort of poultice. But for nearly a week Jumail was hobbling.

When the wind gets too strong an Arab ship does not reduce the area of sail in the European manner by gathering folds in the canvas. Instead, the Arab sailors change the entire mainsail for a smaller one. Changing a mainsail in a rising wind, with the ship pitching and rolling to the waves, is a spectacular manoeuvre. We did it aboard *Sohar* for the first time when we were off Cape Comorin, the southern tip of India. The wind was Force 6, and I could feel the ship labouring under her largest mainsail. *Sohar* was no longer running smoothly, but heeled too much by the weight of the wind. Her bows were beginning to dig into the waves. A short sea, kicked up by the Wadge Bank over which we were passing, struck her hard, and sent sheets of water flying across the waist of the ship. Ida was being seasick. I knew that it was prudent to reduce sail now, and not force the ship too harshly until her rigging broke.

Lowering the mainspar was not too difficult. Its own weight brought it down, and only two men were needed to feed out the main halyard rope steadily to prevent the whole mass of timber and canvas plummeting down like a guillotine. The excitement came as the crew tried to keep the huge, thrashing mainsail under control to stop it from blowing away into the sea or battering itself to rags. Every member of the crew was called into action. They lined the lee rail, and as the great sail descended, curving above their heads like a canvas tunnel, the crew laid hold of it and hung on grimly. Yard by yard they clawed down the huge sail, flinging themselves bodily on the coarse cloth and pinning it to the deck. From time to time the sail gave a mighty flap, and a dozen strong men were lifted clean off the deck by the power of the wind. When the sail was down far enough, the sail handlers triced it up in lengths of ½-inch line. Then the sail was unfastened from its spar, handed below deck, and its smaller version lashed in place. Now the crew went to their hauling stations. The heaviest, strongest men sat on the deck with their legs braced like oarsmen in a racing eight. They would haul on the halyard, the massive rope that pulled the mainspar back up to the mast head. On the foredeck Jumah, the most experienced sailor, would control the wild, dangerous swings of the butt end of the mainspar as it rose. With a series of ringing claps from Eid, and the first roaring lines of their hauling shanty, the hauling crew began to pull rhythmically on the halyard. Abdullah and Khamees Police, standing on top of the huge lower block, leaped up to grasp the moving halyard and pull it down with all their weight. Good co-ordination and the uproll of the ship made the job easier. The spar rose smoothly up and up. The new, small mainsail streamed out to leeward, safely above the wave tops. The mainspar approached the masthead, and with a final lusty roar the hauling crew pulled it home. Jumail and Eid made fast the halyard with some coconut cord, and the sail was adjusted to the correct angle. *Sohar* forged comfortably forward, easier now, and the crew, except for the duty watch, turned in to sleep, dog tired but content.

Traditionally the life of an Arab sailor was very harsh; it was a sobering thought that half of my Omani crew had been in shipwrecks. Jumah had known several ships sink under him; Saleh had been aboard a dhow that went down, and had clung to the wreckage for two days before he was picked up by another vessel. Khamees Police had nearly been drowned when a fishing vessel sank. He was rescued, but he lost his brother. And Khamees Navy had had perhaps the most remarkable experience of all. As a toddler he was aboard a small coasting dhow when it was caught by a gale and anchored off an exposed beach. The gale grew so severe that the men on board decided to send the children ashore. Khamees Navy and his brother were taken on to the beach and placed in shallow graves scooped out in the sand above the high tide mark. Half buried in the sand to protect them from the wind, the children waited until the storm blew out. They were eventually found by Beduin who took them back to their family. The boat itself was lost.

Adam's Peak in Sri Lanka was the landfall the Arab navigators looked for after leaving the Malabar coast. The Peak marked the island of Serendeeb, the largest and most magnificent of all the islands lying off India. The Peak received its name from the claim that when Adam was cast down from Paradise, his foot first touched this mountain peak, and the imprint remains. His next stride was lost, for it was so immense that it carried into the sea. 'Our sailors can see the peak where Adam fell, from nine days off,' wrote a ninth-century Arab chronicler, 'and they steer towards it.' Adam's Peak was *Sohar*'s target too, and on the morning of 21 January we gazed forward, hoping to catch a glimpse of it in the morning sun. It was two days since we had left Cape Comorin, and run south by east through an unusually bad patch of surface pollution. Andrew's collecting sled had been spattered with globules of oil after only a few minutes in the water, and it was evident that more than one ship had been cleaning its tanks off southern India and dumping the waste overboard. Now we were hoping to see the sacred mountain where it was said that a ghostly light flickers over the peak as a mark of its holiness. But the air was thick with dust and haze, visibility was poor, and it was not until *Sohar* was very close inshore that we saw land, and recognized the peculiar hump of the hill known to sailors as the Haycock. *Sohar* was well placed, and only a slight alteration to her course brought her to the old Arab port of call, the harbour at Galle, where the next day we dropped anchor.

Serendeeb, the name the Arabs gave to Ceylon or Sri Lanka, has given the English language the word serendipity, meaning the art of happy discovery. For the Sindbad Voyage, Sri Lanka was just that — a happy discovery. The expedition was to stay there almost a month, and it was to be among the happiest interludes of the voyage.

The marine biologists wanted first of all to count the number of dugongs remaining in the waters off the north-eastern coast of Sri Lanka. The dugong, or sea cow, is a large mammal which was once widespread throughout the seas of the world. Thirty years ago large herds of dugongs were reported to be living in the straits between India and Sri Lanka. The dugong is a herbivore, to the layman a little like a chubby walrus without tusks, and grazes on underwater beds of certain types of sea grass, which extend for many square miles in this region. But the scientists found that the dugong population was sadly reduced. They saw only two specimens, both of which promptly dived because the animals are now so shy of human interference. A major reason for the disappearance of the dugong was obvious. The sea grass beds where the dugongs grazed are now criss-crossed by scores and scores of fishing nets, which present an almost unavoidable deathtrap to the animals. Dugongs are air-breathing, and when they become tangled in the fishermen's nets they drown. The corpse is usually cut up and sold as meat in the fish market. The Sri Lankan fishermen themselves were not to blame: they caught the dugong by accident, and the dugongs damaged their precious nets in their death throes. *Sohar*'s scientists estimated that the dugong population, which until recently had numbered several thousand animals, was now reduced to perhaps less than one hundred or two hundred specimens.

Peter Hunnam, *Sohar*'s specialist in marine conservation, found a mass of other evidence of the increasing pressure on Sri Lanka's coastal resources. Turtles were still being caught and killed, both for meat and to make tortoiseshell ornaments, even though the animal was officially protected by government decree. The tortoiseshell dealers had a convenient loophole. Turtle-killing was still legal in the Maldive Islands, and the Sri Lankan tortoiseshell dealers claimed to be importing their tortoiseshell from there. The beautiful tropical fish off Sri Lanka's coast were also being steadily hunted down. Native divers, some equipped with underwater breathing apparatus, caught and sold these fish to dealers who in turn sent them off as air cargo, thousands of thousands of fish swimming around in plastic bags and aerated water, to aquariums and fish fanciers in Europe and North America. The same fish dealers also handled the fine and rare seashells that were picked off the sea floor by divers. Both divers and exporters admitted that the rarer fish and the most beautiful shells were becoming harder to find. Sri Lankan coral, too, was under attack. The pretty, delicate corals were being plucked to make ornaments; and the massive corals which form the main reefs off Sri Lanka's coast were being broken up with crowbars. Lumps of coral are taken ashore and stacked in kilns between layers of coconut shell, and then burned to produce lime for building. The loss of the coral has stripped the coast of its natural breakwater: where once the coral reefs blocked the main force of the waves, now

A large bull elephant uproots the tree in which Sindbad is sitting
(from *The Arabian Nights' Entertainments*, trans. Edward William Lane, 1877)

the sea gnaws away the sand and the coastline is receding. The jagged
and overturned stumps of drowned coconut trees now poke up through
the coastal shallows where once there was dry land.

While Peter Hunnam collected his data to try to understand the
complex social and economic factors behind the exploitation of Sri
Lanka's coastal resources, I had a simpler question to ask about Sri
Lanka's wildlife. I wanted to find out what happened to Sri Lanka's
wild elephants when they died. The reason for my curiosity was to be
found in the Seventh Voyage of Sindbad. One version of the Seventh

Voyage relates how Sindbad was captured by pirates and sold into slavery, apparently in Sri Lanka. There his new master made him an ivory hunter. Sindbad's task was to go into the forest each day, hide in the top of a tree, and wait for a herd of wild elephants which passed by. Each day Sindbad killed an animal. Then he cut away the ivory, and took it back to his master. This slaughter continued for some time till one day, to Sindbad's horror, the elephant herd surrounded the tree where he was concealed and deliberately knocked it down in order to get at the hunter. Expecting to be trampled by the outraged animals, Sindbad was amazed when the lead elephant picked him up gently in his trunk and carried him through the forest to a place where the bones of many dead elephants lay scattered on the ground. It was the place where elephants go to die, and the elephants wanted only to show Sindbad where he could obtain ivory without killing the herd. Returning to his master, Sindbad revealed the location of the elephant graveyard and was rewarded with his freedom.

Sindbad's Seventh Adventure with the elephants in Sri Lanka may well be a later addition to *The Thousand and One Nights*, though an elephant of Serendeeb is also mentioned in the Fourth Adventure when it is said that the supreme king of Serendeeb rides in procession on a huge elephant, 7 cubits high. Yet the tale of the Elephants' Graveyard is a widespread story which occurs in other fables and other languages besides Arabic. So was there any shred of truth in it, at least as far as Sri Lanka was concerned? With *Sohar* in Sri Lanka, it was a good opportunity to put this question to those people who might know what happened to the dead elephants from Sri Lanka's surviving herds. The obvious people to ask were the last remaining jungle people, the Veddah, and of course the game wardens of Sri Lanka's game parks.

The Veddah are Sri Lanka's aborigines. No one knows when they first arrived in the island, and they are believed to be the oldest surviving population. The Veddah are apparently related to the negrito people of the Andamans, and until recently there were bands of Veddah still living in the forests of Sri Lanka. They were classic hunter-gatherers. They did not have houses, but lived in caves or built shelters in the treetops. They ate the flesh of animals hunted with bow and arrow, jungle fruits and edible plants, and they collected wild honey. They dressed in garments made from leaves and tree bark. Apart from iron knives and tobacco which they obtained from the villages, the Veddah lived in the Stone Age. Today there is only one scattered band of Veddah left. They wear cast-off clothing when they visit the villages, and have intermarried with the village people, but essentially they are still forest hunters and dwellers for most of the year, and roam the last areas of virgin forest in Sri Lanka, where a few wild elephants are also to be found. Yet the Veddah could say almost nothing about what happened to dead elephants. They said they came across the dead bodies of elephants only very, very rarely. Indeed, they knew of only one, or perhaps two, elephant corpses in the past ten years. Where had the other elephants fallen? They did not know. One man claimed he had seen an elephant carrying the bones of a dead elephant through the forest for some distance. Where was the elephant going? He did not know.

The mystery only deepened when the same question was put to the game wardens. Sri Lanka's game parks have a wild elephant population of about 2000. They move in and out of the parks according to the season, and in theory perhaps twenty or thirty animals should die every year. Yet the game wardens said that they found only a very few skeletons. Once again elephant corpses were very rare. It was not that elephant skeletons were easy to overlook. Indeed the wardens said they often found the bones of far smaller animals, such as leopard, that were less numerous than the elephant and far easier to miss. The few elephant bones they found were very obvious and stayed as landmarks for many years. There was only one, partial explanation they could offer. The wardens took me to a natural rock pool below a rocky outcrop, surrounded by scrub and low trees. In the late evening the place had a calm, placid atmosphere. The pool was long and quite narrow: irregular in shape, it was perhaps 40 yards long, and between 4 and 8 yards wide. At one end a small rivulet trickled in to replenish the level, and the water was very still and opaque. The sides of the pool, the wardens told me, were very steep, almost sheer. They knew this because in the dry season the water level dropped several feet, exposing the sides of the rock bowl. Yet even in the worst droughts, when all the other springs and ponds in the area dried up, this rock pool always contained water, so it became the main waterhole in the region for all the wild beasts. Three years earlier, taking advantage of a drought which had reduced the amount of water in the pool, the park administrators decided to clean out the pool. Workmen had climbed down, and begun to shovel up the sludge on the bottom. To their amazement they discovered that the sludge was made of decomposed animal bone, a greyish white ooze. As they dug down, they came across bones, elephant bones, literally tons of them, lying embedded in the ooze. The bones were hauled out of the pond, stacked in piles, and eventually carried away for fertilizer. Five full trailer loads of elephant bones had been hauled away.

But why had so many elephants died in that particular pool? Did they fall in accidentally and drown, perhaps in the dry season while reaching down for water to drink? One unwary step, and an animal could easily tumble in and find it impossible to climb out again. Or did ageing and dying elephants come to the pool to die? Old and weak, they had to stay near water to live, and near the pool they would have found good feeding. But why then had they drowned themselves in the pool, and not died beside it where their skeletons would have been found? No one could tell me any answers; the mystery of the Elephants' Graveyard remained.

Another Sindbad adventure, however, did find a very plausible explanation in Sri Lanka. Perhaps the most famous of the adventures concerns the Valley of Diamonds. The adventure begins on his Second Voyage when Sindbad was marooned on a desert island where he found an enormous egg, belonging to the mythical giant bird the Arabs call the Rukh. When the mother Rukh returned to its nest, Sindbad tied himself to the Rukh's leg and was carried up and off the island as the Rukh flew to its feeding grounds in a distant valley. There the great bird ate the enormous serpents that crawled everywhere in great numbers. Untying himself from the bird's leg, Sindbad found that the floor of the valley was studded with diamonds, a mass of glittering gems. But he was so terrified by the huge snakes which slithered in all directions that he tried to take refuge for the night by hiding in a cave and blocking the cave mouth with a boulder. To his horror he discovered a great snake lying with her eggs in the same cave, and he passed the night in a state of terror. Staggering out of the cave in the morning, giddy with fear and hunger and lack of sleep, he was startled when a slaughtered animal carcass came tumbling down the steep side of the valley, and fell to the ground before him. Then he remembered hearing how in some remote and difficult mountains diamond merchants gathered precious jewels by tossing dead carcasses into a gem-rich valley where it was too risky for them to go on foot. Some of the gems would stick to the flesh, and the carcasses were picked up by carrion birds and carried upward to their nests, where the merchants could retrieve the precious stones. Resourceful as ever, Sindbad filled his pockets and sash with gems, and tied himself underneath a carcass with his turban. A great eagle swooped down, picked up the meat and Sindbad in its talons, and carried him up to the mountaintop. There the merchants, who were Moslems, congratulated him on his amazing escape, and Sindbad shared his rich haul of precious stones.

The tale of the Valley of Diamonds, and how to extract the gems with lumps of meat, is yet another idea that the Arab storytellers could have picked up from other sources. But in the tenth century the Arab writer Al Kazvini, who compiled a whole collection of travellers' yarns, placed the valley in Serendeeb. To this day large quantities of precious stones are mined in Sri Lanka, and the manner in which they are mined may explain several aspects of Sindbad's adventure. True diamonds do not occur in Sri Lanka, but almost every other precious and semi-precious stone is found – rubies, cat's eyes, cornelians, and of course the famous blue sapphires. The island has been a major source of gems for centuries, and these gems are found deep in the valleys, on the valley floors. The precious stones turn up in alluvial gravel and mud which has washed down from the mountains. This mud and gravel is shovelled up from pit shafts sunk into the flood plain. To obtain the gravel, the native miners climb down the vertical, straight-sided shafts by crude ladders. Twenty or thirty feet below the surface of the valley they scrape out small horizontal galleries, and fill their baskets with the gravelly slush. This slush is then hoisted to the surface by rope, carried away to ponds or rivers, and washed in the search for precious stones in much the same way as panning for gold. The location of the mines in the valleys, the straight-sided shafts, the difficulty of extracting the gravel and hoisting it to the surface, even the snakes which love to seek out the cool dampness of the pit shafts, all could have provided elements which link Serendeeb's rich jewel production with the Sindbad story of the Valley of Diamonds. And the early gem merchants would have encouraged such a yarn, for it enhanced the exotic value of their wares, and effectively camouflaged the true source of their wealth.

Today the gem dealers of Sri Lanka are nearly all Moslems and most of them claim Arab descent. They effectively control the production of gems, and have done so for as long as can be remembered. There is no firm date for when Arab merchants first began to trade in Serendeeb, but the Portuguese in the fifteenth century found Arabs firmly ensconced as the middlemen in trade, and the first Moslem shrines in Sri Lanka are said to date from as early as the seventh century. Indeed the oldest of these shrines are located on the south-east corner of Sri Lanka, precisely where ships coming down from India, as *Sohar* had just done, would have made their landfall. *Sohar* herself had anchored within sight of the original Islamic site in Sri Lanka, a ruined mosque built, so it was said, on the burial ground of the first Moslem to have died in Sri Lanka. He was one of eight Moslem sailors who brought the message of Mohammed to Serendeeb. That saint's grave lies among the grass under the coconut palms which surround the ruined mosque. A shallow river meanders past in a gentle curve and empties into Galle harbour, no more than 400 metres away. It is exactly the spot where any sailor would have first landed.

Sohar's Omanis visited the tombs of the Arab sailors who had brought their faith to Serendeeb, and they prayed in the mosques. Then, while *Sohar* was being revictualled, the entire crew took the chance to travel throughout the island. It was an ideal stopover during the long voyage to China. As far as we were concerned Sri Lanka, with its warmth and colour, its gentle people and its easy pace, was still the Fortunate Island. It was easy to appreciate why the Arab chroniclers had written of the King of Serendeeb as among the wealthiest rulers on earth. He lived, they wrote, in the greatest possible luxury. His land produced all variety of scents and perfumes, aloes, aromatic woods and civet. The diamonds found in the streams were used to engrave delicate patterns on ring stones of every sort. Large pieces of crystal were found in the rivers, and excellent pearl beds extended around his coasts. At his capital was a temple so encrusted with jewels that its value was impossible to assess. There the Great King ruled with the help of sixteen ministers, four Hindus, four Christians, four Jews and four Moslems. Even the Caliph of Baghdad could scarcely match the splendour of the Great King and, according to *The Thousand and One Nights*, Sindbad the Sailor brought back a letter from the Great King addressed to Haroun al Rashid and with it costly presents – a cup made of a ruby a span high and lined with pearls, a bed covered with the skin of a snake which 'swallowed the elephant' and had spots the size of a dinar, and which possessed the magical property that anyone who sat on it never fell sick, a hundred thousand miskals of aloe wood, and 'a slave girl like a shining moon'. Sindbad was summoned before the Caliph and recounted to Haroun al Rashid how the King of Serendeeb appeared in extraordinary state processions. Mounted on his huge elephant 11 cubits high, the Great King paraded through his capital, surrounded by his lords and officers. Before him went a spear-man holding a golden javelin, and behind him a mace bearer with a great club of gold whose head was an emerald a span long and as thick as a man's thumb. In the cavalcade around the King, said Sindbad, rode a thousand horsemen dressed in brocade and silk.

The great processions of Serendeeb still exist in a modern form. Nowadays the tradition is honoured by the monthly *pereheras* organized by Sri Lanka's Buddhist monks. Two days before *Sohar* left Sri Lanka, her crew watched such a procession as it paraded through the dark streets. The effect was stunning. Smoke-grimed fire dancers cavorted and whirled with their blazing brands. Men ceremonially cracked great 20-foot-long whips to clear the path. Group after group of dancers spun and twisted to the insistent clatter of drums and pipe, and let loose astonishing leaps so that the bells on their ankles rattled and their silver chest plates clashed. There were devil dancers in masks and coconut fibre suits, slavering black demon dogs, men dressed as women on stilts. Interspersed throughout the procession came rank after rank of Buddhist monks, all saffron robes, shaven skulls, and one bare arm to hold the saffron fan. There were dancers in red and white ribbons, in pantaloons and naked to the waist, in pointed hats and in turbans. A whole troop of mummers, dressed to look like Rajput princes, wagged their flour-whitened faces and hands like dolls. And scattered throughout the procession came the great elephants of Sri Lanka, the elephants the Arabs had spoken of, over eighty of them, marching three abreast with great soft footfalls, swaying over the heads of the crowd. Caparisoned in silk and brocades, the elephants were magnificent, and on their necks rode mahouts in immaculate white. Amid this amazing exhibition, the blur of colours and light and the pounding music, there was no difficulty in summoning back the Arab view of Serendeeb.

Blue surgeon fish

—9—
The Doldrums

Sohar sailed from Sri Lanka with a new photographer on board, Richard Greenhill. He arrived from London to replace Bruce Foster who had now spent more than a year with the Sindbad project and felt it was time to return to New Zealand to see his wife and daughter. My own daughter also went back to school in England.

When I first laid eyes on Richard Greenhill I could scarcely imagine anyone less adapted to be a sailor. He was a great, gangling heron of a man. Tall and lanky, with a beak of a nose, a questing eye, and a stoop to his shoulders, he looked as if he was wading through the shallows hunting for fish as he stepped down the deck with great spindle-legged strides, and his enormous feet planted at an out-turned angle. He was totally passionate about photography and cameras, but he had never been on a boat before in his life. He knew nothing about sailing, and he doubted if he could learn. He wanted to devote every minute of his time to taking pictures, and he turned up with the weirdest collection of cameras and photographic gadgets, many of them home-made one might imagine, as well as an assortment of bits of balsa wood, glue, balls of string, watch springs, safety pins, rubber bands and plastic bags, even toy balloons, with which he hoped to devise yet more photographic gadgets. Everything he did aboard ship was either a near-disaster or a comedy, except for his photography. If he walked across the deck, he tripped over a hatch coaming. If he sat down, a swinging rope's end promptly knocked his straw hat off. If he went below deck, he banged his head on a deck beam. If he put down his mug of tea, it promptly slid into the scuppers the moment his back was turned. He was so maladroit that he could make even a flat calm look as if the ship was pitching in a high sea. Yet Richard never capitulated to *Sohar*'s conspiracy against him. Day after day he lurched and slipped his way around the deck, clicking his camera. By some magic chemistry he developed test rolls of his film in little tubs of fluid, and he never ceased to think up additions to his amazing assortment of gadgets – cameras festooned with balloons as home-made lifejackets, cameras tucked in balsa wood cradles, cameras on the end of bamboo poles controlled by long wires, cameras screwed hopefully to the mast, cameras tied to the strings of kites, cameras linked to telescopes. Nor did darkness deter him. The night was now filled with the repeated dazzle of flash guns and the sounds of Richard tripping over unseen objects in the darkness.

Richard was green with seasickness for the first three days after *Sohar* sailed from Galle on 22 February, eastbound for Sumatra and the entrance to the Malacca Strait. It was a distance of about 900 miles in a direct line across the Indian Ocean, and I hoped to make the passage in less than a month if the wind favoured us. This was the shortest, direct track towards the lands of South-east Asia, and the route that had been used by Arab ships since the eighth century. But everything depended on the arrival of the monsoon winds: March was the changeover time when the north-east monsoon gradually died away and was replaced by the stronger south-west monsoon. On the way to Sumatra any north-east wind would be a head wind, and would be made worse by the west-going current. The combination of head wind and head current would be too much for *Sohar* to make progress eastward, but as soon as the south-west monsoon came everything would change. The wind would turn in our favour, the current would eventually reverse direction, and an eastbound ship could proceed swiftly and comfortably. The golden rule for this sector of the voyage had been laid down by the early Arab navigators. It was to wait for the south-west monsoon before sailing to Sumatra, the land the Arabs called the Land of Gold.

But this year the south-west monsoon was late, disastrously late. We left Sri Lanka at the time when the last of the north-east winds should have been fading, and we sailed hoping to pick up the leading edge of the south-west monsoon as it was drawn across the Equator. In theory we should have experienced unsettled weather, changing winds and brief calms, which would turn into a warm, wet, south-westerly breeze. Instead the unfavourable headwinds continued. Day after day the wind blew from the north-east, interspersed with periods of calm. *Sohar* beat back and forth, gained a little ground, but promptly lost it when the winds died away and the current set her back along her track. On the chart the ship's path made a futile series of zigzags and circles, getting no nearer Sumatra as the weeks passed. It was very frustrating. Seeking to pick up the south-west monsoon earlier, I risked taking *Sohar* farther and farther south, almost to the Equator, but to no avail. The unfavourable conditions continued: headwinds and calm, adverse current, and no sign of a change.

The last fling of the north-east monsoon had a vicious sting. The Pilot Book warned that the changeover season, from north-east to south-west monsoon, was a dangerous period. There was a risk of sudden gales, quick changes of wind direction, and unstable conditions. At dusk on 3 March the air had an ominous feel. All day it had been swelteringly hot; now there was a sullen, thundery atmosphere, and a spectacular display of evening cloud was building up on the horizon, a mass of cumulus cloud boiling up into great pyramids and billows. The sea around us turned a harsh silver, but beneath the thunder heads it was the colour of lead.

The first squall hit at dusk. The impact was like a slap from an open hand, abruptly delivered. The ship shied away, and the sails shivered at the blow. A moment later, and the main weight of the squall hit us. Already off-balance from the first impact, the ship began to tilt. The huge sails, pushed by the sudden increase in pressure, began to force *Sohar*'s head downwind and she began to heel more steeply, in a massive cant. Everything became unstable. We lost our footing on the sloping deck. Men grabbed for ropes as handholds. With an alarming crash, all the items left lying carelessly about during the day's calm slid into the scuppers in an untidy mess of saucepans, tin plates, mugs, hand torches and baskets of fruit, loose dates rolling like marbles. *Sohar* was at an unhappy angle. The force exerted on her rigging was enormous. She lurched and staggered, and the wind brought a hissing curtain of rain across us.

Now the Omanis were at their best. They knew how to handle the situation. With a stamping rush of running feet, all eight of the Omanis raced to the poop deck. They were yelling excitedly, and bubbling with activity. Abdullah grabbed the tiller from Andrew, and with Musalam's help forced the rudder over so that *Sohar*'s head began to swing ponderously upwind. At the same time Khamees Navy and Saleh laid hold of the mizzen sheet and eased it off a fraction. The other four Omanis went to the heavy double mainsheets. With shouts of encouragement they eased out the massive ropes so that the wind began to spill from the mainsail, and the intolerable pressure on the ship was lessened. The great sail bellied and flapped. Massive, soggy thumps of wet canvas reverberated above the hiss of the rain and the clamour of the wind. *Sohar* straightened up, poked her bowsprit towards the wind and, like an acrobat relaxing his muscles, the sinews of the rigging slackened. Again a squall struck. Again *Sohar* tried to wheel away under the blast. And again the Omanis balanced tiller and sail to protect her from the strain. They juggled with the controls of the recalcitrant ship, coaxing her back into a safe attitude. The Omanis were grinning with glee. This was what they enjoyed: the challenge of the sea. The risks of capsize, of ballast shifting, of sails bursting, of a spar breaking loose and coming crashing down on deck, all the dangers and exhilaration of a *boom* under the stress of weather.

It was dark by the time the first line of squalls had gone past us, leaving a mottled night with patches of starlight and larger, dense black masses of cloud. Now we were like men playing blind man's buff with a dozen opponents at once in a darkened room. *Sohar* was the prey, and the squalls were her tormentors. We strained our eyes to windward, trying to pick out the blacker patches of the worst squalls. We listened for the sound of the approaching wind. But the rush of the waves, which were now suddenly much bigger, blotted out all warnings to the ears. Instead it was our noses which became the best sensors, our noses and our skins. You could actually smell the rain sweeping down on us ahead of the squall. And a few moments before it struck with full force, our bare skins also detected the distinct drop in temperature, a sudden chill, just ahead of the rain. Slam! Another squall hit us out of the dark. Once again *Sohar* shied away, rigging and spars protesting under the sudden load. Once again, there was the heart-stopping moment as she heeled over.

'Will she capsize?' I thought to myself. 'Have I left too much sail up for safety? Will it be too dangerous to lower the mainyard in this heaving, bumpy sea? The spar will run amok and injure someone, or a sodden rope, whirling like a flail, will maim a man. Better to ride out the squalls, and see how the crew manages.'

All that night every one of the Omanis, whether or not it was his watch, stood to on deck and worked the ship. They put on oilskins, or rather some of them did – Abdullah insisted on keeping only loincloth and singlet despite the torrential rain which smashed down at the height of each squall. Between gusts of wind they joked and chanted as they waited for the next onslaught, so that they could go leaping into action, handling whipping ropes and dodging the crazily swinging blocks which could have knocked them senseless. The watches changed. The Europeans came and went, some to stand their turn, others to sleep below, stretched out in bunks where the water now dripped down on them, or, like Peter Dobbs, sprawled out on the lower deck, because his usual perch on top of the workbox was directly beneath a small waterfall cascading through the planking. The Omanis, however, stayed on deck all the time, not because they did not trust the westerners to handle the ship, but because *Sohar* was their vessel, they were her sailing crew, and it was their duty to stand by her.

So it was all the more unjust, therefore, that the mishap occurred at dawn, when the Omanis had been twelve hours in action without a single break for rest. Another squall slammed into *Sohar*. And then, just as the wind was clawing at her canvas and she was regaining her footing, an unlucky wave swept under her bow. *Sohar* pitched in sympathy, coming down into the trough with a shudder. The tremor dislodged the heavy belaying pin which held the mizzen halyard. The mizzen halyard went slack just at the wrong moment. The belaying pin fell away, freeing the halyard line. With nothing to hold it aloft, the mizzen yard and the mizzen sail came slicing headlong down to the deck. It was the second most serious accident that I had feared; only the fall of the mainyard would have been more devastating. As it was, the mizzenyard and its sail must have weighed nearly three-quarters of a ton, and now it dropped like a guillotine directly towards the men on the poop. Luckily there were only three of them – the helmsman and a lookout, and Ibrahim the cook who had just crept out on deck to start making breakfast. They were extraordinarily lucky. Plummeting down, the mizzenyard checked its fall, perhaps because of the tug of the wind pulling the sail out to one side. And as the yard checked its rush, the slides which held it to the mast acted as a light brake, and by a miracle slowed its headlong crash. If this had not happened, the falling mizzenyard would have smashed to smithereens the cookbox and the frail gallows frame over the helmsman, and injured him badly. As it was, the crashing yard came down beside Ibrahim with a thump that shook the entire ship from masthead to keel.

Directly below, I heard the ominous crash and felt *Sohar* shudder. A moment later came the piercing clangour of the alarm bell which was being rung furiously. All hands on deck! Emergency! I bolted up the companionway, and emerged into a scene of chaos. The collapsed mizzenyard lay cocked at an angle across the poop deck, a tangle of ropes and blocks surrounding it. Ibrahim was white and shaken by his narrow escape. The sail was thrashing loose on deck. Now the rest of the crew appeared: with a rush they headed for the poop deck, once again led by Omanis. Khamees Police and Eid leaped on the flapping sail. Abdullah and Jumah trapped the loose forward end of the spar and began to get it under control, lashing it against the base of the mainmast. Khamees Navy threw another lashing over the gallows to fasten down the upper end. Swift hands cut clear the dangerous, loose sail and folded it on deck. The situation was under control.

Except for one item: high above our heads at the very top of the mizzen mast now swung the great halyard block, a brute measuring 3 feet by 2 feet square, and carved from a massive lump of timber. The block was loose, swinging back and forth, and occasionally giving the mast a shattering crack that made the deck shiver beneath our feet. Even if the block did not damage the mast, it was clear that it would soon split apart. And it was an essential piece of equipment without which *Sohar* would be partly crippled. Jumping on to the gunnel, I began to pull myself up the shrouds to try to reach the block, and cut clear the bindings that held the main halyard ropes. Once the bindings were cut free, it should be possible to work the block down to the deck. I hauled myself up the rigging cautiously. *Sohar* was bucking in the waves, and the sway of the mast and the dizzy swing of the rigging made it a hazardous business. It would have been very easy to be flipped clear and tossed into the sea.

When I was about two-thirds of the way up, I sensed that I was not alone. I glanced across to the other side of the mast. Swarming up it, racing me to the maverick block, was another sailor. It was, of all people, Jumah! Quiet, pipe-smoking Jumah, the grandfather of the group. Until that moment he had never made a move to climb the rigging. He would sit peaceably on deck, and let Eid and the younger men do the acrobatics up aloft. But now, if his captain was going aloft, he was not going to stand by idly. Jumah went shinning up the rigging like a monkey, a knitted cap perched on the side of his grey curls, sinewy arms and legs wrapped round the cordage. He was unbeatable. Less than a minute later Jumah had pulled himself past me, reached the very top of the mizzen, and with one daring leap in mid-air skipped across the gap, and was sitting astride the block, looking more than ever like a mischievous monkey. I could only gape.

Pulling myself up the last 3 feet, I reached out and handed him my knife, and then slid gratefully back down the rigging to the solid deck. Jumah used the knife to saw through the lashings, and with another

Preceding page *Sohar* sets out from Singapore on the last leg of her 6000 mile journey.
Above Off the coast of Vietnam black clouds churning like smoke herald the approach of one of the many arch squalls that battered the ship.
Below Sails lowered, *Sohar* lies ahull while an arch squall shrieks over her.
Right Five sails were ripped to shreds in a single day

Above 'A minute later Khamees Navy suddenly leaped up on the gunnel, clutched a shroud for support, . . . and cupped one hand to his mouth and let out a high, wavering yell into the teeth of the gale. It was a prayer to Allah, ringing out high and eerily over the ship.' *Below* 'We literally sewed our way northwards. In the lulls between the arch squalls, we mended our sails.' *Sohar* races toward China, trying to beat the onset of the typhoon season

Above A boatload of Vietnamese refugees approaches, seeking help. Short of food and with their drinking water tainted, the refugees feared that the strange sailing ship was a pirate vessel. 'The refugees' main problem was that they were lost. Their compass was damaged, and they had no charts.' *Below* As *Sohar* gives food, water and medical help, Tim Severin explains the right compass course to the refugees who hope to reach Taiwan

Right Seven and a half months after leaving Muscat, *Sohar* makes her landfall on the China coast. Escorted up the Pearl River to Canton, she received an enthusiastic official welcome from the Chinese.

Below right 'There on the quayside stood ranks of schoolchildren waving green and red pompons to the music of a Chinese band. As *Sohar* drew alongside, the noise was deafening. The band played, firecrackers exploded, and the children sang.'

Above 'We stepped ashore to be greeted by Sayyid Faisal and the Chinese officials, and then walked up the aisle of schoolchildren.' Sayyid Faisal (centre), Oman's Minister of National Heritage and Culture, had arrived in a plane of the Sultan's royal flight to head the delegation that greeted the expedition to Canton. From Peking came the Chairman of the Cultural Commission to celebrate the re-establishment of the historic link by sea between China and the Arab world

Left The Omani visitors go to pray at the Smooth Pagoda, Canton's original mosque. Its tower is said to have served as the lighthouse which guided ships coming upriver to the great emporium of China, which attracted merchant ships from Oman, a fifth of the world away

Below Silk and porcelain were the luxury products of China which repai the extraordinary enterprise of the early Arab voyages to the East. Today in the communes around Canton, tray of silkworms with their mulberry-leaf diet are carefully tended for the fine silk which is still a major export

leap jumped back into the main rigging, and shinned down to the deck. He handed me my knife with a twinkle in his eye.

'*Shabash!* Well done, Jumah!' I panted gratefully.

Now it was big Peter Dobbs's turn. Neither Jumah nor I was heavy enough to bring down the block with our weight, sitting astride it. So Peter climbed up, took up his position, lying across the block with all his 14 stone. With each hand he fed the halyard ropes through the sheaves, while down below Abdullah, Eid and Andrew heaved on a downhaul to inch the block lower and lower. Once again it was a hazardous affair. As the block descended, the arc of its swing grew longer and more dangerous. Time and again Peter had to kick off from the mast with his feet when the block threatened to dash him against the mast like a puppet on a string. Finally he was within reach of the deck party. Men grabbed the block. Peter slipped to the deck and sat down, visibly drained by the effort. I felt utterly relieved.

With the wind now blowing at Force 6 to 7, the last of the northeast monsoon set in with a vengeance. All next day the wind blew foul, kicking up a short, ugly sea that reminded me more of the North Atlantic off the west coast of Ireland than the waters of the Indian Ocean. Grey clouds hurried endlessly over our heads. The rain pattered down on the hatch covers. The ceaseless sway and jerk of the mainyard began to gnaw at the canvas of the mainsail. A great split opened up near the tack, and the leading panel of the sail dissolved in tatters.

The following night was also full of thunder and lightning and although the ship rose more easily under smaller canvas, it was obvious that soon we would have to wear ship. The wind had moved even farther to the east, more and more adverse, and was pushing us much too far south. The whole crew fought the mainsail round to the other side of the mast, and *Sohar* once again began to plunge north, the spray from a grey, lumpy sea dashing across her deck. In the afternoon we pulled the tattered number one mainsail up on deck, and everyone went to work cheerfully, stitching and mending, and reworking brailing lines and gaskets. It was strange, I thought to myself, how well people can adapt even to the most uncomfortable circumstances. In the height of yet another squall that morning Terry, the sound recordist, had been at the helm. Neither he nor his partner David Bridges the film cameraman had ever been on a sailing ship before they came aboard *Sohar*. Now, by sheer hard work and enthusiasm, they were turning into prime seamen. As the squall had shrieked across the ship, a whiteout of driving rain beating down the waves and making *Sohar*'s deck awash to the scuppers, Terry was positively enjoying himself. Grinning hugely, his hair plastered down to his scalp by the deluge, his oilskins streaming with rain, he was handling the ship perfectly, turning *Sohar*'s bow upwind each time the wind buffeted her.

'Who would have thought, three months ago, that I would be doing this, at the helm under these conditions!' he yelled happily over the hammer of the rain.

Even Richard, the photographer, was beginning to adapt. Nothing could persuade him to discard his boatlike suede shoes in which he flapped around the deck, but his queer-looking socks were gone and so too was his amazing spotted sun hat which had been picked off his head and sent overboard by a mischievous rope. Now he was sporting a half-hitched loincloth that kept slipping askew like the costume of a pantomime dame, and he was beginning to acquire a tan. It was a far cry from the first-night squall when, worried that he might have tripped and stumbled overboard from the lurching deck, I sent a search party to check that he was all right. The searchers had located him huddled inside Ibrahim's cookbox. Richard was crouching down, hanging on with both hands, and wearing a fully inflated lifejacket. The next morning he asked me to explain how to launch a liferaft.

For another week the north-east monsoon tormented us with a combination of squalls and flat calms. *Sohar* continued to beat back and forth, butting against the headwinds. We wore ship time and time again. *Sohar* could sail upwind as well as a modern family cruising yacht, but the ground she gained was lost in the calms when the current carried us backwards.

Three weeks out of Sri Lanka I began to worry about the rate at which we were consuming the ship's reserve of water and food. With twenty men on board, *Sohar*'s fresh water was strictly rationed. Fresh water was being used only for drinking and cooking. All washing was done in sea water, and much of the water for cooking was diluted, half and half, with sea water. The fresh water supply was kept in four tanks low down by the keel, where it also acted as ballast. Each day 25 gallons of water was pumped up by hand to two kegs kept on deck, and this represented the day's supply of drinking water. When a tank was empty, we refilled it with sea water to maintain the ballast weight. I had calculated that there was enough fresh water in the four tanks to last us comfortably for a month, with perhaps two weeks in reserve; but now I was not so sure. As the north-east monsoon faded, the intervals of calm became longer and longer. During the early squalls it had been difficult to catch rain water on the slanting deck while we were busy preventing the ship from being damaged or capsized. Now the squalls no longer brought rain, and the sun began to parch the deck and crew. After three weeks at sea we had consumed half our fresh water supply, and yet we were no nearer Sumatra than the day we had left Galle. What was potentially far more serious was the fact that *Sohar* had now been driven so that she lay 400 miles downwind of Sri Lanka. Effectively, therefore, there was no way we could get back to replenish our fresh water if the north-east monsoon continued. It would be easier to head down to the Maldives or across to the Chagos archipelago, 600 miles away: it all depended on the wind direction. I looked again at the charts. Should I risk sailing, not to north Sumatra, but southabout via Java and the Selat Strait as the late nineteenth-century sailing ships had done? But this was not the Arab route, and there was an even greater risk that I would put the ship into the dangerous region of calms off west Sumatra where we would be becalmed for months on end, and eventually find ourselves on a lee shore in the south-west monsoon.

No, I decided, we were better to stay where we were, and cut down our water ration still further. Each man began keeping a note of how many cups of water he drew each day. The results were interesting. Some people could get by quite happily on two and a half pints, while others were drinking twice as much. There did not seem to be any relation to a man's size or his build, though it was noticeable that a person drank much more if he had been out in the sun and worked than if he rested in the shade. For the moment, however, the water situation was worrying rather than grave. And it was enough to instruct each man to drink as little as he could comfortably manage, and to keep a careful log of the total daily consumption.

There was one moment of alarm. Andrew, whose job it was to pump up the daily ration of water into the deck barrels, reported that the second main water tank was empty: he could not draw any more water out of it, and the pump was sucking dry. I checked my notes. There had to be something wrong. The tank should have had enough water left in it for another four or five days. Had it leaked, or had my calculations of its capacity been false? In either event, the other two tanks might also be dry, or contain far less water than I thought, so I ordered the suspect tank to be checked. This meant shifting all the main food stores, dismantling the stores area, pulling up the floor-boards, and levering up the lid of the tank. Finally the tank was clear.

As I watched Peter Dobbs reach down and pull up the lid, it was a moment of truth. Either I had misled my crew by miscalculating the water supply and brought them into a very unwise situation, or there was a simpler explanation. The lid came up. At the bottom of the tank lay another 40 or 50 gallons of precious drinking water. It was murky and lukewarm, but it was fresh water. The sucking tube of the deck pump had been blocked by a projecting flange, and had not reached into the bottom of the tank. All was well. We had enough water for the time being. I was quietly relieved, and so too were the crew. No one said anything, but the looks on their faces told me that they, too, had been worried.

In the third week of March *Sohar* lay in a calm so flat that she stood in the shimmer of her own reflection. She was the very picture of stillness. Only a faint ripple radiated out from her hull, which now showed darker patches where the white lime of the anti-fouling had flaked away. Her sails hung limp, sagging loosely from the spars without a breath of wind to fill them. The sea was like hammered steel, and in the water around her rudder post we could see the striped shapes of the pilot fish waving their fins with just the slightest effort to keep station under the becalmed ship. On deck it was so hot that even three months in the tropics had not prepared us for the scorching heat of the calm. Each day the sun arched so high that it stood vertically above the mast, blazing down so that the flaccid sails gave barely a margin of shadow which the crew followed for shelter as they tried to escape the heat. The deck itself was baked until it became too hot to touch, and bare feet which had not worn shoes for twelve or more weeks now wore sandals. Only the leathery soles of Omani feet were tough enough to endure the heated touch of the wood.

There was little work to be done on board. We had already overhauled and mended the sails, replaced any frayed rigging, checked and lubricated the dinghy outboard engines, repacked the stores even from the deepest bilges, done all the hundred and one small chores that would help to pass away the time. Now there was almost nothing left that still needed doing.

A week earlier we had even managed finally to fix the slack rudder. It had again become so loose that it was a menace to the man at the helm. Every time the ship had rolled on a swell, the rudder slammed back and forth on its rope and leather hinges with a great thump, and the massive tiller wagged uncontrollably and threatened to stave in the helmsman's ribs if he was not alert. And when the water flowed along the hull it pushed the whole rudder assembly to one side, made it useless, and rendered steering almost impossible. Looking over the stern I could see where the leather strips and rope lashings, which held the rubber to the stern post, had again stretched or come adrift. I doubted whether the rudder would survive a gale. Another week of rolling in a swell could make it drop off.

'OK. Let's get the job done,' I told Peter. 'I want you to fix the lowest lashing first. Use rope if you find that leather is too difficult to fit while the ship is rolling. But be careful you don't get sliced up by the barnacles.'

Peter and two crewmen inflated the rubber dinghy, launched it, and tied it as a work platform near the rudder. Peter put on mask and flippers, and slipped over the side of the dinghy. We could see him underwater, beginning to work on the lashings. As *Sohar* was moving gently through the water, Peter had tied himself to the vessel with a safety rope so he was being towed along like an underwater sledge. It was a hot, sultry afternoon. The atmosphere was very relaxed.

Suddenly Peter burst to the surface alongside the dinghy. 'Shark!' he yelled. 'Help me out! Quick!' After a second's stunned hesitation, the two men in the dinghy grabbed Peter and heaved him into the boat with a great clatter of equipment. Peter tumbled head over heels on to the floorboards of the dinghy in such a scramble that one of his flippers fell off, and sank down 20,000 fathoms to the bottom of the Indian Ocean. 'A white-tipped shark,' Peter spluttered. 'I was working on the rudder, scraping off the barnacles with my knife so that I could get at the lashings, and I looked round, and there he was. Much too close for comfort. He had come swimming up along the trail of broken barnacles in our wake, eating them. I was just ahead of him. I don't know how hungry he is, but there can't be much else to eat in this part of the ocean.'

We could all see the shark now. It was a modest size, about 4 or 5 feet long, and quite unafraid. Either it was very hungry or very curious, for the animal was cruising back and forth in a menacing way, never more than 50 feet from the ship, and often right beneath the rubber dinghy where Peter was now sitting. We were in a quandary. We could not leave the rudder as it was – Peter had already slackened off the lower lashings before the shark appeared, and now the rudder was half adrift. Yet it was obviously very risky for anyone to go back into the water with the danger of an attack. So we tried to get rid of the shark. Jumah put over a baited line and tried to catch him, but without success, for the shark seemed much more interested by the activity round the rudder. I lowered an underwater firework over the side on the end of a string. It detonated near the shark with a muffled crack. The animal merely flickered at the shock, and then swam back, curious.

After about thirty minutes of waiting it was obvious that the shark was not going to be driven off. Peter was getting impatient. 'Come on,' he said, 'I'm going back in and getting on with the job.' He slid over the side of the dinghy. It was very slow work. Every couple of minutes he had to stop, turn round, and check on the shark which was swimming in erratic patterns, sometimes coming up to within 10 feet of his shoulder. Peter bobbed up again. 'He's hungry all right,' he called up to me. 'He's just gobbled up a piece of leather I cut from the lashings.'

So we devised a plan: while Peter worked on the rudder with Dick Dalley, our newly arrived marine biologist who had joined *Sohar* in Sri Lanka, a third crew member acted as an underwater sentry. The sentry's job was to swim between the underwater team and the shark, staying between the hungry animal and the divers. The shark seemed curious but cautious: it tacked back and forth, but always found the sentry staring at it. The sentry carried a bang stick, a twelve-bore cartridge at the end of a 4-foot rod. The theory was that if the shark attacked he thrust the point of the stick at the animal's nose, pushing home the cartridge, and it exploded with a bang close enough to frighten the animal away. It seemed a doubtful theory, even if the sentry diver was quick and accurate enough to tap on the nose an attacking shark moving at full speed. But luckily the bang stick was not put into action. The sentry found that a better method was to growl at the shark through his snorkel tube. Thus what had begun as a minor crisis ended on a note of comedy. While the divers repaired the rudder, we on the ship could hear the sentry diver growling away like a watchdog as he paddled around in a nose-to-nose confrontation with a hungry but baffled white-tipped shark.

Tim Readman was the sentry diver, or the 'sacrificial diver', as one wag called him. Five months earlier Tim had been working in Muscat for a construction company, and helped to fit out *Sohar* while she was loading. He was so keen to go on the Sindbad Voyage itself that he had given up his job and come out to Sri Lanka to sign on. I appointed him as ship's purser, and he was an excellent addition to the team – stockily built, with curly hair and a ready grin, and a habit of wearing only a pair of very baggy pyjama-style trousers, with a pipe jutting from his beard, he looked like Popeye the Sailorman. With him had come Dick Dalley, the biologist owner of our barnacle 'torpedo', and Nick Hollis, a young medical graduate from London, so that *Sohar* at last had a proper ship's doctor.

Nick was attending to a number of cuts and sores amongst the crew which refused to heal. Insect bites, cuts from coral while diving in Sri Lanka, abrasions from ropes, all mended very slowly in the warm, moist, salty conditions. Sores festered and wept. Tim Readman and Andrew Price looked like strange spotted animals with all the blotches of antiseptic on their legs and arms. Ibrahim was a more serious case. On the passage down from Calicut to Sri Lanka he had jumped to catch a sail and nicked himself accidentally in the ankle with the point of a sheath knife hanging from his belt. The cut had seemed insignificant at the time, but it turned septic. By the time we sailed from Sri Lanka it was a raw, suppurating wound which extended well past his ankle bone, and oozed putrefaction. Nick treated it day after day with drugs, but the response was very slow. Poor Ibrahim was in great pain, and suffering considerably. He grew depressed and began to feel that it would never heal. He could no longer bear to put his injured foot on the deck, and yet he did not give up. He still produced excellent meals, though he could only hop or crawl around the deck, dragging his injured leg behind him. He had considerable courage.

The psychological pressures and strains of being becalmed or frustrated by headwinds was an experience very different from the normal difficulties encountered at sea. Yet in their own way these strains were just as wearing. Instead of short periods of the fear of shipwreck or capsize in the clamour of a gale, we were facing the long, slow, gnawing doubts of boredom, frustration and the ultimate possibility of thirst. There we were, becalmed in the doldrums, hundreds of miles from land, in a very empty part of the world's oceans. Since leaving Sri Lanka, in a month's sailing we had not seen a single ship. We lay off the shipping lanes. There were no fishing grounds or fishing fleets nearby. We could try calling for assistance on the radio, but would anybody bother to look for us or be able to find us? After our experience off Oman where Peter was hurt, it was open to some doubt. So instead we had to come to terms with our situation. And it was satisfying to observe how well the crew was managing to cope. For the Omanis there was no problem. They appeared to have a limitless trust in the conduct of the ship, the reliability of the captain, and the fact that conditions would improve. But for the Europeans it was perhaps more difficult. They could see the water supply dwindling, count the remaining stores of food, note that one item after another was disappearing off our menu as the food stocks were used up. And they had to keep their own counsel. There was nothing to be done, but to remain patient, regulate the daily rhythm of life, and wait and wait. We had truly moved back into the days of sail on ocean passages. Our time scale was longer, slower, and ultimately dependent on nature.

The date of 18 March was an unforgettable one in the lives of everyone aboard. About noon, as *Sohar* lolled gently through the water, a school of mackerel-like fish was spotted near the rudder. A fishing line was lowered into the water, and a gleaming green and blue silver fish was promptly hooked and whisked on board. Three or four more fishing lines quickly hit the water as the Omanis joined in. Obligingly, the shoal of fish continued to feed voraciously, and soon half a dozen fine fish were flapping in the basket on deck, ready for our lunch. Then, just as the next fish was being hauled aboard, a shark rose up out of the depths and swallowed it. The startled fisherman – it was Musalam – found himself hauling in a 4-foot shark instead of a mackerel. The line hissed out through his fingers, burning them, before it snapped and the shark broke free. Now we could see that about two dozen sharks had been attracted by the commotion. They were swimming in to attack the mackerel-like fish, and circling around their prey. The mackerel fish turned away in panic and tried to escape, as the sharks hit them. Thinking quickly, Khamees Police grabbed one of our fresh-caught fish, cut a slice of flesh from its flank, baited a large hook with it, and tossed the lure at the hungry sharks. The bait had scarcely splashed into the sea and begun to sink through the water when we saw a shark swim towards it, close in, and almost lazily suck the bait into its jaws. Khamees paid out the line until the shark turned and began to swim away. Then he struck. In a moment he was fighting against the furious struggles of the enraged shark. The line cut back and forth in the water. The surface of the sea churned up as the shark thrashed about, trying to break loose, but the fishing line was a stout one, and Khamees was heaving in with all his strength, his muscles rippling with effort. Abdullah jumped up on the gunnel to give him a hand, and together they heaved the shark bodily out of the water and up the ship's side. The animal was in a panic. It came tumbling over the rail and struck the deck, and then went cavorting off, arching and twisting its body like a demented spring, its jaws snapping at anything in its path. Pandemonium broke loose as everyone skipped out of the way of those snapping jaws. Abdullah seized a belaying pin and began smashing the shark on the skull to kill it. Khamees Navy danced about, thrusting at the shark with a knife, and taking care to keep his bare toes out of range of its teeth which were chewing at the hatch covers.

No one had been watching Jumah. He had rigged up another shark line simply by tying a massive hook to a length of old rigging rope. 'Yaa Allah!' yelled Abdullah, looking round. Jumah had hooked another shark. Hitching up his loincloth, Abdullah sprang to help him. 'Yaa Allah!' Hand over hand they began hoisting in. Another live shark hit the deck, 80 lb of asphyxiating, thrashing fury which had to be subdued. Thump, thump, went the bludgeons. Khamees Navy had now got himself one of the 4-foot-long windlass bars and was wielding it like a flail, raining massive blows on the shark to stun it while everyone else stood clear. Crash, slap, slither, a third shark came bouncing inboard to add to the chaos. Omanis were everywhere, running back and forth, cheering with delight, baiting hooks, cutting hooks free from shark jaws, hauling yet more sharks aboard, bludgeoning, knifing and shouting. Here was food to last us many days. More and more sharks were swimming up to the fray, attracted by the frenzy and attacking the hooks. They had scented blood, and were in a turmoil. Some bit through the lines and were lost. Others were hooked and dragged aboard, only to be replaced immediately in the sea by another mindlessly hungry shark which swam voraciously in to fill the gap. There seemed to be no limit to the number of sharks in the water. Where once there had been empty ocean around the ship, it was now criss-crossed with the telltale shadows of hunting sharks. Where they had suddenly come from it was impossible to guess.

On deck it was a scene of carnage. There were thrashing, snapping sharks slithering everywhere. They were incredibly difficult to dispatch. They twisted and flapped despite a tremendous battering from the bludgeons and knives. Sharks' blood spattered the deck. Pink foam frothed from their gills. Sharks' tails thrust this way and that, slamming into the cookbox and railings. Sharks bit and snapped at one another, and one shark fastened its jaws on to the tail of the next.

'Bas! Enough!' I shouted at the top of my voice to penetrate the commotion, the yells of encouragement, the thud of blows. I could see that we had enough food now. Besides, life on board was becoming too dangerous. Sooner or later someone's bare foot was going to get too near a snapping shark, and be bitten. In just ten minutes we had caught seventeen sharks and got them successfully on board. We could have gone on catching many more, but it would have been useless slaughter. '*Bas! Bas!*' I yelled again. Finally the Omanis heard me and the excitement began to subside. Men straightened up from their onslaught on the sharks. Clubs and bludgeons fell to their sides. Fishing lines were hauled in and coiled up. The men relaxed.

But this extraordinary day was not yet over. We had stacked the bodies of the sharks forward on the main deck, and were beginning the job of skinning them, when a line of thunder clouds began to advance on us. The clouds were deep grey-black burdened with rain, and this time we were ready for them.

'Quick! Get up the tarpaulins and rig them as water traps,' I ordered. 'Andrew – you and Terry scoop up the rain water as it collects in the tarpaulins. Jumail and Dick, you pour it down into the fresh water tank.'

The rain clouds swept across us and we were enveloped in a wet grey wall. The tropical rain hissed down in torrents. Tremendous cracks of lightning crashed and lit up the murk. The shock of thunderclaps rolled over us. The rain water crew worked furiously – the precious fresh water was cascading everywhere, rushing off the sails in rivulets, whirling across the deck, bouncing off the deck planks in huge drops. More men ran forward to pull up the edges of the tarpaulin so that it made a canvas bath under the run-off from the mainsail. The water poured into the tarpaulin and collected in the central dip. There one man stood, ankle deep in rain water, shovelling up the water as fast as he could with a bucket. The bucket was passed back down a line of eager hands to the main hatch, and tipped down a pipe leading to the water tanks. The rain was magnificent, hammering down spectacularly. Bucket after bucket of it went gurgling down to replenish our drinking supply. Men were grinning and smiling happily, oblivious of wet hair and drenched clothing. This was just what we wanted; in half an hour we had collected enough water to last us four days. A few more thunderstorms like this and our drinking water problems would be solved completely. The thunder reverberated, and the lightning blazed.

'Ow!' yelled Andrew, leaping out of the canvas bath where he had been scooping up water. 'That got me right up the arm!' A nearby lightning discharge had sent a powerful charge of electricity surging through the canvas bath.

All the while Eid and Khamees were working like creatures in a demon opera, kneeling on deck hunched over the shark carcasses. Amid the thunder and lightning, in the grey gloom of the thunderstorm, they were flaying the catch. Snick, snick, snick, their knife blades were disembowelling, skinning and flensing the flesh from bone and cartilage as fast as any fishmonger. As they worked, they chanted a quick rhythmic refrain to match the darting thrust and cut of the knives. The shark flesh was peeled off in wet pink sheets which they slapped down on deck. The waste parts of the skin, head and tail, were tossed over the rail with a heave. The drenching rain washed the deck clean around them, the water in the scuppers changing to bloody red rivulets, then to a faint pink, and finally to the clean fresh look of wet wood. Within an hour they had prepared a quarter of a ton of fine, fresh shark meat, enough food to last the entire ship's company for several weeks. Some of the flesh we cooked and ate that same night; the rest we stacked up by the forward hatch, interspersing the layers of flesh with sprinkled salt to preserve it. When the sun came out we dried the shark meat, draping it over the gunnels to desiccate in the sunshine. The meat decayed slightly, and smelled powerfully, but it provided us with a sure reserve of food.

Over the next week we improved our rain water-catching technique. We kept the tarpaulin ready on deck, and as soon as the first raindrops fell the duty watch quickly rigged the canvas bath. Many of the rain showers came at night, about two hours after dusk, and brought an end to our evening's relaxation. We had taken to hanging a paraffin lamp over the main hatch grating, tying the lamp so that it cast a pool of light over the waist of the ship. There, under the lamp, would gather the off-duty watch to relax after supper. A chess set appeared, and became a regular favourite. Others read or just dozed. A plate of the ever-popular dates was handed round. Farther forward, in the darkness of the foredeck, one could just detect the shapes of the Omanis lounging on the planks and talking softly, or hear the tap, tap of one of the drums playing gently in the stillness of the night. Farther aft, another small hurricane lamp marked the position of the helmsman, steering the ship if there was any wind, or simply perched on the gunnel on lookout. Sometimes Andrew would produce his guitar, and when the Omani drum on the foredeck fell silent one could hear Andrew picking out a tune on the guitar strings. Often the nights were too cloudy for good star sights, but occasionally the sky was so clear that Nick Hollis, who was interested in the star charts, could identify even the smallest of the navigation stars. Then, with the soft breeze, the night was perfect magic. *Sohar* seemed to be sailing in a pool of silver, her great triangular sail black against the stars, and the spinner dolphin which sometimes followed her by day would move ahead of the ship, and curve and cavort around *Sohar*, drawing churning trails of luminous bubbles in the water.

The lamp on the main deck was *Sohar*'s only navigation light, for the red and green navigation lights with which we sailed from Muscat were connected to batteries which no longer gave enough power to illuminate them through the night. Salt air and the rain storms dripping through the deck played havoc with any electrical equipment. Wiring had corroded or was hopelessly damp. The battery charger had given up the ghost, and the reserve charger was only working in fits and starts, barely sufficient to power the small radio set if we were careful, but no more. To report our position we relied entirely on the vigilance of our friends, the radio amateurs in Oman who had organized a listening watch for our signal. Day after day they listened out for *Sohar*'s increasingly weak messages, and began to worry. Picking up our faint reports, they could see that the ship was still not making any significant progress. *Sohar* seemed glued to one small patch of the Indian Ocean.

And on 23 March we almost lost Richard. Once again there was a flat calm: Richard had decided to go swimming off the ship armed with another of his camera contraptions, this time a long bamboo pole. At one end he had fixed a camera, and at the other a lead weight to act as a counterbalance. Now he paddled off, holding up the pole like a periscope – he wanted to take pictures of *Sohar* becalmed. For half an hour the periscope bobbed and circled around the ship, and Richard swam farther and farther away. We began to get worried, and shouted at him to come back, but he remained blissfully unaware. We noticed a line of colour on the water – it was a cat's paw, a puff of wind, the leading edge of a breeze which was coming towards the ship. Soon *Sohar* would be sailing. Her sails gave a warning tremor. Even if we lowered sail, the ship would still be blown through the water faster than Richard could possibly swim to catch up with us. We shouted again. But still Richard had not heard. We yelled again and waved frantically. His head came up, and he waved a friendly reply. He had not the least idea of what was the matter. By now half the crew were jumping up and down on the gunnel, screaming 'Richard! Richard! Get back aboard! Wind! Wind!'

Suddenly, at last, he realized the danger. The periscope wobbled over at an absurd angle as he began thrashing frantically towards the ship. But it was very nearly too late. The breeze had reached *Sohar*, and she began moving through the water, deceptively slowly, it seemed, but faster than a man could swim.

'Throw off the sheets,' I ordered. 'Put her aback.' The ship stalled, and began to drift sideways. The great sail made her almost uncontrollable at this speed, and she began to turn helplessly. She was still moving.

'The rope, Richard! Swim for the safety rope!' Everyone was pointing and yelling. Richard's white, frightened face gazed up. He was still clutching his bamboo pole, and very tired indeed. He made a last effort, a final few thrashing kicks, and managed to grab the safety line.

'Hang on!' He was being towed along behind *Sohar* now, like a half-drowned heron. Even at the speed of a knot or two it was impossible for him to pull himself up the line – he was not strong enough. 'Hang on! We'll pull you in!' We began hauling in the safety line. It was difficult work. Slowly Richard was pulled towards the boat. Now he was level with the rudder, but 12 feet below us. Already the angle of the rope was dragging him upwards, and we could see he was tiring rapidly. Soon he would let go. His knuckles were white with strain, and he was on the verge of panic. Of course he hadn't let go of his precious camera.

'My camera, my camera,' he called. 'Take the camera.' The rest of his words were lost in a gurgle as his mouth went under.

Damn the camera, I thought. He has plenty of others. 'Let it go, Richard!' but he wouldn't. Someone made a quick lunge, and managed to seize the end of the bamboo pole and get it out of Richard's grasp. By now he was desperate. 'I can't hold on! I'm going to let go,' he gasped, thrashing feebly. 'My strength's gone.'

Peter leaped into the stern lavatory pulpit, Khamees Police after him, and leaned right over while Khamees Police held on to his legs – he was just able to reach Richard's arm. He grabbed Richard's wrist, and heaved him up and out of the water by main force. Someone else got hold of Richard's other arm, and he was halfway up the ship's side. A third hand took the photographer by the seat of his swimming trunks, and Richard was lifted into the stern lavatory, safe but shaking with exhaustion. He promised he would never go swimming off the ship again without first obtaining permission.

The cat's paw of wind, which almost lost us Richard, had come from the south-west. It was the first slight sign that the weather was beginning to change, and so the crew began to look hopefully for the clouds that would tell us that the south-west monsoon was on the way.

But the changeover was very gradual. The wind was fitful, swinging to all points of the compass. For an hour or so it might blow from the direction we wanted, and *Sohar* made some progress. Then it died away to a calm or, worse yet, began to blow again from the northeast. The disappointment began to tell. Some of the European crew members showed signs of becoming snappish with one another and fretful, and I began to worry that their patience was being worn thin. The Omanis, on the other hand, were more relaxed. I could see an occasional worried frown, but they appeared to have no doubt that all would turn out well.

People began to make a deliberate effort to keep themselves occupied. Tim Readman started to stitch himself a canvas sailor's jacket; Nick took up fancy rope work; the scientists continued a full routine of daily observations; and Dave Bridges embarked on a complicated project to sew himself a special padded and compartmented case to carry the film camera when we eventually reached Sumatra.

Almost anything served as a distraction, and we even tried to tame a small gull that had been following the ship all the way from Sri Lanka. Like us, the poor creature was far out of range of land, so it stayed very close to the ship, flying around all day, and then fluttering down to land aboard by night. It was a slender little bird, with a well-formed fan of a tail, long, narrow, tapering wings, a white body flecked with dark marks, red legs, and a rather comical round head with a delicate thin probe of a beak. At night the gull would perch by the helmsman, just on the fringe of the light cast by his hurricane lamp. There it would allow itself to be picked up and handled gently, but seemed ill at ease, so we gave it fresh water to drink and let it be, a faint, light-coloured shape waiting in the darkness. In the thunderstorms the gull was desperately worried. It fluttered and scrabbled, trying to keep its perch in the wind and lashing rain, so we picked it up and placed it in shelter on top of the stern locker in the lee of the gunnel.

On 4 April I called the crew together for a meeting on the poop deck. They gathered round, and looked down at the chart I had spread on the grating of the aft hatch. Until now I had deliberately kept the chart from them, and not told them about their position – I was the only person on board to know we had been patrolling fruitlessly back and forth in the same tiny patch of ocean. Now I showed the pencil line of the ship's tracks, circling round and round on itself, never progressing in the calms, headwinds and adverse currents.

'I'm glad you didn't show it to us before,' muttered Tim Readman. 'I would have been too depressed.'

'I didn't want to worry you,' I said. 'We still have some 600 or 700 miles to go, and with the south-west monsoon so late and erratic there is no guarantee that when it finally arrives the wind will blow steadily in the direction we want. We have enough shark meat for food, and we are gathering enough rain water to supply us with fresh water to drink. We can stay out here almost indefinitely. Our only worry is the supply of charcoal. Ibrahim tells me that we have only enough charcoal for another two weeks. So in future we'll have only one hot meal a day in order to save fuel.'

Eid spoke up in Arabic, and Musalam translated. 'He says we should only make tea twice in every twenty-four hours.'

I agreed. 'And if our fishermen can keep up the good work, we'll have fresh fish as well as shark to eat,' I told him.

The Omanis grinned happily. 'Fish, dates, rice, and water. That's correct for sailors,' chuckled Abdullah and, looking utterly unworried, he padded off down the deck, brawny, barrel-chested, with his stubby, splay-toed feet turned out, and a twinkle in his eye.

Hawksbill turtle

—10—

Spar Break

The doldrums eased their grip on *Sohar*. A south-west breeze got up
in the early hours of 5 April and lasted until noon; there followed a
quick burst of excitement as the wind suddenly switched direction,
increased in strength, and caught the ship under full sail. *Sohar* shot
forward like a racehorse under the whip. Suddenly she was creaming
along at 8 or 9 knots, the spray dashing up under her bows, sails
bulging taut, and the whole ship alive with excitement. Cheering, the
Omanis ran forward to hoist a second jib. But barely had they got it
halfway up when the wind seized it and ballooned it out like a spin-
naker to leeward. *Sohar*'s speed increased another knot. She was tearing
along. Looking back, I could see the trailing fishing lines pulled tight
by the speed. There was a loud crash, as a stout bamboo fishing pole
broke in half, snapped by the increased pull of the line.

As the weather changed, so too did the sea around us. We were
witnessing the annual rhythm of the sea, the profound alteration that
takes place as the north-east monsoon dies away to the intermediate
calms and then the south-west monsoon begins to blow. The animals
of the sea responded. Where before the sea around us had seemed flat
and empty, devoid of life except for the constant escort of pilot fish
and the mysterious banding together of the sharks, now there was life
and activity. Sea birds appeared. Flying fish burst from the wave crests,
and skimmed off across the water. The blue, gold and silver flash of
dorado could be seen swimming past the hull. And quite abruptly we
began to catch fish. They were tuna, about 18 inches long, bright silver
and in superb condition. We caught ten or fifteen of these tuna almost
every evening.

The Omanis were delighted. They were all fishermen at heart, and
very skilful with hook and line. There was a great bustle on board, a
checking-over of fishing lines, sharpening of hooks, making of new
feather lures from strips of bright-coloured cloth. Eid filched the spare

deep sea lead and cut up its big lead weight to make small fishing weights. Each Omani had his own box of fishing kit tucked away under the gunnel, but Khamees Police was by far our best fisherman. He was a natural: he would spend hour after hour on the foredeck, enthusiastically casting and recasting his hand line as if he would never grow tired. And inevitably it was Khamees who made the biggest catches. He could catch fish when no one else had a single bite. If someone saw the gleam of a single dorado and called out to Khamees, he would jump to his feet and come leaping down the deck in great exuberant bounds, hurl out his fishing line, and – as like as not – hook the single fish and pull it aboard to a great cheer from the men.

The evening catch of tuna was curiously regular. It took place at the same time every evening, and the size of the fish was nearly always the same. The regularity of this catch was puzzling because *Sohar* was now travelling about 40 or 60 miles a day using the first favourable winds. Yet it seemed that we always had tuna alongside us every evening. It was then that we began to notice a singular phenomenon: the ship appeared to be moving along surrounded by her own huge shoal of fish, which was always there. Whether *Sohar* was becalmed for a day, or received a fair wind and moved 70 miles in twenty-four hours, the fish appeared to keep station with the ship. And there was another curious feature – the shoal always stayed ahead of *Sohar*, never astern of her. The sea birds told us that. By day we noticed there was always a flock of sea birds wheeling and turning, and hunting fish ahead of the ship. Sometimes these gulls would split into two or three smaller flocks, and each flock hunted separately over individual shoals of fish. But always they were hunting ahead of the ship or in an arc extending back as far as her beam. Even when the fish shoals dived or perhaps dispersed temporarily, and the gulls had to fly higher in order to peer down from a great altitude and wait for the fish to reappear, the birds kept their watch ahead of *Sohar* or off to her side.

At night, by contrast, something equally curious happened: as dusk gathered, the shoal of fish moved closer in to the ship. This was precisely the time when the Omanis began to catch tuna, just when the fish were feeding and had come within casting range of the hand lines. Then, for about an hour, we would catch fish, enough for the evening meal and for lunch next day. By dawn the tuna would have gone, presumably moving ahead of the ship. Thus at night if we leaned over the rail and shone a powerful torch into the water, we saw a remarkable spectacle. The beam of the light illuminated fish, thousands upon thousands of them, packed in around the ship on both sides, all swimming parallel, all keeping pace, whether *Sohar* was making 2 knots or 7 knots through the water. It was an uncanny sight. The fish were small, only about 8 inches to a foot long, and we could not identify the species. But they existed in an enormous multitude, and if we raised the torch beam higher and shone it farther away from the hull, it seemed as if the fish in the farther ranks were larger than those close by, and of a different type. We had the distinct impression that *Sohar* was moving forward in a great living mass of fish, with the smallest species close to the hull and the larger predatory fish out on the farther fringes.

It was a phenomenon which I had never witnessed before, and which the marine biologists on *Sohar* could not explain. Possibly, they suggested, *Sohar* represented a fixed point in the ocean for the fish, a point of reference which related to their shoaling behaviour. Or perhaps the vessel attracted its own independent community, with the tiny fish feeding on the weed and barnacles of *Sohar*'s hull, larger fish feeding on the smaller fish, and so forth up the scale until *Sohar* was the focus of a food chain of animals. Of course we could not be sure whether it was the same fish which kept in the shoal all the time. Possibly new fish were joining the shoal, and other fish left it. But one notable fact was to be very apparent for the next fifteen days: *Sohar*'s escort of fish travelled nearly 400 miles with her. It was a sea mystery which found no explanation.

'Captain! Captain!' The urgent cry shouted down the hatch brought me wide awake in an instant, and I rolled out of my bunk. It was the blackest hour of the night, just before dawn; and the cry had been yelled by the duty watch leader, Khamees Police. Clang, clang, clang, the alarm bell was ringing furiously. I grabbed a torch and ran up the companionway, emerging on deck to find that Terry was at the tiller, staring up open-mouthed at the mainspar. I followed his gaze, and saw chaos. The great 81-foot mainspar had snapped in two and now hung like a broken wing, a section some 30 feet long dangling down awkwardly and held up only by the canvas of the sail. The rest of the mainsail was tangled around the mast in a total confusion of canvas and ropes. Every time the ship rolled, the broken spar swept dangerously across the deck, threatening to maim anyone in its path.

Even as I squinted upwards through the flickering rain drops, trying to assess the extent of the damage, there was a horrid soft thump, followed by a gasping cry from up in the bows, as though someone had had the breath knocked out of him. There were calls of 'Doctor! Doctor!' and out of the gloom appeared Khamees Police, half carried down the deck by two Omanis. Khamees looked wretched. He was a poor colour, and clasping his side, giving forth rending coughs that shook his frame. 'Broken rib,' I thought to myself dejectedly – one of my best men out of action, as well as the mainspar smashed. Khamees Police was laid on a deck box, and Nick Hollis began to attend to the injury.

'All non-Omanis on the aft deck!' I called, as more and more of the crew scrambled up on deck. They ran to their stations, and stood waiting for orders. It was essential to bring down the damaged mainspar to the deck as fast as possible without smashing any more of the rigging or causing any further injuries. 'Peter! Dick! Terry! I want you three to control the aft end of the spar as she comes down,' I shouted. They ran to the starboard rail to clear the ropes that controlled the upper end of the mangled spar.

'Down! Slowly down!' I called out to the Omanis.

Already Jumail and Saleh had cleared the main halyard falls and were looking at me for the command to lower away.

'Down! Carefully down.'

They paid out the massive 8-inch rope, and the crippled spar began to slide down the mast, the huge mainsail collapsing beneath it.

'Slowly. Slowly. Eid! Abdullah! Mainstays across to the port rail.'

The two men hurried to rearrange the rigging so that the yard would slide downwards without becoming entangled.

'Musalam! Khamees Navy! Grab the broken end. Be careful. Watch out. Get a rope around it.'

The two men seized the loose end of the broken yard. For a moment it threatened to hurl them against the bulwarks. But then Adbullah with Jumah and Eid rushed to their help.

'Stop lowering! Hold it! More men to the broken section. Get it outboard and clear! One, two, three, heave!' And with a tremendous shove ten men pushed the broken end of the spar out over the side of the ship so that it could fold harmlessly back as the mainspar came down.

Ten feet from the deck the spar jammed – the enormous wet mass of canvas had stopped its descent. 'Cut clear the sail!' Once again it was the grandfather of the crew, the experienced Jumah, who was up and gone in a twinkling. He went swarming up the main halyard, hanging upside down, transferred to the mainspar, and ran along it like a cat until he reached the parrel collar near the mast. There he perched, and began swiftly unknotting the sail lashing ties. I turned my attention to the stern. Clinging to the aft end of the spar which projected 6 feet out over the black water was Terry; his legs were wrapped around the spar, he was hanging on with one hand, and with a knife in the other hand he was sawing furiously at the sail lashings. Every minute was a risk. The wind was blowing a steady Force 5 or 6, and the damaged sail flapped ominously. With each roll of the ship the tangle of ropes slid and shifted dangerously. The neat symmetry of spars and rigging was now a shambles of collapsed ropes and broken timber. *Sohar* was sorely hurt.

Now Tim Readman clawed his way up the slack surface of the mainsail, grabbing handholds of canvas until he was dangling beneath the broken end of the spar, 12 feet above the deck. Reaching for his knife he began to slice away the last of the sail lashings until only one was left. He cut it through with his knife, and came tumbling down spectacularly in a welter of canvas.

'Are you OK?' I called anxiously.

'Fine,' he replied as his tousled head emerged from under a pile of sodden ropes.

'Good. Clear away the brailing lines, and all hands get the sail below deck. I want the mainspar lowered right down, and made fast.'

Another ten minutes of teamwork, and the damage was under control. It was time to take a breathing space.

'Everyone get a cup of tea, and relax. We'll look at the damage in daylight.'

A bleak, wet dawn showed the extent of *Sohar's* injury. The mainspar was shattered. A sudden change in the direction of the wind had taken the mainsail aback, and pressed the entire weight of the canvas against the mast. Luckily the mast itself had withstood the strain, but the pressure had snapped the mainspar – a solid timber baulk a foot thick and hand-picked from the finest spar timber – as though it was a brittle twig. *Sohar* had been crippled as effectively as a butcher snapping the leg bone of a chicken by twisting it against the socket. Now the jagged end of the fractured mainyard projected raw and fresh, the splinters of wood pale in the dawn light. For a moment I wondered whether it would be possible to mend the spar by fishing together the broken parts with a splint of extra timber, but the job would be long and difficult aboard a rolling ship and there was no guarantee that the repair would be strong enough to support the huge mainsail. I squinted down the length of the broken spar, and its length seemed vaguely familiar.

'Dick and Andrew, please measure the longest surviving piece of timber, and let me know how long it is.'

'Forty-nine feet,' came the reply some minutes later.

'Excellent. We'll clean up the fractured end of the broken spar. Then jury rig the ship by hoisting the spare mizzen sail set on the salvaged spar section. It's almost exactly the right size.'

Peter Dobbs and Tim Readman set to work with saw and chisel to round off the fractured end of the spar. When it was ready, the Omanis spent an hour carefully rebalancing the shortened spar so that it hung exactly to their liking. Then the spare mizzen sail was lashed on. Stays and halyards were disentangled and carefully set up in their proper places, and to the strains of our special hauling song the entire crew hoisted the jury-rigged mainspar to the masthead. We gazed up to assess its effectiveness: amazingly, the ship seemed scarcely changed at all. Despite the queer combination of a jib and two mizzen sails, *Sohar*'s rig looked neat and trim. The sails filled out pleasingly, and although her speed was reduced by about a third *Sohar* was moving briskly through the water. By lunchtime, less than seven hours after the spar break, the ship was heading once more towards Sumatra, and once again her crew had proved their competence.

I returned to my calculations of speed and distance. *Sohar* now had about 450 miles to run in a direct line to her landfall in Sumatra, and we had only five days' supply of charcoal left in the lockers. I doubted very much that the charcoal would last out, and soon we were likely to be eating cold food. The main consolation was that now there was little danger of running out of food or water. In the last three days we had collected 200 gallons of rainwater, and the ship's water tanks now held three weeks' reserves. Also the Omanis were still catching at least two-thirds of our daily consumption of food with hook and line, and we were getting along very nicely on a basic diet of rice, dates and fish. In short, the Sindbad Voyage had come to terms with the sea. We had achieved a precious equilibrium: it was an important development. The lesson of the broken spar had shown that we could fend for ourselves despite a major mishap, and that with a well-found ship and plenty of spare rope and canvas in the bosun's stores, we were capable of extricating ourselves from a major predicament.

Over the last four months at sea we had come to understand the

day-to-day requirements of the ship: we recognized the signs to look
or listen for which told us what repairs were due. We knew the
parts that tended to fray or wear out, and needed to be replaced
regularly. We understood the best way to arrange the ropes, to adjust
the sails, to balance the helm so that the ship sailed comfortably. When
the wind changed direction and we needed to wear ship, there was no
longer any fuss or bother. Every man knew his place and his duties,
and the job was done smoothly. Even the night-time rain showers did
not inconvenience us. At the first few drops of rain, the watch on deck
would unroll the canvas covers over the hatches, dowse the deck lamps,
and change into foul-weather clothing. Below decks the off-duty watch
would stow anything that might be damaged by the wet, and rig
themselves little tents and shelters to divert the inevitable trickles and
rivulets which came pouring between the cracks of the sun-dried deck
planks. For an hour or two the rain could be heard hammering down
on the hatch covers, followed by the blessed relief of fresh air which
came wafting down below deck as the shower ended and the hatch
covers were thrown back. Only the stench below decks was difficult
to endure. It was a stifling combination of bilge gas, stale air, and the
myriad smells of ropes, food, human bodies and ship's stores. The
wave of warm, fetid air which welled up the moment the hatch covers
were thrown back was enough to make the deck watch gag: it smelled
of rotting vegetation.

It was little wonder, then, that we spent 90 per cent of our daily
lives on deck in the open air, away from the stifling confines of the
hull. We worked on deck, relaxed on deck, and slept on the planks
under the night sky whenever we could. And by living in the open we
came to be more and more in tune with the sea around us. We began
to remark the subtle changes in the colour of the water, the shape and
size of the waves, the very feel of the ocean itself. We were aware of
the changing patterns of the flocks of our constant companions, the
sea birds, and noted whether they were flying high or low, dividing
into small groups or circling *en masse*. We remarked the arrival of new
species, when skuas and tropic birds first came to join the familiar
gulls. And we reacted with almost the same excitement as they did
when there was a great flurry in the sea, and a hunting whale, about
30 or 40 feet long, came thrusting up out of the depths to pursue the
surface fish, and sent the sea birds into shrieks of frenzy.

We were becoming virtual extensions of the ship herself, responsive
to her movements and moods. When *Sohar* lolled, becalmed in yet

another interval of light airs, we too would laze and doze. But when the wind strengthened and the ship started to hurry forward through the water, we responded in kind: a sense of activity and urgency filled the ship. There was a controlled excitement at the thought of yet another few miles passing beneath her keel. And sometimes *Sohar* rewarded us very well indeed. With the wind a moderate Force 4 or 5 blowing on her quarter, the ship seemed to take off like an express train. Even under her jury jig, she would gather speed smoothly and sweetly until she reached 6 or 7 knots, and there she ran, poised comfortably, reeling off the sea miles that separated us from our landfall, and cleaving through the sea almost as if she was in a well-worn groove.

At such times the Omanis in particular were elated; they would chatter and grin at one another, make small adjustments to the sails, and set their inevitable fishing lines. Long ago I had given up insisting that Saleh or Eid should wear safety harnesses when they climbed aloft. Whenever a sail or halyard jammed they would go shinning up the rigging, quite unperturbed by the risk of falling 50 feet to the deck, and very soon the Europeans followed their example. Peter, the most athletic of us all, could be seen perched at the main masthead, happily working away with Eid, black skin opposite bronze skin, both clad in loincloths and turbans, without a care for the yawning void below them. I learned, too, that with the Omani sailors it was possible to gauge the strength of the wind and the condition of the ship by the volume of the noise that they made as they worked. If they called out cheerily, shouting instructions back and forth, then all was well and *Sohar* was sailing comfortably. But when the shouts turned short and staccato, then the wind was rising. And if the sailors fell silent, I knew they were waiting for their captain to decide what next should be done.

At night, when the wind and rain burst upon the darkened ship, then the Omanis would bob up from the hatchway like genies, buzzing with anticipation, tugging on their oilskins, and revelling in the activity. When it was all over and the squall had passed by, leaving the decks gleaming wet and everyone sodden with the downpour, they would gleefully cook up their 'wet weather special', a sticky ball of about 17 lb of pounded dates kneaded together with cooking oil, heated in a pan, and flavoured with a ferocious amount of raw garlic. Slippery, greasy clots of this mash were picked off with the fingers and swallowed. It was the best way to warm up the body after the cold rain, the Omanis declared, and I agreed. Those Europeans who could not stomach the sticky, greasy sweetness had to suffer. If another rain shower came, and the hatch covers went back on, the reek of garlic below decks even drowned the smell of the bilge gas.

Our extraordinary escort of fish made its presence known even when we were becalmed. Patches of sea around us flecked with the steady plop! plop! of little fish, some 6 inches long, which flipped in and out of the water, presumably as they fed on even smaller fry. And when we went for a swim, and dived beneath the stationary hull, we found a complete colony of sea creatures in the shadow of *Sohar*. Around the rudder constantly hovered a small group of pilot fish. In a crevice near the stern post now lived a different hitchhiking crab. It could be seen creeping along the hull to gather in its daily ration of food or, occasionally, with great daring, it launched itself into the water to seize on a floating morsel and then turned and swam frantically back to its foothold. Always we found remora fish, bland, grey-green creatures with characteristic sucker plates on top of their heads, like the ribbed soles of tennis shoes. From time to time the remora stuck themselves to *Sohar*'s hull so that they were pulled along by the ship, and then they exasperated the Omani fishermen. If a remora took their bait, it would dive for the safety of the hull and would stick itself firmly there. The hopeful fishermen would then imagine he was pulling against a splendid catch, heave and tug until his prey came on board, and find himself with only a modest-sized remora. More effective was the doctor's technique. Nick would hang out of the stern lavatory, spear gun in hand, and shoot remora clean through the head until we had enough for breakfast.

Twice we observed a feeding frenzy overcome the immense shoal of fish around *Sohar*. Each time the flock of sea birds warned us: the birds saw the arrival of larger predators, and began to wheel and call excitedly to one another. Then they grouped and flew very fast some distance ahead of the vessel. Beneath them appeared white flashes of foam where large fish were leaping out of the water. As *Sohar* sailed closer, we could make out that these fish were big tuna and albacore, hundreds of them, hurling themselves clear of the sea and falling back with a splash. Other fish came driving horizontally across the wave tops, skipping from one wave crest to the next. One splendid fish, an albacore almost 3½ feet in length, charged across *Sohar*'s bows like a torpedo, its body shimmering bright silver in the sunshine as it bored through the water with great powerful thrusts. Within minutes we saw the reason for this frenetic activity. Behind the fish appeared the spouts and fins of a large school of dolphins, some fifty animals, who were hunting the tuna. The dolphins had arranged themselves in an arc which extended across a front of maybe 2 miles, and they were driving their victims like sheepdogs herding a flock.

The focus of the arc was *Sohar* herself, and we could see that the dolphins were chasing the fish into a tight box just ahead of us. On both sides of *Sohar* rose and fell the backs of the dolphins as they remorselessly pushed their prey into the killing area, and as they came closer we heard the whistling puffs of their breath. Dolphin after dolphin appeared, some moving singly, but usually squads of three or four animals working in unison and spread out to cover its particular section of the fish drive. As the arc of dolphins tightened, the tuna grew more and more desperate. They dashed in all directions, quite heedless of the ship sailing amongst them. Finally the dolphins completed their feeding manoeuvre. The arc contracted until suddenly there seemed to be dolphins all around us. The hunting circle broke up, and individual dolphins swam around and under the ship, chasing and consuming their victims.

Other hunters were pursuing the tuna. A Korean tuna-fishing boat, rust-streaked and hard-used, thumped its way past us in the morning light, its crew gathered in the stern to gape at the curious sight of a fully rigged Arab sailing ship in these waters. And on the night of 13 April we saw the lights of several small coasters and knew that we could not be far from land. The wind was now constantly in our favour, and *Sohar* was closing rapidly in on her target, the northern tip of Sumatra and the entrance to the Malacca Strait.

Two days later we entered the main shipping lane, a frightening experience. At one moment we were sailing gently towards a line of tankers and container ships which were headed for the Malacca Strait. There was a light breeze, we were scarcely making headway, and we could pick out the hulls of perhaps nine or ten vessels churning steadily across our track. Then a thick line of thundercloud blotted out the sky. A blast of wind and rain swept across *Sohar*, and she began to surge forward through the murk, heading directly into the path of the ships like a blind pedestrian stepping out into a motorway during a rainstorm. It was a sinister moment. We peered through the baffling blanket of rain, looking for the looming grey shapes of the tankers moving like juggernauts through the downpour. With our unwieldy sail arrangement there was very little chance that we could dodge out of the way of one of these monstrous vessels should it suddenly appear out of the gloom. Twice we saw the dark shadow of a large ship plough past us, oblivious of our presence. No one would have expected a sailing ship out here in the entrance to the Malacca Strait, and the radar echo of our wooden vessel would have presented a faint and puzzling mark on the screens of the merchant ships. So I kept *Sohar* sailing at full speed at right angles to the main direction of the big ships in order to cut across the shipping lane as fast as possible. Three hours later we worked clear of the shipping, and as the stars appeared that evening I took a star sight to plot our position. I found that a new current had swept us a little too far to the north so that we would have to sail down on to our chosen landfall, the island of Sabang, lying 10 miles off the north tip of Sumatra.

Next morning the sunrise showed dark hummocks on the horizon which had to be the outlines of Sabang, its neighbouring islands, and the mountains on the main island. It seemed as if we were poised to make our landfall, but the distances were deceptive. Sumatra is the fifth largest island in the world, and everything about Sumatra is on a giant scale. The apparently insignificant island directly ahead of us in fact rose 2000 feet, and the small hill on the mainland was a 6000-foot peak. So what at first glance seemed to be a sea distance of no more than 15 miles between *Sohar* and Sumatra was actually a gap of 40 miles, and those 40 miles became a chasm. Once again the wind died away, and *Sohar* was becalmed. It was as if nature wished to remind us how utterly dependent we were on her.

For another three days *Sohar* drifted, helpless without a wind, turning in the current, and with the very sight of land to tantalize us. We caught fish, we rationed the water, we waited patiently. We even solved the problem of fuel for cooking – the last of the charcoal had long since been burned – because here in the mouth of the Malacca Strait floated waterlogged lumps of timber, the branches and roots of trees washed down from the great forests of Sumatra. Our best swimmers went out for the flotsam, attached light ropes, and we hauled the timber on board. The wood was dried in the sun, and soon we were cooking our meals on it. With rain water, fresh fish and flotsam we had finally become self-sufficient on the ocean. So when *Sohar* came into Sabang harbour, with the help of a friendly cruising yacht, the *Regina Johane*, though we had been fifty-seven days at sea we arrived with full water tanks, ample driftwood for cooking fuel, and two months' worth of salted shark meat on board. To remind us pleasantly of the calendar, *Regina Johane* sent aboard a delicious gift of home-made cake and chocolate eggs. It was Easter Monday.

*   *   *

When one has crossed the sea ... there are some islands inhabited by some people called Langa, who speak no language at all, do not have clothes, and have sparse beards. Women are not seen among them. They exchange amber for pieces of iron. They go before the merchants, outside the island in boats bringing coconuts. Their palm wine is white. When one drinks it (fresh), it is as sweet as honey. If one leaves it a day, it becomes an intoxicating drink. If one leaves it several days, it turns bitter. The natives trade it for iron. They make the exchanges by hand signs. They are very clever swimmers. They succeed in stealing iron from the merchants without giving anything in exchange. . . .

This was how the tenth-century Arab geographer Ibn Al Fakih described the islands where the Arab ships stopped to pick up supplies after crossing the Indian Ocean. The islands guard the approaches to the Malacca Strait, from the Nicobar Islands in the north to the islands of Pulau Weh and Pulau Breeueh just off the Sumatra coast in the south. They are ideal places to take on fresh food and to replenish water supplies after the long passage from Sri Lanka, and in the tenth century the islands would have been inhabited by aboriginal tribes living along the shores or in the dense virgin forest. The Arabs called one of the islands the Golden Island, which has been identified as the island of Pulau Weh, in whose harbour of Sabang *Sohar* had arrived.

We dropped anchor in a magnificent bay, surrounded by the steep sides of hills covered in dark green coconut groves and large areas of forest. In one corner of the bay stood the town of Sabang itself, a workaday place with a utilitarian air and the inevitable collection of warehouses behind the jetty. But the setting was superb. The main buildings quickly gave way to a fringe of small one-storey houses which marked the line of the road that skirted the bay. These houses looked out across the water, and the hillside was so steep that on the downhill side the houses were perched on stilts. Right alongside *Sohar*'s anchorage was a fishing hamlet, a huddle of small houses where a stream ran out into the bay, and the dugouts and small boats of the fishermen were pulled up on the sandy beach. The people of the village had a totally different appearance from any we had yet seen on the voyage. Their faces were Malay, with high cheekbones, straight black hair, brown eyes, and a handsome brown skin. In short they were Asiatics, and we felt abruptly that we had arrived in the Orient.

The population of Sabang was overwhelmingly Moslem. The Golden Island is part of Aceh province, the most northerly part of Indonesia, and Islam has been embraced fervently by the Achinese. The arrival of an Arab ship, bearing real Arab sailors in turbans and *dishdashas*, caused a sensation. When *Sohar* berthed alongside the wharf to take on water the jetty was crowded with islanders gazing at the Omani sailors. Everywhere the Omanis went in the town they were welcomed into homes, and treated with fascinated hospitality. The mayor of Sabang invited the entire crew to attend the wedding ceremony of his daughter, and we were given a demonstration of traditional Achinese dancing. The dancers were children – the girls delicate in long, narrow skirts and tight bodices with wide sashes, and the boys leaping around in baggy pantaloons and short waistcoats, and waving daggers. It was a war dance, the mayor explained as he watched the boys hacking briskly at the air with their knives; and I could not help remembering that the Achinese had earned the reputation of being the most ferocious pirates in South-east Asia.

In their times the medieval Arab sailors had regarded Sumatra with a mixture of awe and dread. Their awe was for the fertility of this immense island and the prosperity of its most important ruler, whom they called the Miharaj, the great Maharajah. His kingdom lay on the eastern side of the island, bordering the Malacca Strait, and was a Hindu one. The Arabs wrote that its settlement was so dense that when the first village cock crowed at dawn, his call woke the cocks in the adjacent village who answered, and the sound would travel from village to village for the distance of a hundred parasangs. The Maharajah himself lived in a magnificent palace which had a pool fed by the tides. As a mark of his wealth, the Maharajah cast a solid gold brick into this pool each morning; and on his death the gold would be recovered and distributed among the royal family to honour the length of his reign. The author of the adventures of Sindbad the Sailor applied the title of 'Miharaj' to any ruler of a distant kingdom who was extremely rich and powerful.

But the sea road to the realm of the great Miharaj was fraught with dangers. If sailing there from the Bay of Bengal, the Arab navigators were fearful of being becalmed off the Andaman Islands. The natives of the Andamans, they wrote, were an ugly race of frizzy-haired cannibals; they caught sailors, and cut them up alive and ate them. Then, too, there were cannibals on the coast of Sumatra, who seem to have found their way into the adventures of Sindbad the Sailor. On his fourth voyage Sindbad and his companions are wrecked on a strange island. The natives, says the story, led the castaways to their village, where they placed food flavoured with herbs before the exhausted men. The sailors ate the food ravenously, but Sindbad himself was suspicious, and despite his hunger he did not eat. He saw how, as his companions ate, they lost their senses and began to roll their eyes and sway like men in a stupor. More and more food was thrust upon them, and they ate gluttonously. In the days that followed, the natives continued to place enormous meals before the sailors, and the unsuspecting visitors became plump and fat. But Sindbad continued to refuse to eat the native food because he had noticed that it contained some sort of drug. While exploring the village one day he came upon the chief and his tribesmen sitting down to feast on a human carcass, and realized that the natives were fattening up his companions for a cannibal ceremony. Too late to save them in their drugged condition, Sindbad fled from the village, and as he ran he passed his companions kneeling on all fours in the fields and cropping grass like fat cattle, watched over by herdsmen.

The possible identification of Sindbad's cannibals with the man-eating tribes of Sumatra lies in the fact that Sindbad's cannibals were said to use a drug in the food they offered their victims. In northern Sumatra the narcotic plant hashish is used as a flavouring in cooking, which may be how the idea of the stupefied cannibal victims passed into Arab folklore. There it mingled with reports of the man-eating tribes of Sumatra, either the Batak peoples of the north or perhaps the fierce warrior tribes of the islands lying along the west coast. These islands lay directly on the route of the Arab ships heading for the port of Fansur, later known as Baroes. Here the Arabs purchased the highest-quality camphor, for which the region was famous. The Chinese would pay huge prices for Fansur camphor when the Arabs brought it to Canton, and to obtain this precious cargo was worth the risk of falling into the hands of the cannibals.

Nias Island was particularly dreaded; its existence was first reported in the ninth century by an Arab writer. When one of the islanders wanted to marry, wrote the merchant Sulayman in 851, '. . . he cannot find a wife unless he has in his hands the skull of one of their enemies. If he has killed two of their enemies, he can marry two wives. If he has killed fifty of them, he can marry fifty wives, according to the number of skulls. The origin of this custom comes from the fact that the inhabitants of this island are surrounded by enemies. He who shows himself the boldest in battle is the most esteemed of all.'

Today Nias still retains strong traces of the extraordinary warrior culture which made such a marked impression upon the early Arab sailors. The origins of the Nias islanders are clouded in mystery, but it seems that they may be related to the hill tribes of Burma and the Naga people of north-east India. How they came to settle in the remote, jungle-covered island of Nias is unknown, because today the people of Nias are not seamen and scarcely use boats at all, but are farmers and gardeners. Their villages, however, are built for war. Each is situated on a hilltop or on the crest of an easily defended ridge. Often the top of the hill has been painstakingly levelled to provide a flat surface on which to build.

The main feature of each village is the broad central street, a wide avenue paved with large flat stones. On each side stand the houses of the Nias islanders, remarkable dwellings elevated on massive treetrunks driven into the ground as pilings, and each with a curved wooden veranda which has been compared in shape to the stern of a Spanish galleon. It is said that these houses were built by slave labour, and certainly it must have required immense effort to raise the intricate geometry of beams and treetrunks which criss-cross the interiors of the houses to support the steeply pitched roofs which, in the houses of the chieftains, rise 45 feet above the ground. The houses lack chimneys, so the interior beams are smoke-blackened with age, and when the cooking fires are lit the dramatic roof peaks seem to exude a thin breath of grey smoke. Outside the houses stand massive blocks of dark grey stone. They serve as seats, as benches, as tables, as podiums for speakers during village meetings. Many of the stones are carved with patterns, while others are incised with the forms of mythical animals which are said to be the protecting spirits which guard the village.

The houses are linked together on each side of the street, so that in the event of enemy attack the defenders can move between them without being exposed to spears and arrows. The hilltop locations of the villages are almost impossible to storm, even though this means that they are extremely inconvenient for the inhabitants. The women have to walk down hundreds upon hundreds of steps cut into the hillside to reach the wells, and then climb back up carrying bamboo tubes filled with water. The same laborious journey is made morning and evening by the menfolk going off to work in their fields and gardens in the lowland. The men carry enormous iron cutlasses which once served equally to clear the forest and to defend themselves, and if one encounters a hunting party setting off after wild boar, the natives make a ferocious sight, armed with 7-foot-long pig-sticking spears, each weapon with its efficient-looking iron spear head honed to razor-edge sharpness. The men courageously fight the wild boar on foot, and wear necklaces of boars' tusks as tokens of their prowess. Also they still demonstrate a war dance which must have been designed to frighten off attackers. They dress up in masks and outlandish costumes padded out with coconut fibre and decorated with clusters of boar tusks, and perform intricate stamping manoeuvres, grimacing and crashing their spears on war shields. Raid, counter-raid and the hunting of heads were the marks of manhood. In the main street of every Nias village stands the training ground for the young warriors. A section of stone wall some 10 feet high represents the defensive perimeter of an enemy village. One by one the young men race down the street, kick off from a small stone placed to give them maximum trajectory, and hurl themselves spectacularly over the wall, to land feet first with their daggers at the ready.

Sumatra also provided a good explanation for another of Sindbad's adventures, the Adventure of the Old Man of the Sea. According to *The Thousand and One Nights*, Sindbad found himself in a land where there was a pleasant forest, rich with fruit trees and flowers. There he came upon an old man sitting by the side of a stream. The old man did not speak, but with gestures indicated that he wanted to be carried across the stream. To oblige him, Sindbad put the old man on his shoulders, and waded across to the opposite bank. But when he stooped down to allow the old man to dismount his passenger refused, and suddenly tightened his legs around Sindbad's neck until Sindbad nearly fainted. Looking down at his rider's legs, Sindbad was appalled to see that they were the legs of a brute, covered in black rough skin. The unnatural creature now beat upon Sindbad's head and back as if he were a beast of burden, and forced him to walk through the forest, carrying his rider who reached up to pluck and eat the wild fruit. Whenever Sindbad tried to rest or escape his tormentor, the creature kicked and choked him into obedience. Finally, after days of this misery, Sindbad placed some wild fruit in a gourd, allowed it to ferment, and drank the wine to relieve his discomfort. Seeing him enjoy the drink, his rider snatched away the liquor and drank it himself. Cunningly, Sindbad gave the creature more and more alcohol until it became intoxicated, reeled and swayed, and relaxed the grip of its legs

The Old Man of the Sea rides on Sindbad's shoulders
(from *The Arabian Nights' Entertainments*, trans. Edward William Lane, 1877)

upon his neck. Then Sindbad took his chance to hurl the befuddled creature to the ground. And as it lay there helpless, he picked up a rock and dashed out the brains of the Old Man of the Sea.

The Old Man of the Sea could have been an early Arab view of the orang-utan of Sumatra, whose habits fit the description of the Old Man of the Sea – the appearance of a wizened old man, the black rough skin of its legs, and the diet of fruit gathered from trees in the forest. The Arab sailors reported all manner of wondrous animals in Sumatra – multi-coloured parrots which spoke the tongues of men, the Sumatran rhinoceros, and perhaps the tapir. The orang-utan would have seemed to be a special race of silent men, no more exotic than several of the wild tribes. And indeed the Sumatran natives would have supported this misconception. In the remote forest villages of Sumatra the orangutan is still considered to be a form of human, dangerous and to be avoided at all costs – quite different from the timid ape known to modern science.

From *The Arabian Nights' Entertainments,*
trans. Edward William Lane, 1877

Malacca Strait

Sohar sailed from Sabang with a brand-new centre section for her mainspar. The crew had searched the forests around the bay for a suitable tree, felled it, dragged it down to the water's edge, and floated it across to the beach. There the bark was stripped away, and the timber was trimmed to shape. Now the spar was as good as new, as we set out into the Malacca Strait which the Arabs had called the Sea of Selahit. It was the fifth of the Seven Seas on the Arab sea route to China, and as they sailed down it the Arabs passed the kingdom of the great Miharaj on their right-hand side, and the Port of Kala, possibly modern Kedah, on the left. They would trade to Kala for tin, precious wood and iron before carrying their cargoes towards the China Sea. Now, on the same route, I decided it was wiser to keep *Sohar* close to the Sumatra shore. In the Malacca Strait the winds are notoriously fickle; they can blow from all directions of the compass, but prevail from the south in the summer months and so would give *Sohar* a headwind. Obedient to the wind the current also runs foul, northward through the straits. The best way to negotiate the Strait, it seemed to me, was to use the combination of the tides and the land and sea breezes to work the ship southwards.

So *Sohar* embarked on a fascinating piece of sailing, quite unlike the long blue water passage we had made from Sri Lanka to Sumatra on the deep ocean. Now we were hugging the land, almost a part of the lush tropical island shore. We made a modest, steady progress, 30 or 50 miles a day according to the conditions. Often we lay becalmed, or met an adverse wind and current. Then we would let go the kedge anchor in perhaps 60 fathoms of water, and ride to it until the tide changed or the wind swung in our favour. We cleared Sabang on 7 May, after a last-minute delay when we had to plug several leaks in *Sohar*'s hull. The ship had now been four months afloat without any attention to her underwater body, and inevitably the long haul across the Indian Ocean with the constant flexing of the planks in the sea had opened slight cracks between the planks. It was nothing to worry about, but it was a nuisance to have to pump a foot or so of water from the bilges every three or four hours. The main problem seemed to be a crack between the keel and the first plank, the garboard strake. So my spare bed roll was ripped up, and the cotton stuffing was mixed with mutton fat to make a wadding which the divers poked into the cracks to seal the leak. The inflow of water stopped very quickly, and my only worry was that *Sohar*'s hitchhiking friends, the hungry crabs, should acquire a taste for mutton fat and prise out the wadding for their food.

By 14 May we had worked our way along the north coast of Sumatra, and had turned into the Strait, still hugging the shore. The dramatic line of hills which had marched parallel with us now fell away to swampy lowlands, and at night we could see the flames of the flares burning on the Sumatra gasfields. Small open fishing boats with outboard engines scuttled out from the coastal villages and set their nets in our path. The fishermen would throw a weighted clump of palm fronds into the water, wait for the curious fish to assemble around them, and then circle the fish with a light net to scoop them up. Often these little boats turned aside and came to stare up curiously at the odd spectacle of an Arab sailing ship making her way slowly through these waters. We took the chance to beckon the fishermen closer, and for a small sum bought thirty or forty fish for our supper.

The water in the Strait was a rich, thick, warm soup, coloured with silt brought down from the rivers draining the interior of Sumatra. Logs, uprooted palm trees and all manner of flotsam turned and bobbed in the tide. Frequently we saw groups of hunting dolphins. A grey humpback whale surfaced right alongside us one day to take a closer look at the silent ship before submerging again in a great swirl of opaque water. And an odd-looking sickle fin, very thin and curved, which no one could identify, tacked and sliced around the ship for a couple of hours. Andrew logged a number of sea snake sightings, and Dick, who was still taking his daily count of the number of new barnacles that appeared on the trailing safety line, announced that between 100 and 150 new larvae fastened themselves to the rope daily, which compared with perhaps ten or twenty larvae each day in the Indian Ocean, and was a good example of why the warm, rich waters of the Malacca Strait are considered to be the original breeding ground for many of the marine species found in the Pacific and Indian Oceans.

One afternoon, Richard, our photographer, appeared on deck with a kite, which he proposed to use to lift his camera above the ship for aerial pictures of *Sohar*. As he began to assemble the kite, virtually the entire crew of *Sohar* tiptoed quietly up and arranged themselves expectantly on the opposite gunnel in a spectators' gallery, and waited for the fun to begin. Unconscious of his watchers, Richard finally got his kite assembled, and climbed into the starboard lavatory which he had selected for his launch pad. The mizzen sheet promptly gave a warning tremor, and flicked Richard's straw sun hat off his head. Richard clutched wildly for the hat, but it was gone. The watchers gave a contented chuckle.

Next Richard tied to the kite an enormous reel of string which must have contained half a mile of thin, tough nylon line. He attached the string to the kite in a suitably confused granny knot that brought grins to the faces of the silent spectators. Then he stood up, swung the kite over the edge of the ship, gave the string a jerk, and the kite began to fly up handsomely. But Richard had miscalculated the strength of the wind, which was much stronger than he had imagined. The kite began to soar away at speed, pulling the line briskly through his fingers, so that it began to burn his skin. He let out a yelp of pain, and began a wild rumbalike dance in the lavatory, shifting the string from hand to hand, trying to stop it running out, but with no success. His loincloth slipped away and nearly fell off entirely. The watching crew rocked with mirth. The enormous reel of string now fell over onto its side and ran amok, bumping round the poop deck, its line stripping off crazily. Like a spindly marionette, Richard's dance went on. Finally the string ran out, and to everyone's satisfaction Richard discovered he had forgotten to tie the end of the string to the reel. The free end of the string flicked clear, slid out through Richard's fingers, and the bright yellow kite, now no more than a speck in the sky high above *Sohar*, sailed gaily off towards Sumatra while Richard gazed up in dismay.

But Richard was not defeated: he had a second kite. He went below to get it out, and this time reappeared with a pair of special leather kite-flying gloves to protect his hands. Naturally he had brought a stock of several pairs of these gloves, but had omitted to wear any of them on the last attempt. Now wearing gloves, so that he looked like the White Rabbit in *Alice in Wonderland*, he relaunched his kite and this time succeeded. Up it flew, stable and firm, and hovered over the ship. With a look of profound satisfaction Richard went to attach his camera to the kite string. Preparing the camera was a complicated business. First he wrapped it in a plastic bag, then he tucked the bag into a crazy looking balsa wood cradle. Finally he tied a balloon to the cradle to act as a lifejacket if the whole contraption fell into the water. Arranging all this paraphernalia took half an hour, and by the time the camera was ready to go aloft, it was also time to wear ship.

'Richard, I think you'd better bring the kite down,' I said. 'We're going to have to wear ship, and the mizzen spar will foul the kite strings. You can put the kite up again later for your pictures.' Richard went off to attend to his kite, and I thought no more about it.

We began to wear ship. Halfway through the manoeuvre I glanced across to where the kite had been flying. To my astonishment I saw that instead of pulling in his kite, Richard had merely hauled it in close to the ship, and left it flying about 20 feet in our lee where now it was certain to be entangled in the sail. Richard realized his error at the same instant. With a strangled cry he ran to the kite string and tried to untie it from the gunnel before the sail swung across. Of course he had fastened the string with a knot that stubbornly refused to come undone. He plucked off his gloves and threw them to the deck. Still the knot stayed jammed. Now the sail was beginning to swing across the ship. To make his task easier, Richard decided to cut away the reel of string. He fumbled for the penknife which hung on his belt, and with deadly certainty slashed through the kite string. Unerringly he cut it, not between the reel and the knot on the gunnel, but between the knot and the kite itself. The freed kite's string flicked lazily away down the deck, as the second kite escaped to freedom.

Sohar was running directly downwind, so the string was dragged along the entire length of the deck, just a trifle faster than Richard could move. He stumbled down the deck behind it, making futile snatches. The string danced tantalizingly away, just out of reach. Richard reached the bows, tripped and pounced at the same instant. His fingers just failed to catch the string, and the end vanished overboard. Then to everyone's amazement Richard climbed unsteadily up on the gunnel, cast a despairing look around, and – all arms and legs – hurled himself overboard after the kite in a shattering belly flop.

'Richard, come back!' I bellowed. 'Throw him a rope. Get him back aboard! Quick!'

The ship was gliding through the water. Already it was moving past Richard who was thrashing away clumsily, and was level with the midships. The end of a rope was thrown down to him. He grabbed for it, and was hauled dripping wet on deck. He stood there dejectedly, peering forward for his missing kite.

'There it is!' called someone, pointing at a waterlogged yellow diamond floating in *Sohar*'s path.

'Andrew. You are our best swimmer. Off you go. But tie a line to it. Don't try to swim back with the kite. You'll not be able to.'

Andrew dived overboard, a light line trailing behind him. A few moments later we had retrieved Richard's toy. He accepted it happily, and next day, to our relief, destroyed it utterly when it nose-dived into the sea as *Sohar* was doing 7 knots, and the kite crumpled into pieces.

Shaving the Sumatran coast to catch every breath of wind brought exciting moments. Far away to our right we could see the clouds boiling up over the distant mountains of the plateau. The air had a heavy tropical warmth and a slight edge of menace. In the mornings we were frequently becalmed, with the tide pulling against us as the ship lay to a light anchor. Then as the afternoon wore on the unstable air mass over Sumatra heated up, and the clouds began to tower upward. The western horizon was daubed with the threatening underbellies of cloud. Black shafts of tropical cloudbursts mauled the mountain slopes, and we could hear peals of thunder rolling out across the swamps. As the afternoon faded the thunder grew heavier and more frequent. Flashes of lightning began to play over the mountains, sometimes flickering for several seconds behind them so that the crests were sharply defined in hard silhouette. Then, just before dusk, the wind and the rain reached us. Up would come the anchor, as the entire crew laid hold and chanted and stamped back along the streaming deck, their wet clothes plastered to their bodies, and there was a purposeful bustle as the sails were spread and adjusted, and the ship began to glide through the water.

Then the black night squall would sweep across us, and everything was reduced to an inky darkness as the tropical rain hissed down. *Sohar* surged forward, and the lookout would crouch under a tarpaulin by the bowsprit, squinting forward into the blackness trying to pick out the shapes of fishing boats or the line of foam that marked the crest of a mudbank. At the very core of the thunderstorm we would sail through the most incredible visual displays, as the constant roll and flash of lightning bounced and reverberated inside the bodies of the clouds. Jagged lines struck down on the sea beside us and – most impressive of all – occasionally burst over our heads like an artillery barrage. Sometimes the discharges were so close that they produced a sharp, flat crack like a giant whip, the lightning strike appeared to burst apart like shrapnel, and bright morsels of static went whizzing over the ship with tremendous speed so that one literally ducked as if a rocket was being fired across the deck.

The lookout's job was vital. *Sohar* was committed on her course, rushing down the coast with the tide under her and the night wind in her sails. The swampy lowland coast sloped very gently out to sea, and the silt from the rivers was deposited in a maze of mud banks and sand bars over which the tide sucked and swelled in currents and eddies. Some of the mud banks were uncharted because they shifted their position so rapidly. There was little time to manoeuvre around any obstacles in her course, and every second of warning was vital. There were shoals, fishing boats, and lines of nets set in the tide run, but most dangerous of all were the fishing houses which the Sumatrans built on the offshore mud banks. They were solid structures, raised on heavy pilings well above the surface of the sea, and with a trap door through which large scoop nets could be dipped into the water, or the fishermen could set a series of fishing lines. To protect the occupants from the tropical weather, a shed was usually built on top of the platform; this shed could be the size of a small house, so that the whole structure was a permanent feature. Luckily the fishermen lit very bright lights to attract the fish, and these lights warned us of their presence. But it was not always possible to distinguish between a string of fishing boat lights, and a line of lights marking a mud bank with fishing huts perched on it.

Then the vigilance of the lookout and the quick reactions of the deck watch were all-important. *Sohar* would go tearing down on the line of lights. I would be called by the watch leader, and together we would peer at the fast-approaching line of lights. Should we go around them or between them? How fast was the tide? What was the depth of water? How much leeway was the ship making? A whole stream of questions raced through my mind, and then with the decision came the need for fast, quick action by the sail handlers. 'Wear ship!' There was the sound of running feet, the swift casting off of sheets, the call of '*Lessim! Lessim!* Ease away! Ease away!', the hauling in of the mainyard. Saleh or Abdullah would scamper around the gunnel carrying the mainsheet to its new position. There was the tearaway squeal of the mainyard block running out, as the sail swung round to its new position, and cries of '*Yah Allah! Yah Allah!*' as the mainsail was sheeted home. A final yell of '*Mawal!* Make fast!', and *Sohar* would swing away on her new course.

It was a remarkable contrast to our first fumbling attempts after leaving Muscat with a novice crew. Now we could wear ship in under ten minutes, in a strong breeze, and in the pitch dark. Even so, my heart was often racing. One slip, and *Sohar* would have gone smashing into a fishing house in a tangle of spars and wreckage. It only needed one rope to jam, or the sail to catch round the mast, and the ship would be out of control. It never happened, but we came alarmingly close to an occasional fishing hut, and I often wondered what the Sumatran fishermen must have thought when they saw *Sohar*'s ghostly outline swirl by. Out of the darkness would have come the outlandish shape of an Arab *boom*, its huge triangular sails like bats' wings against the night sky, a ship absolutely silent except for the creak of her ropes and the sound of her hull pushing through the water. Pointing straight at the fishermen with her lance of a bowsprit, the strange apparition must have seemed set for a terrific impact, until with a squeal of blocks her sails began to rise and swing across. The shape of the vessel would have altered as she changed course to avoid collision and came swooping past. And as abruptly as she had come, she would vanish into the gloom of the night. It was unlikely that any Arab ship had been in those waters in living memory, so the effect on the Sumatran fishermen must have been awe-inspiring.

The trickiest part of the Malacca Strait was the channel of the South Sands, the choke point of the entire Strait, where the shallows from both Malayan and Sumatran sides reach out to leave only a narrow channel between them. Through this channel has to pass all the shipping moving up and down the Strait, and here too *Sohar* was obliged to abandon the Sumatran shore and make for the Malayan coast, or risk being enmeshed in a maze of shallows and mud banks on the Sumatran side. It was a manoeuvre which the early Arab navigators had treated with respect, and Ahmed Ibn Majid, the master navigator of Sur, had warned of the dangers of the South Sands passage in the fifteenth century. So it was ironic that the South Sands was the one point in the whole voyage to China when *Sohar* came closest to running aground.

It happened at night. We were attempting to slant across the gut of the narrows, keeping a sharp lookout to avoid the heavy shipping, when the fickle wind swung round.

'Captain! Captain! Course south-west!' called Khamees Police who was the watch leader and had the helm at the time.

The course was quite wrong, I thought to myself. It would bring us over the Sands.

'Take soundings.' The lead went down.

Its line ran out a short distance, and the helmsman gave a sharp cry. 'Four fathoms!'

My God! We were right on the edge of the Sands. The bank sloped up very steeply from the edge of the channel. If *Sohar* was caught there in a rising gale, we would be battered to bits. It was all happening so quickly. There was not even time to wear ship. The wind was still changing direction.

'Let go both anchors,' I yelled.

The moments seemed to drag by. A man ran forward to cut the anchor lashings. The ship ploughed forward inexorably. The helm was having no effect. The wind was right astern now, pushing *Sohar* to the very edge of the sand. Splash! The kedge anchor went down, and it seemed that there was only a couple of seconds when the chain was falling vertically, before the anchor hit bottom and the speed of the chain slackened. The anchor cable took up an acute angle, leading back under *Sohar*'s hull as the ship was blown forward by the wind. 'Let go the main anchor!' Men struggled to clear it. Splash! Three and a half hundredweight of our best bower anchor went down. Again, only a momentary rumble of chain. 'Ease out both cables gently together. Dick! Take soundings with the lead.'

'Four fathoms. Four fathoms. Three and a half . . . .'

'Make fast both cables.' We were right on the edge of the sand bank now. 'Dick, leave the lead just bumping on the bottom. We'll see how the tide runs.'

By now everyone was on deck and we waited anxiously. The wind was indeed picking up strength. The sound of the sea had changed around us: instead of the deeper rumble of real waves we heard the high-pitched hiss of small, light waves running over the shallows. If the wind grew stronger, we would be among breakers. After twenty minutes I checked the lead line. I pulled in nearly half a fathom of slack before I felt the weight of the lead, and could bounce it on the bottom. It told me that *Sohar* had lost 3 feet of water under her keel. Either the tide was running out, or the anchors were dragging, and *Sohar* was being wind-driven down on to the sands. Certainly the ship lay at a very unhappy angle. Her head was downwind, and her two anchors streamed out behind her stern – she felt all wrong. The situation called for emergency measures. Normally one does not manhandle heavy anchors in small dinghies at night time. There is a risk of capsize, of a man being dragged down and drowned when his foot or hand is trapped in chain flicking out at speed from a dinghy, and it is difficult to render assistance in the dark. But I felt that we had no choice. We had to get *Sohar* off the sands as soon as possible and by brute strength if necessary.

'Peter, I want you to take the rubber boat with the best crew, and take soundings around the ship.' Peter Dobbs, Tim Readman and Peter Hunnam vanished into the darkness in the rubber boat. As they took soundings with the spare lead and flashed a torch back at the ship, Nick Hollis took compass bearings on them from *Sohar*. Directly astern of us, along the path by which we had entered the Sands, was the only place where they found deep water and safety. We would have to lay out an anchor in that direction. The boat crew came back, and we began the awkward, dangerous task of preparing the kedge. We eased out one cable, hauled in on the other, and recovered the big grapnel anchor. The grapnel was carefully lowered down into the rubber boat, and perched on a board laid across the little dinghy. The rubber boat struggled back out into the darkness, this time following directions called out to it from the ship. It reached the end of the scope of the anchor cable. Big Peter seized the end of the board, and tipped it up like a slide so that the anchor tumbled into the water. Now the entire crew ranged down the length of *Sohar*'s deck. Only Jumah was absent, tending the second anchor cable. '*Minataw, minataw* – who are you? who are you?' sang the crew, taking up the hauling chant and beginning to heave back on the rope to the kedge anchor. The rope came in quickly at first, then the anchor took hold, the strain came on, and the crew was heaving and grunting in unison to pull the reluctant ship out of trouble. Jumah eased out on his rope inch by inch. Gradually the crew dragged *Sohar* out of danger by their muscle power. Twice more we laid out an anchor, hauled in, and *Sohar* was floating clear. I checked the lead line. The bottom of the channel fell so steeply that in a distance of only 65 yards we were now anchored in 20 fathoms of water. *Sohar* was safe for the rest of the night.

In Ibn Majid's day the Arabs had established a trade network throughout the vast archipelago of South-east Asia: Omani and other Arab ships traded down both sides of Sumatra, visited Java, and penetrated as far as Borneo and the Celebes. There was a constant coming and going of Arab vessels, which used the monsoon winds to reach the Indonesian islands and then worked around the archipelago using the local weather patterns. Interestingly, Singapore was already on Ibn Majid's list of ports visited for trade. So it was a port for Arab merchant shipping long before Sir Stamford Raffles encouraged its development. In Ibn Majid's time Malacca was the most important port in all South-east Asia, and *Sohar*'s brief visit showed how very convenient the site and layout of the city must have been in its heyday.

Malacca lies very handily in the narrows of the Strait. Already the shallows on the Sumatran side had forced us to cross to the Malaysian shores; there, coasting comfortably down the attractive green coastline, the town of Malacca with its prominent hill was very evident. A small island gives a comfortable lee if one does not wish to enter the river mouth; and there are no rocks or shoals to deter the newcomer. *Sohar* sailed quietly along the 4-fathom line until she was convenient to the port, and there dropped anchor. The two rubber dinghies were inflated and launched, and headed for shore. We were expected. Polite, hospitable harbour officials cleared our documents, and I explained that we would only stay long enough to revictual the ship. Shopping could not have been easier. The dinghies proceeded up the narrow river, past a row of Indonesian *prahus* unloading sacks of charcoal, under the bridge, and between the attractive red-tiled Chinese houses which crowded both banks and gave the place the air of a tropical Venice.

Malacca's market was built right on the river bank, where fishing boats could bring their catch direct to the stalls, and canal craft from the interior could unload vegetables and fruit. *Sohar*'s dinghies joined the swarm of boats clustering around the market steps. There were smiles and waves; the boat owners took our mooring lines and made them fast, and *Sohar*'s people stepped ashore as if they had been marketing in Malacca all their lives. In just half an hour Tim Readman, the purser, reappeared behind a rickshaw piled high with pineapples, star fruit, dried mushrooms and vegetables, with two live chickens perched on top. The local bank manager kindly invited six of the crew to join him and his family for a Chinese lunch; he was astounded when the *Sohar* men, who were admittedly the largest of the crew members, demolished a banquet calculated for twenty. The bank manager was even more impressed when three of his voracious guests admitted over the wreckage of the meal that it was their second lunch of the day.

Then it was back to the ship to hoist anchor and take *Sohar* down the Strait the following afternoon. Everyone was in an excellent mood, with the exception of the two chickens who were looking distinctly gloomy on the foredeck, perhaps in anticipation of Ibrahim's cooking the pair of them. Also, our weather luck had finally changed: at long last *Sohar* was finding a favourable wind just where, by rights, we should have been having difficulties. The wind was with us, blowing fresh off the land and pushing us on our way. Every sign told us that the Strait was closing in around us – the tide was running faster and stronger in the narrows, and the two-way stream of shipping was bunching up and growing more dense. I had calculated a generous three days' run from Malacca to Singapore, but *Sohar* covered the distance in less than half the time. At 1 a.m. on the second night we saw the massive glow of light illuminating the night sky, which was Singapore's huge blaze of city lights. The first hint of dawn saw us running, mainsail squared across the ship to take full advantage of the following breeze, down the main Singapore shipping channel. The only snag was that we were sailing against the traffic flow.

I tried anxiously to call up the Singapore pilot on the radio to warn him that big ship captains should not be startled to see an Arab ship under full sail rushing down towards them on the tide. I need not have worried. Singapore, too, was expecting *Sohar*. The biggest port in the world, with the most shipping movements each day, had already heard about the sailing ship from the Sultanate of Oman. A police launch came racing up, followed by a boat from the harbour authority. A trim Chinese Singaporean in gleaming white uniform skipped up our boarding ladder, clutching a walkie-talkie and large-scale harbour chart. 'I am your pilot,' he said, shaking me by the hand, 'but I don't know how I am expected to pilot this ship. It's a new experience to be aboard a sailing vessel. Just tell me what to do. And don't worry about the fact that you are going the wrong way down the channel. I think we can say that these regulations don't apply to your ship.'

So, with the senior pilot barking orders on his walkie-talkie to clear our path, *Sohar* sailed majestically through the great mass of shipping assembled at Singapore, past row upon row of moored merchant ships, under the bows of supertankers, past oil platforms and refrigerator ships. A battered freighter flying the yellow-starred red banner of the People's Republic of China gave us a series of greeting blasts on her siren. A great, square container ship made way, and we turned into the home anchorage. The pilot had a surprise for us.

'Anchor here only long enough to prepare your ship. The government of Singapore has organized a reception ceremony for you. And the harbour authority is giving you a special berth.' More police boats and harbour craft appeared, the inevitable television crews, and a tug which almost dwarfed us; together they escorted *Sohar* into her berth. On the quayside was a cheering crowd. A team of Chinese dancers whirled and stamped to the booming of an immense drum and the clash of cymbals. A pair of Chinese lions pranced on human legs, and as we tied *Sohar* to the quay a line of Malay girls stepped forward and sang a traditional welcome. It seemed only appropriate that we should reply. As *Sohar*'s fenders squeezed up against the quay wall, every member of *Sohar*'s crew climbed up on the gunnel where we responded to the greeting with a rousing chorus of our mainyard hauling song. From the grins of the crowd it was clear that our Singaporean hosts were delighted.

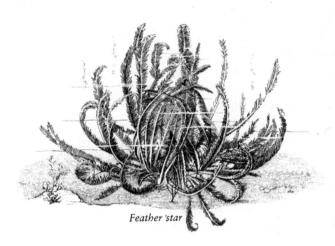

Feather 'star

—12—
South China Sea

There remained only two of the Seven Seas of the early Arab searoad to China, but by all accounts they were the worst. In these last two seas, wrote the Arab geographers, you met the great storms, the tempests which were beyond all power of description. Here the gales sent a ship to her doom, and the waves battered her to pieces. A ship might be saved by cutting down her mast and throwing overboard her cargo, but usually it was only the help of Allah which stood between the vessel and destruction. In these terrible waters black devils appeared out of the waves and walked the decks of the ship. And at the very height of the foulest storm a strange luminous light might be seen high in the rigging. If it took the form of a shining bird, then it was a sign that the ship would be saved.

The China Sea would be the worst, wouldn't it? the Omanis asked me. Wasn't it true that here one met *tufan*, the storm wind? I supposed that the Arab word *tufan* was the same as the Chinese word 'typhoon', and tried to reassure them. The whole theory behind the sailing programme so far had been to stay at the leading edge of each sailing season as we progressed. We had left Muscat as soon as the north-east monsoon had settled in our favour; we had sailed from Sri Lanka and endured the long delays of the doldrums in order to reach Sumatra with the very first winds of the south-west monsoon. We had pushed on down the Malaccan Straits with the land and sea breezes so as to arrive as early as possible in the South China Sea. By arriving so soon I hoped to reduce to a minimum the risk of running into a typhoon, but it was impossible to avoid the risk altogether. Typhoons can occur in any month of the year, but the main season begins in July, and the frequency increases to its maximum in September or October. *Sohar* had shown that she was a stout and well-found ship, and I thought there was every chance that she would ride out a typhoon if she was properly handled, but it was an experiment that I preferred not to try.

We sailed from Singapore on 11 June, bound direct for the China coast and determined to make a fast run. It had been a good visit to Singapore. We had seen the city, and had been treated most hospitably by the government and by private hosts, and in return we had entertained visitors on board, though they had been rather shocked by our damp, confined living conditions. There had been surprisingly little work to be done to the ship. Tom tried to get our radios working again – the corrosive bilge gas had played havoc with their internal parts, and both the small amateur radio sets were increasingly ineffective. Similarly the little generator was being kept alive only by careful nursing. Of the modern equipment, only the outboard engines for the rubber dinghies were in first-class order, carefully maintained by Peter Dobbs and Tim Readman.

By contrast, all our traditional equipment was in excellent condition. We had been rerigging and replacing ropes whenever needed, improving the carpentry, and restoring chafed gear. The rudder now hung solidly on its chains, and the Omanis had given the hull a glistening coat of oil. *Sohar* looked smart and fit for sea. Her only weakness that I could see was her canvas and her lower planking: after months of being alternately soaked and sun-dried, stowed and set, the sails were very worn. Their handmade canvas had served us well, but it had seen tremendous use. Also, the ship had now been at sea without any attention to the underwater parts of her hull for half a year, and understandably her seams were leaking. Twice a day we had to pump her bilges. We swam below her and stuffed in more mutton fat and cotton, but to do the job properly *Sohar* needed to be hauled out of the water and given a complete new coating of lime and mutton fat, smeared on by hand.

The first four days out of Singapore were magnificent. The sea was superb, bright blue with small white caps and scatterings of flying fish skimming ahead of the bows. The breeze blew warm and steady from the southern quadrant. The sky was flecked with puffs of cotton wool cloud, and *Sohar* reeled off mile after mile in a most satisfying manner. We were achieving 90 to 100 miles a day with scarcely a need to touch the sheets, the mainsail stayed set square, billowing out comfortably and spilling a cool breeze down on to the foredeck. The entire crew was relaxed, confident and tough. These ideal conditions, Jumah told me, were like those encountered on the run to Zanzibar from Oman on the Africa trade – day after day of fair weather and following winds, nothing to do but relax, never the need to wear ship all the way from Oman until one raised the African coast. Sailing to China, he added with a grin, was rather different. You could sail twenty times to Zanzibar, and never encounter such exciting conditions.

On the fourth night out of Singapore, Peter Hunnam's voice woke me. It was 3 o'clock in the morning, and I was asleep on deck in my usual spot near the tiller. 'Looks as if we'll have some rain,' he said.

'No rain, only wind,' came Khamees Navy's reply.

Half-asleep, I got up, rolled up my mattress and carried it below, put on oilskins, and came back on deck expecting the same sort of night squall which we had experienced in the Malacca Strait. I was wrong. The blacker patch in the night sky moved closer, and the wind blew harder. *Sohar* was wearing her small mainsail, and I was not unduly worried; she had weathered plenty of squalls before. The wind continued to increase. Now the sail was shuddering ominously. Out of the main strength of the wind came a sudden violent gust, full gale force. The rigging let out a great groan and there was an alarming cracking and popping sound from the wooden structure of the ship. The sea to windward was becoming increasingly confused. Out of the dark raced a line of short, steep rollers. As they swept under the hull, *Sohar* began to pitch and roll more heavily. The weight of the main spar exerted a pendulum effect and the ship heaved and laboured under the strain. Abruptly one wave surged under the ship and pitched her over on her side; the angle was enough to put *Sohar*'s lee deck under water, and the sea came bursting in through the scuppers. From down below came a rumbling crash and several thuds as loose boxes and barrels cascaded across the ship. Like disturbed ants, the entire crew came clambering up on deck, dressed in oilskins, clutching on to ropes and gunnels. On the weather side several men had been thrown out of their bunks.

The main spar was bending alarmingly every time the ship lurched and staggered. I had under-estimated the wind: we were caught with far too much sail up, and it was going to be very difficult to reduce sail safely.

'Brail up! Brail up!' I yelled. The crew scurried forward to the brailing lines which would pull the mainsail up to its spar. But even with five men hauling on each brailing line it was useless. The friction on the ropes, the weight of the wet canvas and the power of the wind made it impossible to hoist up the mainsail. The task was simply beyond our strength.

'Come on! Heave! Heave!' screamed Peter Hunnam. The crew flung themselves at the brailing lines with a frenzy that indicated that they realized that unless something was done, there was a danger that *Sohar* might capsize or break her mast. Now the storm line was right on top of us. The din of the wind and the slapping of the ropes created a pandemonium of sound, a raw fury. The slick figures of the crew were lit up again and again by flashes of lightning. Suddenly one of the brailing lines began to move.

'Heave! She's moving,' came a cry. But it was a delusion. With a thunderous crack the whole rear edge of the mainsail, 50 feet of double stitch canvas, was ripped asunder. The tear ran up the sail in an instant. A moment later the whole rear edge disintegrated into shreds, a lashing ruin of torn canvas. The useless brailing lines dragged only strips of cloth to the yard. The mainsail was a total wreck, 1600 square feet of canvas blown away in an instant; the last rags of material flew away downwind into the black night like departing spirits.

There was nothing to be done now but try to limit the damage. 'Mainspar down. Leave the brails. They are useless.' Someone untied the main halyard stoppers, and the great ropes were paid out. Bumping and thudding against the swinging mast, the yard came swaying ponderously down. Six months ago the feat of lowering the mainyard in half a gale would have been utterly unthinkable. Now, with experience, the job was still dangerous but well within our capabilities. There was no need for orders. Everyone knew exactly what was needed to bring the huge spar under control. Saleh and Jumah were lying spreadeagled on the foredeck, flat on the planks, looking upward and ready to pounce on the fore-end of the spar as it swooped over their heads, throw a restraining rope around it, and bring it under control. Terry was at the stern with another rope, ready to lasso the aft end.

'Slack away. *Lessim. Lessim.*' In the first light of dawn the spar and its shattered sail came down. Men rushed to secure the shredded remains, and to hoist them inboard in case we could salvage the remnants. Others swung themselves like gymnasts on to the spar itself, and with wet fingers began to unknot the lashings which held the sail in place.

By full light the ruined sail was free and clear. The wind was easing, and under jib and mizzen *Sohar* pushed more comfortably forward. I looked at the scene. On the deck lay the sodden mass of the old sail; pulled over it was the spare mainsail which we had already brought up on deck as a replacement. But that task would have to wait. Scattered along the sail like dead men lay the crew, sprawled bodies fast asleep from total exhaustion. They were oblivious to the rolling of the ship, the sodden canvas on which they lay, their soaking oilskins which they had not removed. They were completely worn out. Sailing a ship to China could not be called an easy life.

Lunch was a sorry affair of cold porridge and tea, as poor Ibrahim had been seasick. Then it was back to work, and much to be done. One gang cleaned up the mess below decks. Burst sacks of peas had shot their contents everywhere. There were piles of water-sodden tarpaulins, bananas rolled into mash, bruised and rotten pineapples, half-opened tin boxes spilled. Even the main food locker, a quarter of a ton of it, had been shifted a foot out of position by the lurching of the ship. All this had to be tidied up, while on deck the rest of the crew fastened a replacement mainsail to the yard.

By 2 o'clock in the afternoon the new mainsail was ready. Below decks was reasonably tidy, and the remaining loose items had been stowed or lashed down securely. *Sohar* was still ploughing forward solidly under a jib and mizzen sail alone.

'Hurry up and get the mainsail well secured,' I called to the deck crew. 'There's a lot more wind coming.'

The western sky was like nothing I had seen before. Advancing towards us, at sea level, was a dark black mass of shadow extending clear across the horizon. Above the shadow towered a vertical wall of grey cloud, as dark as smoke from a blazing building, and churning with upcurrents of air. The top of this ominous cloud wall was as clean and straight as if sliced off with a knife. Behind it rose another cloud wall, a lighter shade of grey, and behind this again two more cloud walls as if a giant had been stacking vertical grey plates of cloud. Beneath this strange cloud formation the sea had already turned a peculiar blue-black, ripped through by the white tops of waves lashed by the wind.

'Thank God we've got the mainsail down and secure,' I muttered to Tom. 'That night squall was a blessing in disguise. We are in better shape to take this. But I expect it's the jib that will smash now.'

They were prophetic words. As the cloud banks swept over us, the wind roared to gale force, and the little jib which had seemed such a puny handkerchief of a sail became a monster full of power. The wind filled it under terrific strain and the jib bellied out downwind.

'Look at the bowsprit!' exclaimed Peter Dobbs. 'It's bending. It can't stand the strain. It's going to break.'

You could actually hear the creaking noise, even above the gale, as the massive bowsprit was twisted to one side, and the fibres of the timber groaned under the stress. The bowsprit was bent sideways like a stiff fishing rod. Just then, a moment before it seemed inevitable that the bowsprit would snap, the jib sheet broke with a sharp report like a shotgun being fired. Instantly the jib streamed out downwind. There were five or six loud cracks as it flailed like a whiplash, and then the entire jib disintegrated. It was shredded in an instant. All that was left of the trailing section of the sail was a ribbon of canvas sewn to the bolt rope.

'Get the pieces aboard. Salvage what you can,' I yelled above the howl of the wind. The shattered remains of the jib flapped into the sea, and were fished out by the foredeck crew. Less than a third of the canvas remained.

'Put up the small jib,' I ordered. The tiny heavy-weather jib was brought on deck, and fastened to the main halyard. It was an absurd little scrap of canvas, more suited to a family cruising yacht than a full-sized sailing ship. 'Up she goes.' Eight men were needed to pull on the jib halyard in this gale. The remainder of the watch held down the jib on the foredeck until the strain came down on the halyard, then let go, and the jib shot out to leeward, filled, and hung there, rigid with the wind, and far below its correct position. The eight men on the halyard heaved away with all their strength. The rope refused to move, and a tiny bulging jib hung there, taunting them. Even as it hovered, I could see the ominous strains appearing in the cloth.

'OK. Bring her down.'

It was no use. We could not get the jib down fast enough. In the thirty seconds it took to haul down the jib, it ripped right across the base. It was the third sail damaged in the same day.

Now the wind was slicing off the tops of the waves, blowing them out in white spume. The waves themselves no longer had crests. They were ripped off as soon as they appeared, and the seas rolled down on us in a series of short, steep walls. There was rain too, being blown horizontally across the streaming deck so that it was impossible to look upwind since the rain lashed one too painfully across the eyes. The wind was now so strong that it was difficult to stand on the gunnel to survey the ship's condition; it was easier to crouch on deck, in the shelter of the bulwarks out of the reach of the wind blast. *Sohar* herself seemed happy enough, riding sideways to the gale, and only an occasional lurch put her scuppers under. I ordered the crew to don lifejackets, not so much for fear of capsize – I was confident that *Sohar* could ride out the gale – but in case anyone should be swept overboard by a loose rope or slipped and fell from the rolling ship.

Just then the mizzen sail exploded. It was a new sail, our best, neatly stitched, specially cut down to a small size, and made of first-quality canvas. But the gale was too much for it: with a noise like a thunder clap, the mizzen sail split. The retaining sheets snapped, and what had been a smart sail, iron-hard with wind two seconds before, was now just scraps of canvas, banging and slapping in torment. It was the fourth sail to be destroyed. A minute later Khamees Navy suddenly leaped up on the gunnel, clutched a shroud for support, and with the wind flattening his rain-soaked loincloth to his legs cupped one hand to his mouth and let out a high, wavering yell into the teeth of the gale. It was a prayer to Allah, ringing out high and eerily over the ship, a strange unreal sound in the bedlam of the gale. The rest of us, streaming wet in our oilskins and crouched down on deck below the line of the gunnel, looked at one another. Was Khamees praying to his God in praise of his works, or was he praying for an end to the lashing of the gale? We could not tell.

That evening the gale was gone, and we were left with a grey, lumpy sea. At last we were able to hoist our mainsail, replace the jib and mizzen, and set about repairing as much canvas as we could salvage. The rate of destruction was more than the ship could sustain: two sails were destroyed utterly, and two more would take several days' hard work to repair. But at least the crew weren't utterly daunted. They were quiet and self-confident, and there was still plenty of good humour. But I feared that eventually these conditions would knock the stuffing out of them too. Below decks they were having to put up with the constant strain of damp bedclothes, dripping beams, wet clothes and tumbled chaos. No wonder that a thousand years ago the Arabs had considered the passage of the South China Sea the worst experience of all on the trip to Canton. Yet the squalls which *Sohar* was suffering were nothing to the experience of riding out a typhoon.

Sohar now ran the gauntlet. The strange, black squalls which hit her were a local phenomenon known as arch squalls. They raked her again and again, twice on 16 June, three times on 17 June, four times on 18 June, twice on 19 June, and once on 20 June. We got to know the drill very well indeed. Each time the ominous stacked cloud banks appeared, we scurried to lower and make fast our precious mainsail, the last we had. We dreaded that it would be destroyed or that our elegant new mainspar, fresh cut in Sumatra, should snap. This sail was our ship's driving force, and we needed it badly if we were to reach China before the main typhoon season was on us. We were acutely conscious that every day we spent out in the South China Sea increased the risk of being embroiled with a typhoon, so we literally sewed our way northwards. In the lulls between the arch squalls, we mended our sails. Jib and mizzen, leach and foot, bolt ropes and panels, we stitched and stitched to keep the sails aloft. As each arch squall swept over us, we watched for the slightest tear in the jib and mizzen sails that kept us moving. Occasionally we lay ahull without a single scrap of sail, and let the gales and rain sweep over the stripped ship; and always, as soon as the squall passed, every member of the crew took up his position on deck and laboriously we hauled the great, creaking mainspar back aloft so that we could press on northward. We were moving along very well: 90 miles one day, 110 miles the next, 135 miles on the best day's run, with the safety line drawing a fine tail of spray through the water as we rushed along.

During the second arch squall on 19 June a curious phenomenon occurred, something which I had often wondered about but never experienced: a whirlwind passed directly over the ship. It was not a large whirlwind, merely the spinning vortex of air which can sometimes be seen out on the leading edge of a bad squall, a twisting column of spray which usually seems to avoid a ship. But this time the whirlwind came spinning right up to the vessel, boarded *Sohar*, and passed on over the lee rail. It was over in an instant, so there was no time to react or take precautions. At one moment the whirlwind could be seen quite distinctly, twisting and spinning crazily as it advanced about 50 metres ahead of the rain line. It hit the ship fair and square at about 30 m.p.h., passed clean across the poop deck, and went spinning away down wind. When the whirlwind was actually aboard there was a brief, extraordinary sensation. We were conscious of a terrific wind speed, impossible to calculate but lacking any true weight so that there was a startling, almost fresh feeling to the air which must have been revolving in a complete circle around the vortex at two or three revolutions a second. Our cheeks were stung smartly in quick succession, once on each side by the spray, as the vortex passed over and the wind direction changed through 180 degrees, and then the water spout was gone. But in that split second, the very instant that we had actually stood in the eye of the spiral, there had been an uncanny moment when all the noise amd roar of the gale had ceased. Instead, just for that moment, our ears had been filled with a strange, high-pitched whistle, so unlike the usual uproar of the wind that it almost sounded like silence.

Bunks were soggy with rain. Fingers were white and wrinkled with hour after hour of stitching wet canvas. *Sohar* was a wretchedly uncomfortable place to live during these days. Yet the morale of the crew seemed to soar higher and higher, partly because we knew that we were on the last leg of the voyage, and that *Sohar* was devouring the final miles, but partly because the discomfort and hard work was a challenge which brought out the best in the crew. Everyone was working splendidly. Each man turned out on deck without hesitation to tackle the grinding, muscle-aching chores of keeping the ship driving forward. The men helped one another unselfishly, and even found time to keep a weather eye on poor Ibrahim who was being tossed around unmercifully at his open hearth in a great rattle of pots and pans, and a cascade of rice and curry. Several times he managed to do his cooking only with a member of the crew hanging on to his waist like a human safety line to prevent him from sliding into the scuppers.

Richard, too, excelled himself by nearly dismasting the ship in a manoeuvre that baffled all of us. *Sohar* was running briskly downwind at the time, the mainsail set square, and Abdullah our crack helmsman at the tiller. All was well, and Richard had climbed into the stern lavatory. Long ago he had been warned never to touch any of the ropes on the ship, but when Abdullah tried to adjust the helm to keep *Sohar* running true, he found the tiller was immovable. He looked across and was aghast to see that Richard, for some reason he never explained, had taken the loose ends of the tiller lines into the lavatory with him, and tied them in a great knot to the inboard end of the safety line. The whole tangle was a hopeless muddle, and the tiller was effectively lashed solid. It was like driving a car with the steering locked, and there was a serious risk of being back-winded and snapping the mainspar, if not breaking the mast. Abdullah's roar of rapid-fire Arabic, almost the only time on the whole voyage he really let fly, brought a thunder of running feet as all the other Omanis came racing to untangle the mess, cast off sheets, head the ship out of danger, and generally save the situation.

Amid the pandemonium could be heard little cries from a semi-naked Richard, bobbing up from the lavatory in alarm, and ducking down again like a half-plucked chicken. 'What have I done wrong? Is the ship going to sink? Oh I am sorry. I really am.'

The Omanis forgave him. Once they had sorted out the situation, they faced him and with mock seriousness chanted, 'Oh Reechard,' and mournfully shook their heads. They knew they would never make a sailor of him.

The only compensation for the wretchedly damp and uncomfortable conditions below deck was that our fellow passengers liked it even less than we did, and we had long been waiting for them to regret taking the passage with us. These fellow passengers were a motley collection of crawling, scurrying, creeping, buzzing and food-stealing creatures which had stowed aboard *Sohar* at all her various ports of call. We could trace our progress by the newcomers to our company. There had been an initial batch of cockroaches which had come aboard in Muscat, probably in cartons of food, and brought with them their travelling friends, the chirping crickets. These had been reinforced by a fresh cockroach influx in Beypore, plus a swarm of fruit flies. The fruit flies, true to their reputation, bred ferociously, and for four or five days out of each port we would be plagued by cloud upon cloud of them, mindlessly flying into our nostrils or drowning themselves in the dregs of the tea mugs. But when the fruit ran out, so too did the fruit flies. We liked to think they died miserably of starvation.

There was no such luck with the cockroaches. They bred and bred and bred. They crawled and scuffled everywhere, in the food, in the dark nooks and crannies, in the bilges. There was no way to get rid of them. We tried cockroach traps and chemical sprays, but all were useless. At night we could feel them crawling over our faces as we slept, and a quick stab of a torch beam in the dark invariably picked out the shape of a questing cockroach, feeling its way round the deck beams and bulkheads. We became experts on cockroach behaviour. After a good spray round with insecticide killed most of the adult generation, we observed how a new generation replaced it, born of eggs secreted in hiding places. We learned to distinguish between our bilge-raised cockroaches, which were a bright, almost pinky orange colour from living so long in the darkness, and the healthier mahogany variety that took their exercise in the sun on deck. The problem with the latter, we discovered to our disgust, was that a fine fat deck cockroach on a dark night was indistinguishable in shape and colour from a juicy date.

In Sri Lanka the cockroaches had been reinforced by the first generation of mice, which also joined in the breeding game and soon were scurrying around the food lockers. Finally, we had been boarded in Sumatra by rats, but they were comparatively discreet travellers. They kept themselves to themselves, and we saw them only rarely, usually at night when they passed quickly along the caprail of the gunnel which they used as a runway. It was the cockroaches we really loathed, and so it was with some pleasure that we observed how they too disliked the damp and the rolling motion of our run up the South China Sea. When *Sohar* heeled far over, and the water came squirting in fine dribbles on the inside of the hull, we were delighted to see them run in panic, seeking to get above the high water mark: it was evident that they hated getting their feet wet. Best of all, when *Sohar* changed tack and the hull leaned over in the opposite direction, so that the bilge water slopped up the new lee side, all the bilge cockroaches, who had been living comfortably on that side, had to move their accommodation. Up one side of the hull, across a deck beam and down the other side of the planking would march a line of disgruntled cockroaches. Terry, lying on his bunk with a sea boot, would smash a few into oblivion. But of course there were always more to come, more hidden eggs ready to hatch into new cockroaches, yet at least it was satisfying to know that the cockroaches were not having an entirely luxurious cruise.

By 25 June we had negotiated the passage between the Paracel Islands and the Macclesfield Bank separating Vietnam from China. There was now a sense of exhilaration on board. We had only 300 miles to run to reach the mouth of the Pearl River, and *Sohar* was sweeping forward fair and true with a fine following south-west monsoon. It seemed that perhaps we would beat the typhoons. Tropical storms were reported on the radio, but they were safely off our present track. As *Sohar* rushed forward, occasionally swooping down the front of the following seas in a graceful slalom, there were cries of 'Go *Sohar*! Go *Sohar*!' from the Omanis, as they cheered her on, and lively bouts of clapping and singing as they practised the songs that they were preparing for our Chinese arrival. The refrain of one song went 'Welcome to the young men of China, we have come to bring you greetings'; and another, 'This is the Sultan's ship; we are on it, and sing this song for you.' Eid would lead each line in a hoarse voice. Jumah called the refrain in a high-pitched answer; and sometimes all eight men would leap to their feet to clap the rhythm, stamp their feet on the deck, chant and dance to the rattling, thumping beat on the drums.

The next day brought a beautiful pale pink dawn, a gentle breeze, and a welcome sighting of other ships: a pair of container vessels passed us, hull down and probably heading for Hong Kong. As the sun rose higher the breeze faded, and *Sohar* was barely creeping along when, a little after midday, a very different sort of vessel was spotted, approaching us directly from astern. It was a low, small motor launch, a suspicious sight, for it was well beyond any coastal fishing grounds, and through the binoculars we could see that there were only men on board. I remembered the grim warnings we had been given by the harbour authorities in Singapore. They had told us that pirates were operating less than 50 miles from their harbour, attacking tankers as they slowed down to pass through the narrows, coming alongside in small fast launches, boarding, and robbing the crews. Farther north, it was estimated that there were some fifteen thousand pirates in the South China Sea, mainly fishermen who had taken up looting and murdering the Vietnamese refugees known as the Boat People. Now these pirates were attacking yachts, and any small boats which could be taken by surprise.

Without an engine, and therefore at the mercy of motorized attackers, *Sohar* was such an obvious prey that I now asked Peter Dobbs to prepare *Sohar*'s defences. In addition to the three Kalashnikov assault rifles which Peter had collected from the armoury in Muscat, we had three Browning pistols, all the necessary ammunition, and a couple of cases of tear gas grenades. I had hoped that this lethal collection would never be needed, but just in case it was we had held regular gun drills ever since sailing from Muscat. Under Peter's careful instruction we had cleaned and oiled the guns, stripped and reassembled them, and blasted into fragments a series of orange boxes, empty bottles and other targets as they bobbed in our wake. Observing Musalam as he operated the slide mechanism of his assault rifle and expertly clicked home a fresh magazine, I felt that with his fierce scowl, hairy chest, turban and rakish moustache, he looked much more a pirate than anyone who might care to attack us.

Our visitors in the approaching motor boat must have thought the same: they were not pirates, but their potential victims. They were Vietnamese Boat People. Approaching *Sohar*, they had already taken the precaution of hiding their women below decks. The next instant a rubber boat shot out at high speed from behind *Sohar*, and came roaring to intercept them before they came too close. On board the rubber boat were Peter Dobbs and Tim Readman, heavily bearded and armed to the teeth, with orders to stop and search the small craft to make sure that it was genuine. On board they found seven men, four women and seven children, including babes in arms. All eighteen souls were crammed together in a little boat some 25 feet long and 11 feet in the beam, with an underdeck space, apart from the engine room, barely 28 inches high. The refugees came from the Vietnamese port of Quiahoa and had been at sea for eight days. They were hungry and very thirsty, for although they had fresh water in five plastic jerry cans, the cans had previously been used for diesel fuel and their drinking water was tainted. In order to drink they were sucking up the water through a thin plastic tube – even the toddlers. By an incredible stroke of luck they had sighted *Sohar* as she glided along, and had approached this strange apparition, a medieval sailing ship in the South China Sea, to seek help.

There was plenty we could do to assist them. Nick, our doctor, went aboard. He reported that the refugees were in good physical condition, though some of the children were suffering from sunburn, and one toddler had a withered limb, probably a recent case of polio. All the refugees were at risk of suffering severe exposure because they had nothing but the clothes they stood up in, and these garments were already beginning to fall to pieces. They could not avoid the sun by going below decks for there simply was not enough room for them. Nick treated the burned children, sterilized the new water supply which *Sohar* sent across to replace the fouled water in the jerry cans, made up a sugar and salt mixture for the infant in case the child developed enteritis, and put together a general first aid kit for the rest of the refugees' voyage. Luckily one of the young women who had emerged from hiding knew enough English for Nick to explain the medical kit.

Meanwhile a steady shuttle service with the dinghy ferried across tins of food, a big sack of Omani dates, glucose, a bag of rice, and a roll of sail canvas with needles and thread so that the refugees could rig up awnings against the sun. There was also some soap, for the refugees were filthy from their cooking charcoal which was scattered all around the deck. Their charcoal was almost exhausted, and *Sohar* must have been almost unique in these waters in that she could replenish their stock. Tim Readman checked over their hull and engine, and reported that both seemed to be in excellent condition, and there was enough fuel to get them to their goal, which was Taiwan. The refugees' main problem was that they were lost. Their compass was damaged, and they had no charts. I drew a sketch map of their journey, and marked out the course they had to sail. Their compass proved to be a salvaged US Navy compass card floating in a bowl made by cutting open a plastic oil can and half filling it with diesel fuel. The fuel had slopped out, and the card was sticking, so it was easy to top up the oil and check that their makeshift compass was accurate. The real drawback was that no one aboard the little craft had any knowledge of seafaring. Their skipper was a young man of about twenty-one who had only the haziest notion of how to operate his craft, but through the girl interpreter he seemed to understand which way to steer and how many days they would have to travel.

'Thank you! Thank you!' became the main phrase in their vocabulary, as *Sohar* sent across as much stores as the little motor launch could absorb. The women and children tucked into the food with cries of appreciation. We had plenty to spare and were delighted to help. When someone opened a bag of dates, there was a fresh upsurge of astonishment. 'Thank you!' Their eyes sparkled. By our *Sohar* calculations we reckoned they had enough dates to feed them for two months. As a final gesture, the crew members of *Sohar* took up a quick collection of spare clothes on board, and passed it to the refugees. One Vietnamese man wore nothing but a greasy black raincoat. 'Thank you!' they called again as they stood up to wave goodbye.

'Good luck,' we replied, and 'Remember Oman!' Khamees Navy called after them as their boat chugged away. They had some six days to run before they reached Taiwan, and had a very good chance of making their landfall.

Spinner dolphin

—13—
China

At 8 a.m. on 28 June we sighted China. Dead ahead lay a well defined, grey peak. Some of us cheered, and the Omanis broke into excited chatter. Eid came running up the deck to slap me on the back. Everyone was standing up and peering forward to catch a glimpse of the land.

'I thought I saw something at about seven in the morning,' said Khamees Police, 'but nobody believed me.' Khamees had the sharpest eyes on board, so he was probably right, and the prize of first sighting China most likely went to him, the cheerful marine police corporal from Sur. Now there could be no doubt about our landfall. There it was, a regular cone of mountain rising from the horizon, the indisputable evidence of China, and our destination after seven months' voyaging since leaving Muscat. 'Ooeeeah! Ooeeeah,' the Omanis began to sing a victory chant, their voices rising and falling. A highly charged, almost electric feeling of excitement gripped the entire ship's company. We had done it. We had sailed *Sohar* to China. Thump, thump went the drums, there were enormous happy smiles on all sides, hands were clapping, and feet stamping out a thunderous victory dance. 'Ooeeeah! Ooeeeah!'

Some landfalls are disappointments after the long effort and anticipation of an extended voyage, but *Sohar*'s arrival on the China coast was magical, a heady combination of exuberance and the downright pleasure of looking forward to visiting a country that we had sailed nearly 6000 miles to reach. How many fleets and ships, I wondered, had seen that same looming grey peak at dawn, as they made their way north on the winds of the monsoon, eagerly searching the horizon for the distant glimpse of China? Over the centuries there had been Chinese traders returning from South-east Asia, Indian merchant ships, squadrons of Portuguese caravels, fast-moving tea clippers, and convoys of Dutch and English East India Company ships. For all of them that mountain, Taiwan Shan, had been the beacon standing over the mouth of China's southern gateway, the Pearl River. Up that river lay her great southern entrepôt, Canton. Perhaps the author of the seventh adventure of Sindbad the Sailor had possessed a faint notion of China, lying on the farthest limit of his knowledge, for he had written that on his seventh voyage, after being wrecked in the most dangerous sea of all, Sindbad had found a people so strange as to be almost beyond credence. The menfolk changed into the shapes of birds one day every month, and flew up into the sky. Persuading one of them to carry him on his back, Sindbad rode up into the sky with him on a dizzying flight, until he chanced to call out the name of Allah, the spell was broken, and he was taken abruptly back to the ground.

The bird people of the mystical Islands of the East are found in Arab books of wonders; they are harpy-like creatures with brilliant plumage and bewitching faces. Possibly it was this notion which overlaid the earliest reports of the first trading voyages to China to produce the strange country of Sindbad's seventh adventure, for the story tells that Sindbad made his fortune there by selling logs of aloes wood, and in fact the Chinese traders of Canton paid enormous prices for aloes wood imported from abroad. Indeed the first Arab to reach China, according to the written records, was an Omani, Abu Ubayda, who in the mid-eighth century traded to the Orient for aloes wood. Certainly the Arab geographers and merchants knew a good deal about the China trade: to them China was the only kingdom to be compared in size, magnificence, social order and power with India and all its princes. In the Arab view of world geography China began where India left off, and extended to the very farthest limits of the known world, to a mysterious land, perhaps Korea, whose people sent presents to the Emperor of China, and without whom the natives believed that the rain would cease to fall.

In Canton, as the Arab merchants and navigators knew, the overseas trade was highly organized. A Chinese port officer came to look after their wares. Their cargo was to be off-loaded, inventoried by Chinese officers, and placed in special government warehouses. There it was left in bond, under lock and key, and not touched until the last of the foreign ships had arrived in port and the sailing season was declared to be at an end. Only then were the government warehouses opened, and in this way the Chinese authorities avoided wild fluctuations in market prices according to shipping arrivals. The state took, and generously paid for, one-tenth of all the goods that had been imported, and the remainder were then free to be sold on the open market.

A millennium later I hoped that the same efficient welcome would be waiting for *Sohar* as she sailed her way towards the mouth of the Pearl River. The Chinese Ambassador and a Chinese government official had attended our departure ceremony from Muscat, and *Sohar* had been formally invited to enter China by the government of the People's Republic. Yet it all seemed a long time ago, and there had been no official contact between the ship and the Chinese authorities.

Gradually the land ahead became clearer. It resolved itself into a chain of rocky islands, with sage-green vegetation on rocks of light brown which stretched away to the north-west. Far away to our right we could identify the aptly named twin peaks known as the Asses' Ears. Our course was set for the entrance splendidly named the Great West Channel, but the mouth of the river was so large that it was difficult to know where to steer. Apart from Taiwan Shan and the Asses' Ears there were no landmarks to identify, no towns, no lighthouses, nothing. The huge estuary seemed deserted. Offshore a handful of fishing boats wallowed by at a cautious distance, ignoring us, and trailing long lines on the end of outrigger poles. Hull down, a solitary small freighter emerged from the river, barely discernible, and turned away to the north. Otherwise there was no sign of any activity. Only the hills of the islands watched us arrive, a little bleak and mysterious. As if to emphasize the air of timeless calm we picked out a single dilapidated fishing village in a cove beneath the peak of Taiwan Shan: it could have been there for one century, or for ten centuries. Through the binoculars we saw no signs of activity among the low houses. There were no people, no boats, no dogs. And on Taiwan Shan itself was the round golfball of a radar tracking station, which seemed to be watching over us like a solitary, baleful eye.

Sohar kept her course. The ship was gliding between the islands now and the water had turned the colour of fudge. By some trick of the light the scenery took on a peculiarly Chinese air – the puffy clouds of late afternoon were tinged with a particular golden pink against the sky. Blacker clouds, trailing rain showers, seemed to be ink-washed on to the horizon, and the distant mainland hills ranged one behind the other in outlines which evoked the traditions of Chinese landscape painting, even without the boxy shapes of small fishing junks in the foreground to identify the scene.

From the chart I selected a likely-looking anchorage in the river mouth where we should spend the night. The spot was sheltered from the south wind behind San-chiao Shan Island, and I wondered when was the last time an Arab sailing ship passed that way. Four hundred years ago? Even more? According to the Arab chronicles, the China trade was almost ruined in AD 950 when a Chinese army sacked Canton, killed the foreign traders and burned their houses. But the Arab traders must have gone back to renew the link, cautiously seeking out old trading contacts and reopening the China trade. For another six centuries Chinese porcelain was finding its way to Oman, probably by sea and perhaps aboard Omani ships. The history of the commerce is woven so deeply into a confusing tapestry of entrepôts, goods exchange, rival trading nations and contradictory claims that modern archaeology is only just beginning to fill in the absence of reliable written records. What was certain, however, was that as *Sohar* entered the 'Great River', as the Arabs called the Pearl River, she was celebrating a link between China and Oman which went back at least a thousand years. As *Sohar* edged forward over the tide eddy at the flank of the rocky island it was a symbolic moment for ship and crew, and I hoped to myself that our arrival, private and unobserved, would have done credit to the original Arab sea captains who had won through to China.

We entered the little anchorage under sail alone, a feat we would not have dreamed of attempting when we were an inexperienced crew back in Muscat. Now, with Saleh at the helm, *Sohar* nosed her way into a little bay, enclosed by a small amphitheatre of low hills. A small Chinese fishing junk was already anchored for the night at the back of the bay; there was no one to be seen on board her. *Sohar*'s anchor squad went forward to prepare the main anchor; a sailor stood by the mainsheet ready to cast it off. The rest of the crew were waiting with the brailing lines.

'Brail up!', and up went the great mainsail, its canvas pulled to the mainspar in loose folds. There was still enough wind on the canvas and the spar itself to keep *Sohar* moving gently. She edged forward towards the stern of the fishing boat.

'Stand by the anchor!' 'Let go anchor!' With a rattle of chain, *Sohar*'s main anchor plunged deep into Chinese mud.

The Omanis took a ten-minute break for their evening prayer, and then we lowered the great spar with a final grinding and squealing of wood on wood as the spar slowly settled like a traveller wearily lowering himself into a creaking armchair at the end of a great journey. As the last of the evening light faded, another Chinese fishing junk came into the bay: it seemed a favourite place to spend the night. We lit two riding lights and hung them on the stern and the bowsprit to join the lanterns of the Chinese boats. The fishermen took absolutely no notice of us. They did not stare or wave or even react to the strange sight of an Arab dhow in their cove. *Sohar* settled down to her anchorage, quietly and without fuss. She swung on her cable to the wind, until her bowsprit pointed to the Southern Cross. And then the ship was at peace, a great bird settling on a branch after a long, long migration.

Dawn brought a rain-laden sky which threw down periodic heavy showers that soaked the deck. The crew, relaxing after the final passage, rose late, so it was not until midday that we hoisted anchor and set off to search for an official Chinese contact. The river mouth was still devoid of life, and there was a curiously unreal air to the whole scene. The little islands looked more and more like sketches from Chinese drawings, their stark silhouettes and sparse tufts of bushes etched in hard outline against the grey horizon. It was almost as if we were sailing across the pages of a Chinese picture book. We had expected to be intercepted by a Chinese guard boat, perhaps a customs launch or pilot boat, but there was absolutely nothing to be seen, only the distant fishing junks which ignored us entirely. We were well within Chinese waters, 10 miles inside the Pearl River estuary, and yet we might as well have been 100 miles out in the open sea for all the reaction we caused.

At lunchtime we anchored within 100 yards of an island which had some sort of a military installation on it, and we saw soldiers in green drab uniforms take notice of us and run back over the hill crest. Then their sergeant appeared, stared down at us, and he too ran off. Finally two officers came hurrying along the path, still in their shirt sleeves, and stared at us for some time through binoculars. But they did nothing. So again we hoisted anchor, and this time I set course for La-sa-wei Island which I judged from the chart to be a likely spot for a pilot station.

On the way we finally disposed of our weapons. As instructed by the Sultan's armed forces, we got rid of the guns so that they could never be recovered. We stripped down the Kalashnikovs and tossed the pieces one by one into the opaque waters of the Pearl River. Then we dumped overboard the canisters of tear gas, thankful that we had never had reason to use the ship's armament. Scarcely had the last weapon splashed overboard than we saw a Chinese gunboat racing at full speed towards us. *Sohar* was trudging her way through a nasty, short, blustery sea, and the gunboat was making very heavy going. She rolled and pitched abominably, and at times her hull leaned over at an alarming angle. It was a very old-fashioned looking craft, with a tall, narrow hull like a World War I torpedo boat, and her bridge was jam-packed with sailors gazing in wonder at the strange sight of an Arab sailing vessel. We hoisted a Chinese courtesy flag, and tried to make radio contact as the gunboat tore round and round us in spectacular tight circles and her officers inspected us. Had anyone told the Chinese authorities that we were coming, or were we about to cause a diplomatic embarrassment? There was no reply to our radio calls. Then the Chinese gunboat began signalling to us with a lamp. There was a scramble for pencil and paper, and Musalam, a signaller with the Sultan's navy, began to call out the letters. They didn't seem to make any sense. What language was being used? Was the message in international code? Perhaps we should reply. A modern signal lamp is not a piece of equipment found aboard a medieval sailing ship. So we made do with a piece of cardboard placed over the bulb of our best deck torch, and flashed back a message. 'Please repeat.' Flash, flash, flash – back came the Chinese instructions. We puzzled over the letters, and still we couldn't understand what was wanted. We made gestures, shrugging to show we were puzzled. The gunboat continued to circle around us, now entirely festooned with curious Chinese sailors. The only thing to do was to drop anchor and wait. *Sohar* edged closer to La-sa-wei Island, down went the anchor a second time, and apparently the gunboat was satisfied, for it tore off at high speed, leaving a spectacular wake behind it.

We spent an uncomfortable night, the ship rolling on the exposed anchorage, and at last Tom managed to make a radio contact. Our link with the Chinese authorities was circuitous. Our message went first to a radio amateur in Hong Kong, who relayed it to a friend in the Hong Kong and Shanghai Bank. This friend then telephoned the bank's representative in Canton, who in turn contacted the Canton city authorities who sent a message back down the same tenuous link. Yes, the Canton authorities were expecting us. They were delighted we had arrived safely; all was being made ready. But there was a major typhoon warning in effect. *Sohar* was to leave the exposed river mouth at once, and come up river to a proper typhoon shelter. The Canton harbour authority was sending a tug downriver at full speed to assist us.

I could scarcely believe our luck. By driving *Sohar* hard up the South China Sea we had succeeded in avoiding the worst danger of all. We had entered the Pearl River and reached safety, barely forty-eight hours before a big typhoon hit the area. All the sails we had arduously repaired after the arch squalls, all the weary hours spent rehoisting the great spar and gaining a few more miles' progress, had paid off. Next morning, as the sky began to darken under the outer edge of the typhoon cloud system, a Chinese tug was seen hurrying down towards us from the north. Our radio crackled into life.

'How do you do? I am Mr Liu from the Chinese Foreign Office,' said a voice from the tug in impeccable English. 'I have come from Canton to meet you.'

'How do you do,' I replied, falling in with the formal mood of the moment. 'My name is Tim Severin, and my crew and I have come from Oman to greet you.'

Our passage up the Pearl River was a light-hearted introduction to our Chinese hosts. The tug was under orders to tow *Sohar* to safety as fast as possible, for the Canton authorities were very worried that the ship would be damaged by the typhoon. Now that she had come all the way unscathed from Oman, the Chinese did not want to see *Sohar* sunk in their waters. So the Cantonese tug crew passed us a warp, and began to tow us briskly up the river to the old port of Whampoa, where foreign ships had traditionally been made to wait until they received clearance to enter Canton itself. The tug crew was a lively band of cheerful, friendly sailors who had not the slightest inhibitions about their job. Halfway up the river, at midnight with the rain drenching down and the wind gusting strongly as the outer fringe of the typhoon reached us, the tug boat men decided to change from towing *Sohar* to lashing her alongside the tug. The manoeuvre was a hilarious shambles. The tug crew got themselves into every conceivable tangle and mishap. There were yells and shouts, men slipped dramatically on the tug's steel deck and took slapstick falls, knots came undone, ropes were snagged. The magnificently fat Chinese bosun fell overboard with a shattering splash and, barely able to swim, dog-paddled back to safety, only to jump back into the water to retrieve his sandals which were bobbing away in the flood. A minute later he was back on deck, rushing up and down in his dripping shorts and straw hat, yelling instructions and waving his arms.

The control button for the deck winch on the tug was poorly insulated so that it gave an electric shock to whoever touched it. With the typhoon rain and the steel deck beneath their wet feet, the Cantonese technique was to prod gingerly at the button with a short wooden stick, so when the winch ran amok and had to be stopped in a hurry the frantic lunges at the control button became a comic fencing lesson. With each failure to stop the winch, the stick was passed from hand to hand like a relay baton. Eventually the rope was stretched so taut that it was certain to snap, and the entire crew scuttled off to safety, hiding behind the superstructure of the tug and peeking out like naughty children. Watching all this and trying to keep a straight face, it suddenly became obvious that the tug crew were enjoying the pantomime as much as we were. Someone on *Sohar* let out a chuckle, and in an instant everyone, Chinese, Arabs and Europeans, were roaring with laughter. In one moment all formality and reserve were swept aside. Khamees Police leaped aboard the tug with a tray of dates as a gift. Their dripping bosun, the chief comedian, gracefully accepted a date and sat down by accident on a hot stove top. Clouds of steam burst from his underwear as he leaped up with a yelp of pain and the broadest of grins.

The Chinese authorities succeeded in making *Sohar*'s visit to Canton a total success. After seven and a half months at sea we were overwhelmed by the warmth of the reception that awaited us. At the quayside in Whampoa we were greeted by dignitaries of the city and the province of Canton, and also by the Omani Ambassador to China who had come down from Peking to meet us. Our Chinese hosts had arranged a special programme for us. *Sohar* was to be left at Whampoa under Chinese care while the crew were taken to visit the city and its surroundings; if we wanted to see anything in particular, we had only to ask and the necessary arrangements would be made. There were coaches, guides, interpreters in English and Arabic, hotel accommodation, everything we could possibly wish for. And we were not to worry about the ship. Policemen would guard her, and the harbourmaster would provide extra mooring lines. During the whole of our visit we were to be honoured guests.

The kindness was memorable. Musalam, Eid and the other Omanis were whisked off on a tour of the beauty spots and tourist sights. The marine biologists were taken to fishery research stations, fish farms and universities. Nick Hollis had a chance to see surgery performed under acupuncture in the city hospital. As a civil engineer

Tim Readman visited construction sights to watch how the Chinese did their building. For my own part I was taken to examine ingenious canal boats of a traditional design used to carry live fish to market. Their hulls were drilled with holes to let the water run through, so the boats became moving fish tanks. And one particularly rewarding afternoon was spent aboard a Swatow coasting junk moored in a typhoon shelter on the river. Over thimble-sized cups of acrid Swatow tea the crew explained their trade to me. Without compass, engine or chart, they sailed their vessel from one port to the next, ducking in and out of river mouths, using tides, carrying on the age-old commerce of the China coast. There were eight to ten men on the crew, including a pair of apprentices doing a year's training. With a good wind their junk could make 5 knots, but if the wind rose to Force 7 there was a risk of it being swamped, so they always ran for shelter.

Their ship was lovingly maintained, and as her ribs were cut from camphor wood, her hold smelled delicious. It was a happy contrast to *Sohar*'s odorous bilge gas. *Huilai 108*, as she was named, belonged to the production team of Huishui Water Transport Commune, and there was still much that was traditional about her. She was caulked with a mixture of tung oil, lime and rice stalks. She had no engine, but depended on her great fans of red-dyed sails, and her planks were nailed, edge to edge, in the traditional Chinese fashion. Son followed father on the crew, taking his job when the parent retired, and when I asked how the ship was run, and whether the crew reached communal decisions about how to handle her, I received a matter-of-fact reply: 'Oh no, the captain or first officer has the authority.'

Throughout our visit our Chinese hosts were evidently fascinated by *Sohar*'s mission. That men should have sailed nearly 6000 miles in an engineless boat to visit their country was a novelty to them. Our hosts appeared both flattered and appreciative. They seemed to understand the effort that had been necessary, and that *Sohar*'s crew had worked their way to China by muscle power, patience and sheer application to the job in hand. These were qualities the Chinese valued, and in particular they appreciated that the success of the voyage had been largely due to teamwork. Perhaps the historical perspective which *Sohar* brought with her was a little more difficult for our Chinese hosts to comprehend. They were so proud of Chinese modernization programmes that it must have been puzzling to have visitors who deliberately recreated a thousand-year-old trade voyage. Yet one could easily detect the constant patterns of Chinese life. As in Sindbad's day, Canton was still a major outlet for Chinese trade. The thousands of businessmen who came to Canton's trade fair were the modern equivalent of the Arabs, Indians and Persians who had come a millennium earlier. On the communes around Canton millions and millions of silkworms still munched mulberry leaves and spun the silk which had been exported to the medieval world. Now the Omani crew of *Sohar* purchased glittering swatches of silk to carry home to their wives and families in the Sultanate. And on a visit to the Chinese porcelain factories we found that the production lines were painting little stylized palm trees on coffee cups that were destined for the Arab market. One day the shards of these cups would presumably add another layer to the fragments of medieval Chinese porcelain that the archaeologists are excavating in the countries of the Arab world.

At the University of Canton the historians very kindly consulted the Chinese chronicles for me, and to my delight they found a report of a sewn ship seen in Canton harbour by a Chinese official in the late eighth century. 'Their merchant vessel,' wrote the Chinese official, 'is without nails. The only material they use to set the parts of the ship together is coconut fibre. . . .' It was proof that ships held together with coconut string had berthed in China's ports when Haroun al Rashid was Caliph in Baghdad, and the Tang dynasty ruled China.

Towards the end of the Tang dynasty, in the late ninth century, it was said that there were as many as 10,000 foreigners living in China, and it is very likely that many of them were Moslems. The mosque which they supported is said to be the same mosque where Canton's surviving Moslem population still go for prayer every Friday. Today the Smooth Pagoda, as the Chinese call it, lies at the city centre. But the city's shape has changed, land has been reclaimed, and originally the mosque stood near the river bank. There, it is said, the mosque's tower served as a beacon for merchant shipping coming up the river. Certainly the mosque has a most unusual form: it looks exactly like a lighthouse.

The Smooth Pagoda Mosque was, of course, a place of pilgrimage for *Sohar*'s Moslem sailors. They prayed in the mosque, and gave thanks for the success of the voyage, and the call to prayer was made by an aged Chinese Moslem in a formal lace cap. Today there are

4300 Moslems left in Canton, and each Friday some of them assemble to worship in their mosque. The Moslems' customs are respected by the government; the mosque is under state protection; Moslems are given special rations and restaurant facilities so they can keep their dietary laws; and in a land where cremation is the norm, the Moslems have the privilege of burying their dead.

There was one final ceremony to perform: the official greeting of the ship by the government of China. It was set for 11 July, and on the previous day Sayyid Faisal, the Minister of National Heritage and Culture of Oman, arrived in a gleaming aircraft of the Sultan's royal flight. With him came an Omani delegation, representatives from the Army, Navy, Ministry of Defence and Ministry of Foreign Affairs. From Peking came the chairman of the Cultural Commission of the Government of China, his vice-chairman, various departmental heads of China's Foreign Ministry, and a host of dignitaries. They all assembled at the quayside in central Canton.

Meanwhile *Sohar*'s crew had been taken back to our ship in Whampoa, and just after dawn a tug came to take us upriver. All the small craft about us were fluttering with flags and banners. *Sohar* was dressed overall with the Chinese flag at her mizzentop, and three huge Omani flags at main masthead, bowsprit and stern. She looked very colourful, if slightly travel-worn. As she eased out into the Pearl River, a gunboat of the Chinese Navy was waiting to escort her. The entire crew of the gunboat stood rigidly to attention along the rail, ready to salute, and a signaller was poised at her flag halyard. There was an awkward moment as I realized that I had no idea who should dip their ensign first, the gunboat or *Sohar*, but as the two ships drew level I could see the agonized look on the face of the Chinese first officer. It was clue enough. Obviously the visitor should begin the honours. Eid, perched precariously on *Sohar*'s rudder head and wearing his best *dishdasha*, dipped the Omani flag. The gunboat responded, the Chinese sailors cheered, and their ship blasted off her siren. *Sohar* replied with a brisk clanging of her brass bell. Then we were off upriver to see our reception committee.

It was an impressive sight. The main wharf had been cleared. A big freighter had been sent out into the river, and there on the quayside stood ranks of schoolchildren waving green and red pompons to the music of a Chinese band. As *Sohar* drew alongside, the noise was deafening. The band played, firecrackers exploded and the children sang. We stepped ashore to be greeted by Sayyid Faisal and the Chinese officials, and then walked up the aisle of schoolchildren preceded by dancing Chinese lions.

On the podium there were speeches of welcome, of thanks, and references to the re-establishment of the long-standing friendly relationship between Oman and China. Finally it was my turn to speak on behalf of *Sohar* and her crew. I spoke of the extraordinary help that had been given so generously to make the Sindbad Voyage possible, of the sponsorship and co-operation that meant our ship could sail the Seven Seas of Arab geography once again, and of this impressive welcome ceremony. As I spoke, I remembered the remarkable moments and people of the entire project – the elephants hauling timber in the forests of India, the shipwrights labouring in the searing heat of Sur, the labour of careening ship in Beypore, the long tedium of the doldrums, the near-grounding on the South Sands in the Malacca Strait, the battering of arch squalls in the South China Sea. I knew that in a few days *Sohar* would be returning downriver to Hong Kong, and then be shipped back to Muscat where she would become a monument to Oman's seafaring history. She had fulfilled the purpose for which she had been built.

Her crew were there in front of me, and I felt a pang of regret when I realized that this would be the last time that we were all together as a team. We had done what we had set out to do: we had traced the origins of the Sindbad stories nearly a quarter of the way round the world – in India, Sri Lanka, Sumatra and now in China. Our great adventure was ending, and soon we would disperse to our homes.

In the front rank stood the Omanis, splendid in coloured turbans and gleaming *dishdashas*. How they managed to keep their kit so clean that they always came ashore in superbly pressed gowns I would never understand. Behind them stood the Europeans, all heavily bearded, all bronzed and looking immensely tough and competent. Together they had formed a superb crew. To their right I could see the lace caps of Canton's Moslem community, invited for the special occasion. Then there were ranks of schoolchildren, crowds of spectators, bandsmen and the lion dancers.

Behind them, again, rose the mast and rakishly tilted spars of *Sohar*. She was unique: no other ship like her had been seen on the Pearl River since the greatest days of Arab seafaring. I could make out the 20-foot-long crimson pennant of the Sindbad Voyage flying from her main halyard. The pennant's forked tail was waving jauntily, so that the emblem of the golden flying bird could be seen. And I remembered the last time that crimson and gold pennant had flown, when we had set sail from Muscat. At the same moment I realized that if my crew and I were safe and well on Canton's quayside, and if the voyage had been a success, then it was thanks to one ship – *Sohar*. She had made our voyage a reality. Now her voyage, like Sindbad's Seven Voyages, would become another tale.

The Texts

The Sindbad Voyages

For those interested in reading the Seven Voyages of Sindbad the Sailor in their entirety the most readily available version in English translation is Penguin Books' *Tales from the Thousand and One Nights*, translated by N. J. Dawood. First published in 1954, its numerous reprints show just how popular these stories remain. *The Thousand and One Nights* include not only the Sindbad stories but also the tale of Aladdin. If it can be found, an earlier translation by E. W. Lane (3 vols, 1839–41) gives a suitably romantic flavour to the tales with its nineteenth-century vocabulary, useful notes, and some excellent drawings. There are, of course, many other translations, abridgements and adaptations including a very idiosyncratic one by the Victorian traveller-linguist, Sir Richard Burton, who concocted a special archaic English for the purpose. In *The Art of Story Telling* (Leiden, 1963) Mia Gerhardt has made a literary analysis of *The Thousand and One Nights*, and identified several of the sources for the Sindbad story cycle as well as listing the variants.

The point should be made, however, that there is no definitive version of *The Thousand and One Nights* either in Arabic or English or any other language, because after eight centuries of being worked and reworked, they exist in a number of versions. As far as Sindbad's voyages are concerned, the different forms are broadly similar, with the important exception that Sindbad's Seventh Voyage has two endings: in one version Sindbad has the adventure of the Elephants' Graveyard, and then returns to Baghdad; in the second version he has his adventure with the elephants, then goes on to another adventure in a land of people who once a month sprout wings and fly. Sindbad survives a ride on the back of one of these bird-people, marries a local girl, and brings her back to live in Baghdad.

Early Arab Voyages and Vessels

The starting point for any study of the history of long-distance Arab voyaging is still G. F. Hourani's *Arab Seafaring in Ancient and Early Medieval Times* (Princeton, 1950); and G. Ferrand's collected early Arab texts about the Orient remains the most convenient point of departure into the Arab geographical writings about the East. Ferrand's collection, published in Paris in 1913–14, is called *Relations de voyages et textes géographiques arabes, persans et turcs rélatifs à l'Extrème Orient du VIII au XVIII siècles* (2 vols).

Since these foundation studies, significant contributions have been made by T. M. Johnstone, Esmond Martin, A. H. J. Prins, R. B. Sergeant, Paul Wheatley and David Whitehouse.

G. R. Tibbetts's studies of Arab navigational techniques are all-important; in particular his *Arab Navigation in the Indian Ocean before the Coming of the Portuguese* (London, 1971) is essential reading.

New editions of the works of the main medieval Arab geographers – Idrisi, Masudi, Ibn Khurdadbeh and others – are now appearing or in preparation, and are complemented by G. S. P. Freeman-Grenville's edition and translation of *The Book of the Wonders of India, Mainland, Sea and Islands* by Buzurg ibn Shahriyar of Ramhormuz (East–West Publications, London and The Hague, 1981), which is a revealing source for some of the background material to the Adventures of Sindbad.

Two other recent books are of special note: *Oman, A Seafaring Nation*, published in 1979 by the Ministry of Information, Oman, and largely prepared by Will Facey, deals specifically with the history of Omani shipping, while Clifford Hawkins's book, *The Dhow* (Lymington, 1977), is by far the best study of Indian Ocean dhows in general. Both books have excellent bibliographies.

Sohar

Dimensions

As designed, *Sohar* had a nominal hull length of 80 feet, a beam of 20 feet 4 inches, and a waterline length of 63 feet. Her designed draught was 6 feet, with a sail area of 2900 square feet, arranged as jib 370 square feet, main 1625 square feet, and mizzen 815 square feet.

Construction

Work began with the laying of the ship's 52-foot long keel, 12 by 15 inches in section. Next the bow piece, 36 feet 3 inches long, and the stern piece, 18 feet long, were fitted. The lower strakes were then formed to shape and sewn in place to the height of the fifth strake. Each strake was 8–12 inches broad, and between 2¼ and 3 inches thick depending on its position. No stealers were used. The strakes were normally divided into four or five sections, between 5 and 15 feet long, butted end to end with tongue and groove joints. The edge-to-edge surfaces between the strakes were flat; that is, there was no step or groove, though every 18 inches or so a locator dowel was used. The entire form was held together with coir stitching, done with four-strand cord. Stitch holes were approximately 4 inches apart, and placed 2 inches from the edges of the strakes.

After the fifth strake was in place the floor frames were lashed in, again with four-ply cord. Frames were 4 × 6 inches in section, and the majority were grown frames. Planking then continued up to the twelfth strake, when the futtock frames were lashed in place. The futtock frames fell into the 2-foot interval between the floor frames, and were not joined to them. Planking then continued up to deck level, after which the topside frames were fitted. Again, these topsides frames were not linked to the futtock frames but fell in the same plane as the floor frames. In layman's terms this meant that each 'rib' of the ship actually came in five independent pieces which could work separately. Two main cross beams supported the main mast partner on either side, and took the weight of the 61-foot forward-sloping main mast, shaped from a single treetrunk. The 46-foot mizzen mast stood vertically. Deck

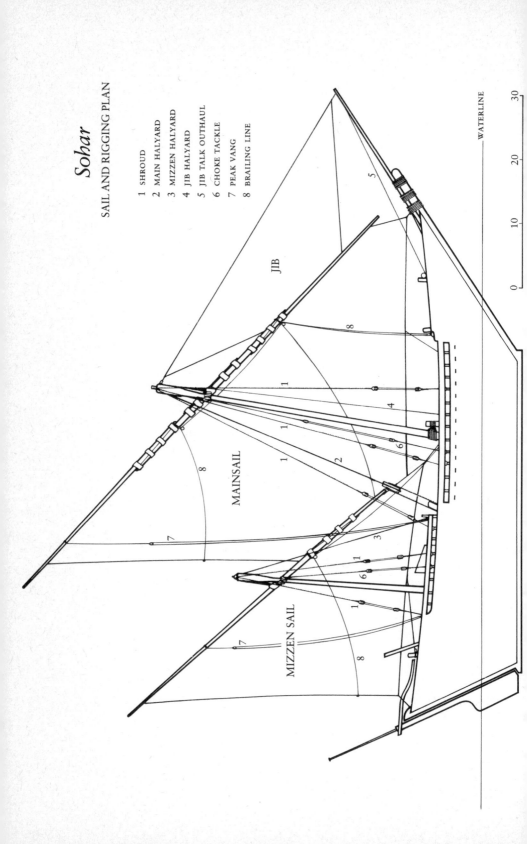

Sohar

SAIL AND RIGGING PLAN

1 SHROUD
2 MAIN HALYARD
3 MIZZEN HALYARD
4 JIB HALYARD
5 JIB TALK OUTHAUL
6 CHOKE TACKLE
7 PEAK VANG
8 BRAILING LINE

JIB

MAINSAIL

MIZZEN SAIL

WATERLINE

0   10   20   30

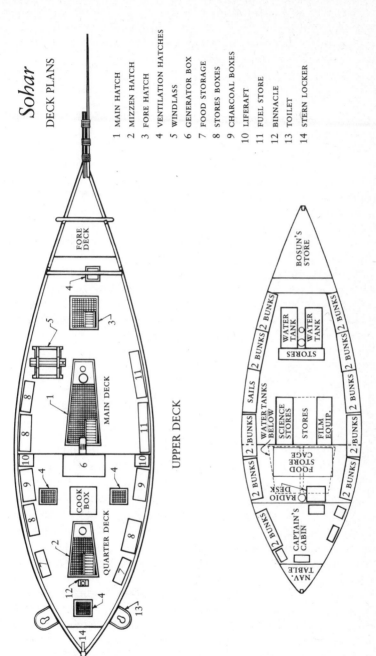

Sohar
DECK PLANS

1 MAIN HATCH
2 MIZZEN HATCH
3 FORE HATCH
4 VENTILATION HATCHES
5 WINDLASS
6 GENERATOR BOX
7 FOOD STORAGE
8 STORES BOXES
9 CHARCOAL BOXES
10 LIFERAFT
11 FUEL STORE
12 BINNACLE
13 TOILET
14 STERN LOCKER

FORE DECK

MAIN DECK

COOK BOX

QUARTER DECK

UPPER DECK

BOSUN'S STORE

2 BUNKS | 2 BUNKS

WATER TANK
WATER TANK
STORES

2 BUNKS | 2 BUNKS

SAILS

2 BUNKS

WATER TANKS BELOW

SCIENCE STORES

STORES

FILM EQUIP.

2 BUNKS

2 BUNKS

FOOD STORE CAGE

2 BUNKS

RADIO DESK

CAPTAIN'S CABIN

2 BUNKS

NAV. TABLE

LOWER DECK

planking was 2¼ inches thick. Ballast was 15 tons (later reduced to 12½ tons) of sandbags.

Sails and Rigging

The blocks for *Sohar*, including the huge lower main block which stood chest-high to a grown man, were all hand-carved from solid pieces of timber, with wooden wheels and wooden pins. The rigging specification was very precise, and ranged from 8-inch circumference rope for the main halyard to 2-inch rope for the lighter stays. All stays were running stays. *Sohar* was first rigged with coconut rope, but this was partially replaced with manila rope as the voyage progressed and the vessel reached countries where manila rope was available.

The first set of sails were made of 18-oz, No. 3 quality cotton canvas, handsewn from strips 24 inches wide, and edge-roped. These sails were replaced in India with larger sails (the mainsail was increased to over 2000 square feet) made of 22-oz and 24-oz cotton canvas in yard-wide bolts. A third mainsail of approximately 1800 square feet was sewn by Minicoy islanders and proved very satisfactory during the last week's run up the South China Sea. This sail was made of 20-oz canvas, and from 18-inch-wide strips.

The 75-foot mainspar of *poon* wood came in three overlapping sections. When this spar broke in the Indian Ocean its replacement (timber unknown) was increased to 81 feet to allow more variation in setting the bigger mainsails. Similarly the original jib boom, projecting 11 feet, was increased in Beypore to 16 feet to give more headsail.

Sailing Performance

Lacking sophisticated instruments to measure the ship's performance (there was not even a functioning modern log) *Sohar*'s performance figures are only generalized. Her best day's run was 130 miles, noon to noon, in the South China Sea. Her maximum speed was perhaps 8–9 knots. On the other hand she was often becalmed, set back by currents, or suffered from appreciable leeway. Her average voyage speed was therefore a little better than 2 knots over the entire route from Muscat to Canton. This is almost exactly the same as the speed of ninth- and tenth-century Arab merchant ships on the same run, calculated from the early texts.

Sohar's windward ability was to point about 45 degrees off the wind. Her leeway added 10–25 degrees, so that she sailed at an effective 65–70 degrees off the wind; but she needed at least a Force 4 wind to do so. She tended to gripe to windward, and there was much juggling with different sizes and positions of headsails. The mizzen was actually cut down in size and reshaped while at sea between Sri Lanka and Sumatra.

The Omani crew paid a great deal of attention to the correct point of suspension for the mainspar, and also to the exact position of the mainsail along the length of the spar. Despite our experiments I am sure that we never extracted anything like her best performance from *Sohar*; the possible combinations of sail sizes, sail positions and spar angles are legion, and it would take more than a lifetime to work through them all under particular conditions of wind, sea state, lading and ballast. On the other hand I was chiefly concerned with sailing the vessel as safely and sensibly as possible, presumably much as an Arab merchant captain would have done. *Sohar*, treated in this manner, served us very well indeed, and in heavy weather in the South China Sea felt a very safe ship.

Sohar's sewn structure survived the voyage in excellent condition. With a new set of sails she could have been turned around and set out for Muscat at the start of the next north-east monsoon in China. Her traditional anti-fouling had protected the hull effectively against shipworm, whereas unprotected timber, especially sapwood, was riddled by teredo.

A final note on safety: *Sohar* carried liferafts, lifejackets, radio and flares for the safety of her crew, and there were three big anchors, plus heavy modern cable, for the safety of the ship. Luckily, none of these items was ever called upon in a life-or-death situation, but I would not have set sail without them.

Acknowledgements

In Ireland: Andrew Dillon; John O'Dwyer

In London: HE the Omani Ambassador; Averil Bloy Slade; Rosie Bunting; John Curd; Patrick Deuchar; Gecoms; Harold Harris; Constance Messenger; Jenny Moseley; Don Shearman; Barbara Wace

In Oman: HE the Minister of Defence; HE the Minister of Imformation and Youth Affairs; HE the Minister of Communications; HE the Under-Secretary for Defence; HE the Chinese Ambassador; Sultan of Oman's Navy, especially Commodores Mucklow and Gunning, CONB, and the Commanding Officer and staff of Sur Training Centre; Royal Oman Police; especially CO Marine Division and the helicopter pilots of Air Wing; Commander Eric Hollin; Seif Behlany and staff; British Bank of the Middle East, especially Frank Paul, Ian Gill, Keith Cumming, Peter Parsons and Mr Sanpat; Mulraj and Bipin Nensey; the Sindbad Net of the Royal Oman Amateur Radio Society; Alison MClay; Carol Ventura; Emma Biles; Dr Paolo and Germana Costa; Julian Paxton, Neil Edwards; Colin Briden; Tarmac; Travo; Airwork, especially Harry Glover and Jim Treloar

In Bahrain: Ali Ibrahim al Malki; Abdulla A. Karim; Bill Eve

In India: John Cheriyan; Dr S. Jones; Antony Kadavill; R. T. Somaiya

In Sri Lanka: Pat and Rhianon Vickers

In Sumatra: The Major of Sabang; Lubis; Mobil Oil; Schlumberger

In Malacca: Koon Leck Keong

In Singapore: S. C. Lim

In Canton: HE Huang Zhen, Minister i/c Commission for Cultural Relations with Foreign Countries; HE Vice-Chairman Wang of the Commission for Cultural Relations with Foreign Countries; the Mayor of Canton; HE Ibrahim al Subhi

In Hong Kong: CO HMS *Tamar*; James Dreaper; Trish Harwood; Nanette McClintock; Sami Nasser; Peter Smith

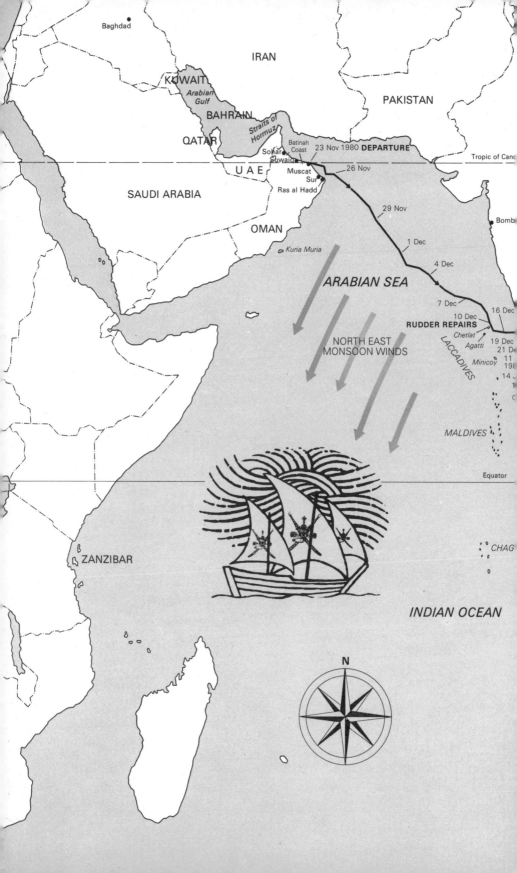

Baghdad

IRAN

KUWAIT

Arabian Gulf

BAHRAIN

QATAR

Straits of Hormuz

PAKISTAN

Batinah Coast

23 Nov 1980 **DEPARTURE**

Sohar

Suwaiq

Muscat

Sur

Ras al Hadd

26 Nov

U A E

SAUDI ARABIA

OMAN

29 Nov

Tropic of Cancer

Bombay

1 Dec

4 Dec

Kuria Muria

ARABIAN SEA

7 Dec

16 Dec

10 Dec

RUDDER REPAIRS

Chetlat

Agatti

19 Dec

21 De

11

198

14

LACCADIVES

Minicoy

NORTH EAST
MONSOON WINDS

MALDIVES

Equator

CHAG

ZANZIBAR

INDIAN OCEAN

N